THE INDONESIAN
DEVELOPMENT
EXPERIENCE

The **Institute of Southeast Asian Studies (ISEAS)** was established as an autonomous organization in 1968. It is a regional research centre dedicated to the study of socio-political, security and economic trends and developments in Southeast Asia and its wider geostrategic and economic environment. The Institute's research programmes are the Regional Economic Studies (RES, including ASEAN and APEC), Regional Strategic and Political Studies (RSPS), and Regional Social and Cultural Studies (RSCS).

ISEAS Publishing, an established academic press, has issued more than 2,000 books and journals. It is the largest scholarly publisher of research about Southeast Asia from within the region. ISEAS Publishing works with many other academic and trade publishers and distributors to disseminate important research and analyses from and about Southeast Asia to the rest of the world.

THE INDONESIAN DEVELOPMENT EXPERIENCE

A COLLECTION
OF WRITINGS
AND SPEECHES
of

WIDJOJO NITISASTRO

FOREWORD
BY
EMIL SALIM

LSEAS

INSTITUTE OF SOUTHEAST ASIAN STUDIES
SINGAPORE

First published in Singapore in 2011 by ISEAS Publishing
Institute of Southeast Asian Studies
30 Heng Mui Keng Terrace
Pasir Panjang
Singapore 119614

E-mail: publish@iseas.edu.sg
Website: <http://bookshop.iseas.edu.sg>

We acknowledge Penerbit Buku Kompas for granting permission to produce a selection of articles originally published in Bahasa Indonesia in the book *Pengalaman Pembangunan Indonesia: Kumpulan Tulisan Dan Uraian Widjojo Nitisastro* with Foreword by Emil Salim, co-edited by Tina Widjojo Nitisastro (Jakarta, 2010).

ISEAS Library Cataloguing-in-Publication Data

Nitisastro, Widjojo,
    The Indonesian development experience : a collection of writings and
    speeches.
  1.   Indonesia—Economic conditions—1945–1966.
  2.   Indonesia—Economic conditions—1966–1997.
  3.   Indonesia—Economic policy.
  I.   Title.
HC447 N73   2011

ISBN 978-981-4311-75-5 (soft cover)
ISBN 978-981-4311-83-0 (eBook PDF)

Photograph of Widjojo Nitisastro on the spine and page vi from the *Tributes for Widjojo Nitisastro by Friends from 27 Foreign Countries* published by Penerbit Buku Kompas. Reprinted with permission.

The cover design is based on the original Bahasa Indonesia version of the book as conceptualized by AN Rahmawanta.

Typeset by International Typesetters Pte Ltd
Printed in Singapore by Photoplates Pte Ltd

To my grandchildren

WITA (Sawitri Miriani)
MIRA (Emiria Wijayanti)
RAFI (Rafi Pradana Widjojo)

May this concise economic history bring
benefit to you and your peers

WIDJOJO NITISASTRO

Contents

Part V EQUITABLE DEVELOPMENT

Part VI INDONESIA AND THE WORLD

Foreword

As Indonesia entered the 1960s, its economy nosedived into an alarming exponential degradation. The cost of living index in Jakarta hit 100 per cent per year from 1962–64 before "shooting up" to 650 per cent from December 1964 to December 1965. The prices of daily necessities went up every day and Indonesia was trapped in spiral hyperinflation.

Building the nation

The main reason behind the hyperinflation was the uncontrollable increase of the volume of money driven by a deficit in the State Budget. There was a strong linkage between the increase in the deficit and the overflowing volume of money. Even if some 45 per cent of the total State Budget were to be channelled for military purposes, the impact on the economy in terms of increasing the flow of the volume of goods and services would not be that big. Its impact on boosting state revenue would be equally insignificant because most of the revenue would be spent on war preparation. The problem was the combination of the bulging revenue deficit, the allocation of revenue for unproductive purposes, and the rise of the volume of money. These things together had triggered the hyperinflation.

The trade and service balance of payments in the 1960s also showed an alarming rise in deficit. As exports and imports dropped, there was a need to repay our foreign debts. All of these things had nibbled into our foreign reserves which tumbled from US$326.4 million (1960) to US$8.6 million (1965).

Almost half of the total US$2.4 billion in foreign debts was spent by the Indonesian Armed Forces (ABRI), making it a power to be reckoned in terms of military equipment, weapons, fighter jets and warships, a leading edge for a developing country with a meager income. But this was unavoidable because the head of state had made a political decision to prepare for a war to win West Irian back into Indonesia's fold. Later, the "crust" Malaysia policy, was adopted. The war drums were then beaten even harder to fight the "Capitalist and Imperialist Blocks" in the then Cold War era.

In this "war economy" situation of the 1960s, emotions were fanned and patriotism whipped up. It was during this time that Sukarno embarked on nation and national character building, a process through which the minds of the people were infused with thoughts of nationhood and singular awareness of the motherland. His talent for boosting the spirit of the people with his fiery oration justified him a place in history when the nation was consolidating itself, but not without the relegating of economic development down in the priority scale.

As the nation solidified itself, a new generation emerged with dreams of a prosperous and affluent Indonesia. The Indonesian revolution had brought forth a new generation with many of its members educated in universities. If the "war economy" condition were not addressed, the disillusionment among university communities would accumulate, not only among students but lecturers alike; all of whom were becoming more critical of the direction of the nation due to their dream of an accomplished and productive Indonesia.

On the global political stage, the wars that had raged primarily in Vietnam, China and Korea had subsided and shifted into economic development. Indonesia was not spared by the spirit of the age that swept over Asia in the 1970s.

After the war, new countries were born in Asia and Africa, all of which were developing countries that had to deal with their economic backwardness. Whereas, initially economic school of thought focused on microeconomy, the spirit of the age in the 1950s had demanded it to shift it into focusing on solutions to developmental economy problems relevant to developing countries.

It was in 1950 that the University of Indonesia opened its School of Economics (FEUI). The school's orientation was initially continental Europe because it was dominated by Dutch professors.

The nationalist fervor sweeping the country in the 1950s did not spare the campus of the University of Indonesia. There was a need to train Indonesian professors to run FEUI and at the same time shift its education orientation from Western continental to the more relevant school of thought which was development economy. It was for this purpose that a program was launched in which dozens of lecturers were sent abroad in batches, particularly to the University of California at Berkeley.

A dispute with the head of state in the 1950s had prompted the dean of the School of Economics, Professor Soemitro Djojohadikusumo, to leave the campus. In the ensuing political chaos, FEUI was handed over to Professor Djokosutono who was assisted by first batch FEUI alumni, including Widjojo Nitisastro. The overseas study programme for lecturers continued from one year to another so that by the end of 1960s all of the subjects at FEUI were taught by Indonesian lecturers with an international standard of education. FEUI's orientation in education was to develop the intellectual capacity of students to understand economic science for policy formulation for developing countries in general and Indonesia in particular.

Building the economy

One of the FEUI alumni sent to the University of California at Berkeley to pursue his doctoral studies was Widjojo Nitisastro, who later became the head of FEUI upon his return.

As Indonesian leaders drenched themselves in war frenzy and political madness to win President Sukarno's trust, economic rationality fell into greater jeopardy. A strong view that economics was not important had gained currency among government circles; so much so that books on economic theory by Keynes were burned.

It was in this kind of situation that Professor Widjojo Nitisastro presented his inaugural speech as a professor of economics titled "Economic Analysis and Development Planning" at FEUI in August 1963. At that time, the common rhetoric of the nation was splashed with vocabulary taken from the compulsory "Seven Basic Elements for Indoctrination", but Widjojo Nitisastro employed "barren" scientific words while putting development issues into economic analysis perspectives imbued with basic elements, such us efficiency, rationality, consistency and decision making processes, among the alternatives which played a central role in development planning methodology. This rational approach has since been part of his policies, which were to be implemented by the upcoming New Order government.

This rational economic approach featured prominently in FEUI's ideas proposed by Widjojo Nitisastro on "The New Path in Economic, Financial and Development Policies" to the Provisional People's Consultative Assembly, which convened in 1966. This convention later issued MPRS No. XXIII/1966 Decree on "Reform of the Foundations of Economic, Financial and Development Policies" containing clauses from FEUI's contribution of thoughts, which were written in terse language.

In this thinking, the ideological foundation of development was Economic Democracy, which did not allow the free fight liberalism, etatism or monopoly that undermined public interests. In the short term, a stabilization programme to control inflation and a rehabilitation programme to build infrastructure were given particular priority. Focus was then shifted to long term development using a priority scale in the sectors of agriculture, infrastructure, industry, mining and oil. The line of thought on our journey to build a just and prosperous society was simple but put down in lucid and rational language. There was no hidden "message from sponsors" nor ideological stowaways. The substance of the document was a reversal of the model and system of development that had brought the Indonesian economy to its knees for correction purposes by means of clear and measured economic rationality.

Most interesting is that this economic rationality applies to various economic systems. China, under Mao Zedong, sought to make the great leap forward into an industrial country driven by the communist ideology, but was met with a failure in the 1960s because that nation applied command economy rather than economic rationality. On the other hand, Deng Xiaoping applied economic rationality without being intervened with by communist ideology, while purposely applying market economy. It was proven more effective for the economy as the Chinese people were able to respond to economic stimulants created by the market albeit without abandoning their communist ideology.

The same went with economic development in the United States in the 2000s when its housing credit system was no longer based on economic rationality, but was driven by the greed of creditors who created numerous irrational credit guarantee derivatives. Lenders' failure to pay back their subprime credits ended up in the domino-like collapse of the creditor companies, credit guarantors and colossal banks, one by one, because they did not take into account economic rationality.

From the above examples, it is clear that economic rationality, as revealed by the market, is an important element, but incomplete. The setting of prices based on the liberal supply and demand system does assure prevention of waste and scarcity of goods. Behind this price fixing system are forces that can cause disequilibrium between supply and demand that end up in price distortions. It is in this connection and from the point of view of planning methodology that "prices" fixed by the market need to be intentionally corrected so that goods allocation and other sources are directed to achieve the goals of development.

Hence, unlike the Chicago school of thought, that holds on to the 1976 Nobel Prize winner Milton Friedman's free market capitalism for economy, Widjojo Nitisastro, on the other hand, saw the need of planning to influence the market through intervention in supply or demand. Widjojo Nitisastro's line of thinking is to develop economic analysis in order to understand development issues that will in turn correct the market through development planning by the means of policies allocating production factors to achieve the goals of development. This is the essence of economic planning through the market.

His position as Chairman of the National Development Planning Agency and later Coordinating Minister for the Economy, Finance and Industry during the New Order Government allowed him to exploit his economic analysis potential for Indonesia's development planning.

Top Priority: Food Self-sufficiency

A development process does not occur in a social vacuum but in societal groups with different interests. Factors of production can be allocated to accomplish development goals for specific societal groups. A huge fund allocation for the agricultural sector, for example, will benefit those societal groups in that sector. If it is allocated in industrial or mining sector, those societal groups associated with industry or mining will reap more benefit than groups in other sectors. This is why, it is very important to determine the allocation of production factors to achieve development goals that will offer the biggest benefit for the public.

But, how to determine the specific target if the economy is being plagued by high inflation, economic chaos, a dysfunctional market and a crisis-ridden government and political institutions?

When hyperinflation bites, the first thing to do is to stabilize and rehabilitate the economy to overcome it. The stabilization policy and economic rehabilitation, which were immediately carried out in 1965–66 had to be based on economic principles balanced between revenue and income, export and import, and between the flow of goods and the flow of money, as well as employment opportunities and population growth of productive ages. There was also a need to bring back the principle of efficiency in using economic resources, the principle of justice in dividing the burden and the cake of development and the principle of the need of investment for economic growth. Implementations of these principles were absolute because Widjojo Nitisastro was convinced that they were part of the inner logic of the economy.

Numerous policies came to birth out of these considerations, such as the state budget balance principle, policies to balance exports and imports in trade, in-country investment policy to off-set deficit in capital balance, policy to arrest excessive money supply to balance the flow of goods, intensification of labour-intensive programmes to accommodate the overflow of workers entering the labor market.

When the hyperinflation could be brought under control, it was time to shift to a planned development model. Hence, the first Five-Year Development Plan (Repelita) was launched embracing the 1968–72 years, with the agricultural sector taking a central role, particularly food production. Agriculture is the dominant factor in rural areas. Villagers constituted the bigger part of the population but they belonged to the lowest income bracket. Indonesia has farmers, arable land, irrigation and knowledge about prime seeds, fertilizer and integrated pest control. We have huge potential to increase our rice production. Indonesia's staple food is rice but it has been the biggest rice importer from the world rice market for years. It is fitting, therefore, that the first Repelita primarily focused on food self-sufficiency in agriculture which, at the same time, was expected to also jolt other sectors back to life.

The public works sectors were expected to support the development, rehabilitation and expansion of irrigation channels. The agricultural sector developed the pattern of "mass guidance" in five-point efforts, including prime seeds, fertilizer, integrated pest control, and irrigation in the appropriate season. The Logistics Agency (Bulog) ensured the stability of rice prices through the buffer stock policy, which meant buying rice when the prices were down and selling it when the prices were up. The industrial sector prioritized the growth of the fertilizer industry. The bank provided credit for agricultural business deals. And so it went, on and on, all sectors offered their support to the agricultural programme in such a way that this multi-sectoral approach would reach a critical point when a solid based was established further development could be pushed ahead.

The road toward food self-sufficiency was not without obstacles. A food crisis occurred in 1972. Rice prices shot up. Rice production was on the decline, compared to in previous years. The heavy 1971 rainy season had given rise to floods that devastated an extensive area of paddy fields thereby reducing rice production, while by the middle of 1972 the dry season was so severe and long that there was no rain until November.

Normally, if rice stock in the market dropped, Bulog would release its buffer stock into the market. But the amount of rice purchased by Bulog in 1972 had been below that of the previous years. To ensure that the rice would not rot in a short time Bulog had made sure that it only bought good quality rice. In addition, Bulog altered its purchasing procedures in 1972 to boost its competence in rice trading. These measures had reduced the volume of rice stockpiled by Bulog, thereby reducing its ability to flood the market with rice in order to lower the prices.

Following intensive efforts to forge cooperation with friendly countries, Indonesia was able to import a huge amount of rice to curb price hikes, thus overcoming the 1972–73 rice crisis.

This experience strengthened the government's resolution to exert all efforts to achieve rice self-sufficiency. Thank God, rice production then steadily increased reaching the self-sufficiency level in 1984 and allowing the country to win an award from the Food and Agriculture Organization.

What is interesting about this rice self-sufficiency is that it was achieved not by a state-owned company or coercive measures of the government but by the rice farmers themselves who made good of the incentives and facilities provided by the government under the market planning system. The government was gaining a lot of valuable experience in the implementation of food production planning. Unfortunately, Agriculture Ministry officials and regional government officials had developed a tendency to inflate the figures for rice production, while the figures provided by the Central Statistics Agency eventually exposed the drop in rice production compared to the previous years. Because the reports about rice production contradicted one another, Bappenas Chairman Widjojo Nitisastro asked all government officials to use the "rice prices during harvest season" as the production benchmarks in the regions and not the "officials' predictions of rice production". Reliance on the inner logic of the economy was heavier than on "official reports by government officials", especially when the officials were reluctant to report a "drop" in rice production compared to previous years.

Another important lesson was that the spotlight on agricultural sector development had propelled rural growth. This was especially accelerated when the Presidential Instruction for Village Development (Inpres) was issued through which profits from oil and gas price rises were specifically allocated for village development programmes. Thus, more development efforts were exerted that touched on the livelihoods of villagers, which in turn significantly facilitated the government's endeavors to reduce poverty.

Poverty reduction

As head of the Economic and Social Research Institute in the 1950s, Widjojo encouraged students to do research in villages, such as a critical view monograph in fifty villages, field research on transmigration in Lampung, development of cooperatives in West Java villages, and the urbanization problem in Jakarta, as well as other subjects. A thematic thread and problems faced by villagers and the poor became evident from the research studies he led. For Widjojo, poverty reduction is not something that should only be discussed in seminars or be blown up out of proportion, but must be brought to fruition through serious commitment by decision makers. This commitment should be reflected in policies and actual programmes to be consistently implemented regardless of the economic condition.

When opportunity knocked to influence the government's policies by drafting five Repelita from 1968 to 1993, poverty reduction became an interminable thread as could be seen from the nature of development policies comprising:

First, development efforts focusing on solid rural economic development and supported by social networking development. Fundamental to the improvement of the livelihood of the people was the implementation of nine-year compulsory education throughout the country. This policy was supported by a nutrition improvement programme, a health care programme and a family planning programme made stronger by the Community Health Clinics (Puskesmas) and the Integrated Services Posts (Posyandu), as well as by providing access to the villages through infrastructure improvement through the building of roads, bridges and through clean water provision that would have a positive impact on poverty reduction efforts.

Second, as a response to the steep depreciation of the US dollar coinciding with the fall of oil prices in the world market in 1986, the government embarked on economic reformation measures by devaluing the rupiah, upholding flexible foreign exchange rate regime management, reforming fiscal and tax and financial sector policies, deregulating trade and industry, establishing a stock market, and numerous other measures to boost non-oil exports. Amid the economic reformation, protection was rendered at all times to the state budget linked to the agricultural sector, human resources development and development in the regions.

Third, swift economic reformation measures to counter the international economic crisis in 1986, had managed to recover investment and employment in the manufacturing and agricultural sectors. Emphasis was then given to labour intensive industries apart from developing the agricultural sector. A variety of policy packages gave birth to a process of rapid growth in the agricultural sector, along with the development of labor intensive industries. All of this led to the increase of employment opportunities that would result in poverty reduction.

Development policies focusing on poverty reduction were mentioned in the World Bank Annual Report in 1994 when it said that the percentage of absolute poverty in Indonesia fell from 60 per cent to 15 per cent of the total population in the period from 1970 to 1990. Whereas, in China absolute poverty went down from 33 per cent to 10 per cent during the same period. Translated into figures, the number of people who lived in absolute poverty in Indonesia dropped from 60 million (1970) to 26 million (1993) when the country had a population of nearly 190 million people.

Interestingly, the poverty reduction was achieved alongside an increase in people's incomes. When Indonesia began its development in 1968 Indonesia's income per capita was US$50 per person, and Indonesia was categorized as one of the poorest countries in the world. After 25 years of planned development with an average growth of seven per cent per year, Indonesia reached an income per capita of $650 (1993) or an increase of 13 times. With this achievement, Indonesia had proven that growth could be accomplished in tandem with poverty alleviation, if it were conducted in a structured way and based on the inner logic of the economy, while focusing on poverty reduction by means of rational policies in influencing market prices.

The Role of the Global Economy

This achievement would have been more pronounced if the global economic climate had been more favorable. A conducive condition for the economic development of developing countries would have been better realized if access to the markets of advanced economics were opened for their export products, such as textiles and garments, which were blocked by non-tariff barriers stipulated in the Multilateral Fiber Agreement. Although advanced countries love to preach in global forums about the merit of free competition for development, in reality, developing countries are facing non-tariff protection and have to compete with the subsidized agricultural products of advanced countries. Likewise, it is very difficult for developing countries to obtain transfer of technology to boost their production because they have to pay steep prices to buy "intellectual property" rights.

But most importantly, industrial countries should realize that they should exert prudence in maintaining their financial stability in the global economy lest they will adversely affect developing countries' economies in terms of currency depreciation that can shake the stability of exchange rates in developing countries. With the advent of the global economy, the age in which the economic model dictates the shielding of a country's own national interests has come to an end. The problem is that there is no global economic institution that has the authority to run the global economy in an objective and neutral manner. International institutions that administer global economic affairs, such as the World Bank, the International Monetary Fund and the World Trade Organization, adopt a "one dollar one vote" rule. Hence, those advanced countries, which make the biggest contribution to the international institution, will win most of the votes. Whereas developing countries are left out of the process of decision making in such international economic institutions.

Being conscious of this imbalance, and with political and financial support from the president, Widjojo Nitisastro set up a countervailing force, by initially setting up the South Commission (1986–90) and consolidating it further in the South Center (1990–99), which was led by Mwalimu Julius K Nyerere, President of Tanzania, and was based in Geneva, Switzerland. The threesome, Widjojo Nitisastro; Gamani Corea, former Secretary General of the United Nations Conference on Trade and Development 1974–84; and Dragos lav Avaramovic, Central Bank Governor of Yugoslavia (1994–96), were the masterminds and driving forces behind the South Centre, which drafted the Non-Aligned Movement (NAM) economic agenda in the 1990s, such as NAM's Economic Agenda for Priority Action 1992–95 and policy papers of the NAM Ad Hoc Expert Group on External Debt. In the 1990s, Indonesia embarked on an initiative to send its former ministers to Africa to assist the execution of aid programmes in South-South countries in the Tokyo International Conference on African Development (TICAD) 1994–96.

One continuous thread in Widjojo Nitisastro's efforts on the international stage was to uphold an equal level playing field in trade between industrial and developing countries. It would be unfair if industrial countries subsidized agricultural products in competition with agricultural products from developing countries. It was unfair if industrial countries offered aid to developing countries, while at the same time prodding the latter to pay back their debts, without any hunch that the dollar, yen or euro values had actually soared. The conditions set out in loan agreements did not take into account the changing exchange rate of currencies, bank interest and world economic conditions. That's why Indonesia fought for fair and civilized principles in development efforts. Industrialized countries needed developing countries and vice versa. Extortion of one country by another country should have never happened in a global economy. An awareness of the need to support each other in terms that were favourable to both industrial and developing countries should bring us into a cooperation based on fair and civilized principles.

This line of thinking gained currency in all developing countries, so much so that the World Bank and the International Monetary Fund eventually came into awareness that resolution of developing countries' foreign loans had to be conducted in a fair and humane manner.

The urge to nurture cooperation based on a fair and civilized principle came after Widjojo Nitisastro caught a glimpse of the wave of world economy in the 1980s, which had developed into a haphazard cycle, which became detrimental to cooperation among countries in setting up a sound global economy.

The world plunged into a disturbing economic depression from 1980 to 1982 before recovering in 1983–89. A major disturbance in the exchange rates of industrial countries flared up during the economic depression in the 1980s, which adversely affected the Indonesian economy and other developing countries already burdened by their obligation to repay their loans in line with the soaring exchange rates of foreign currencies. Coinciding with the changes in the foreign currencies exchange rates, the price of oil plummeted from US$25 to $8 per barrel (1986). Afterwards, oil prices went up and down and were very difficult to foretell. At the same time, the prices of most of export commodities from developing countries nosedived and actual interest rates in the global market went up.

In the 1980s, the state budget and current account deficit in the United States balance of payments rose steeply. On the other hand, the current account of the balance of payments of Germany and Japan, had soared to recovery level. Therefore, it is imperative for industrial countries to find a solution out of these imbalances without adversely impacting developing countries' economies.

In the 1960/1970s capital trickled from advanced countries to developing countries, but it reversed the trend in the 1980s. Flow of capital shifted from developing countries to advanced countries because developing countries had to pay back their debts and interest. This phenomenon gave birth to a severe foreign debt crisis, particularly in Latin American countries. The worst hit African countries were those to the southern part of the Sahara Desert where life quality plunged to its lowest point, exposing a dreadful humanitarian tragedy.

But the 1980s also saw the rise of the Four Dragons, comprising South Korea, Taiwan, Hong Kong, and Singapore. Asian economies were predicted to soar, with Thailand and Malaysia next in line. The Philippines and Indonesia were seen as nominees for the ascending countries in later years.

As "new stars" in development were born, protectionism, particularly in the form of non-tariff barriers under various pretexts, flared up in the global economy.

Widjojo Nitisastro's account on economic development gives us an understanding that the up-and-down cycle of the global economy during the 1980s is an inseparable part in economic life. Hence, it will always be there in upcoming decades. But, Indonesia does not have to be worried because history shows that the nation has the resilience and the capability to overcome countless cycles of this economic crisis. An important prerequisite is our unwavering commitment to the economic principles of inner logic of economic life, and it is capable of influencing market forces through systematic, unyielding, and consequential development planning intended to reach development goals that embrace the interests of the majority of the people who still live in poverty on our road toward realizing a just and prosperous society.

Reflection

This book is titled *The Indonesian Development Experience* and subtitled *A collection of writings and speeches of Widjojo Nitisastro*. What is being presented are pieces of historical fact that have been experienced by someone who has had the opportunity to take part in developing Indonesia. I wish to find the undercurrent thread in Widjojo's rich and widely spread pieces on events and experiences unveiled throughout 25-odd years in order to put them in a framework that tells us about Indonesia's experience in facing the challenge of development.

In drafting this framework, we can make out the logic of a rational economist who is driven by the fighting spirit of a son of the motherland who has a strong commitment to developing the economy for the sake of the common people, those who live in poverty, the majority of whom live in backward villages.

The chance to translate the commitment into action was not a "gift" from somebody, but it had to be seized with an unbending courage and a conviction of the soundness of the proposed economic concept, whose emergence was spurred by the commitment. The next task was to find a leeway in the political community to "sell" the concept without resorting to "prostitution" of personal integrity.

As soon as the opportunity gave way to this commitment, it was pertinent to raise spirits, to disseminate the concept and the commitment as widely as possible in society before exerting all out energy and personal capability to instill in the minds of colleagues the "get things done" mentality in the grueling labour of turning the concept into a reality.

The account recorded in *"The Indonesian Development Experience"* came to an end in 1993, marking a span of more than 25 years of a calling humbly answered by Widjojo Nitisastro to work tirelessly toward Indonesia's development. It was an era filled with the spirit of the age pregnant with prayers, work, performance, perspiration and tears.

An era has come to an end and a new spirit of the age has unveiled itself to be replaced by a new generation. Hopefully this book will assist the new generation to capture the soul and spirit of the new age with a nobler and more dignified dedication and commitment in pursuant of the betterment of our people to live among a fair and civilized society of man in the 21st century.

Emil Salim
8 February 2009
Jakarta

Introduction

Allow me to convey my deepest appreciation to Professor Dr Emil Salim who, on this occasion, wrote the Foreword of this book that will be of utmost benefit to the reader, particularly, the younger generation who will carry on the development of Indonesia.

This book consists of thirty articles and speeches collected during the past decades and divided into six parts:

I.   The Indonesian Development Plan
II. The Implementation of Indonesian Development
III. Facing Various Economic Crises
IV. Foreign Debts Management
V.   Equity and Development
VI. Indonesia and the World

Each part of the book comprises several chapters, each of which contains original articles and accounts.

Each CHAPTER is opened by an INTRODUCTORY NOTE, prior to the article or original account, which has been freshly written to cast some light on the background of the article or the original account.

I. PLANNING OF INDONESIA'S DEVELOPMENT

1. Economic Analysis and Development Planning (1963) is the title of my inaugural lecture as professor of economics at the Department of Economics, University of Indonesia, in 1963. The opinions expressed in the lecture contradicted those held in government circles and part of the community who believed that economics was useless and that it was mere "textbook thinking" and should be thrown out.

2. **Imprudent Economic and Financial Policies (1966)** is based on a lecture given at a huge gathering at the University of Indonesia campus in 1966. The event was a Seminar on Economics and Finance organized by the Indonesian Students Action Front of the Department of Economics of University of Indonesia (KAMI FEUI), in January 1966.

3. **Restructuring Indonesian Economic Fundamentals with Economic Principles (1966)** is the title of a lecture given at another huge gathering at the University of Indonesia campus. This event was a Symposium on the Awakening Spirit of '66: Exploring a New Path, organized by the Indonesian Scholars Action Front (KASI) and the University of Indonesia in May 1966.

Both of the big gatherings were a show of support for the huge student demonstrations against the G30S/PKI rebellion and less than firm response from the government.

4. **Contribution of Ideas of the Department of Economics, University of Indonesia, to the Session of the Provisional People's Consultative Assembly (MPRS) in 1966** is a contribution of thoughts in support of the 1966 MPRS Session. (Note: There was no MPR at the time, only Provisional MPR or MPRS). The FEUI people who drafted the contribution included Moh. Sadli, Ali Wardhana, Subroto, Emil Salim and myself, all of whom were professors at the Department of Economics, University of Indonesia.

5. **Comparison between Articles of the Contribution of Ideas of the Department of Economics, University of Indonesia, to the Articles in the Decision of the Provisional People's Consultative Assembly No: XXIII/MPRS/1966.** This comparison shows a striking resemblance between ideas contained in the Contribution of Ideas and those in the MPRS Decision No. XXIII/1966.

6. **The Essence and Consequences of MPRS Decree No. XXIII/1966 (1966)** is an attempt to convince the people that the decree, which boils down to a total correction of the previous management of the economy, was highly important.

7. **Challenges in Increasing Food Production in Indonesia (1968).** In 1968 the Indonesian Institute of Sciences held a workshop on food

production and invited the National Academy of Sciences of the United States. I was asked to present the keynote speech at the workshop that was held in the framework of preparing the REPELITA Five Year Development Plan on the sector of food production.

8. The Basic Framework of the Repelita (Five-Year Development Plan) (1968). This paper containing the main ideas of the REPELITA was drafted with the purpose of facilitating exchanges of views with various parties.

II. IMPLEMENTATION OF INDONESIA'S DEVELOPMENT

9. Progress and Challenges of Indonesia's Development (1990). At a lecture delivered at the Walter and Phyllis Shorenstein Symposium at the University of California, Berkeley, I described a number of development challenges faced by the Indonesian government, among others: the need for equity and social justice to go in tandem with the rapid growth of the business sector.

10. Some Features of Indonesia's Economic Development During the Last Twenty-Five Years (1993). The Japanese government, which organized an international conference on Development in Africa, had asked me to talk about "Asian Experience and African Development". The Japanese initiative was heartening because Japan is one of the richest countries in the world and as such it pays special attention to the suffering of millions of people in Africa.

On that occasion I highlighted the numerous similarities between Indonesia and African countries in terms of the challenges they face, including their diverse populations. Several of my colleagues, who also attended the conference, had ample opportunities to meet and share their views with delegates from a number of African countries. The conference was followed by visits to several African countries by Professor Sadli and Professor Emil Salim. Their African experience reinforced their conviction about the need to fight for debt relief for countries dogged by massive debts in their meetings with officials from the World Bank and the International Monetary Fund in Washington D.C. and in their meetings with government officials in industrial countries.

They came up with strong arguments not only because they had seen a lot of suffering in a number of African countries, but also because they came from Indonesia, a developing country that had escaped the shackle of foreign debts and whose development had won international recognition.

11. Oil and the Indonesian Economy (1985). The Indonesian Petroleum Association invited me to give a talk at its convention commemorating the centennial of the oil industry in Indonesia on 8 October 1985. In my address I said: "Indonesia is a country blessed with an abundance of natural resources, however, rich natural resource endowments are no guarantee for rapid economic growth."

12. Making Tough and Painful Decisions (1991). The turbulent economy of the world has been going on for years, affecting virtually all countries. But it is mostly the developing countries that have borne the brunt of it. Hence, it is an absolute necessity for leaders of developing countries to be persistently vigilant and to avoid any doubt in making the necessary decisions, however difficult or painful they may be. President Soeharto never showed the slightest hesitation in making decisions, no matter how tough and bitter they would be. Two of his many decisions will be described below, the first was made in 1968 and the second in 1986. The first decision was related to the increase of fuel prices (BBM), while the second one was linked to the devaluation of the rupiah in September 1986, although he had said in January of that year that the rupiah would not be devalued. He said during the announcement of the devaluation: "I consider it to be the upper ground morally, and that it is more responsible to tell it like it is to the people, while consciously making this painful decision for the sake of long-term development planning, than refraining from making the painful decision merely for the sake of saving my face because of the statement I had made earlier."

13. Responding to Various Development Proposals (1997). Studying the attitude of Bapak Sudharmono S.H. in handling the various matters he faced over the years would be a good idea for those who are in charge of approving, rejecting or improving various kinds of proposals to build development projects; or of purchasing goods and/or equipment; or of hiring contractors; or of providing certain goods or services, etc. His methodical way of working brought about great benefits for the country and the nation. We need to view him as an exemplary person and worthy guide not only for the Indonesian people but for people in other developing nations as well.

III. FACING VARIOUS ECONOMIC CRISES

14. The International Monetary Crisis (1971). An International Monetary Crisis emerged in early 1971, culminating in August of that year, when the United States detached itself from the 1941 Bretton Woods Accord on defining the industrial countries' monetary exchange rates. This disruption affecting industrial countries had a huge impact on developing countries

15. Food Crisis (1972). A food crisis occurred in 1972. Rice production plummeted, rice prices soared. The government rice stock was severely limited. Importation of food was next to impossible. This account is a Government Explanation on steps being taken to overcome the food crisis.

16. Pertamina Crisis (1975). The Pertamina Crisis broke out in 1975. The government promptly took a number of measures to solve it. The following is the Government Explanation on the issue during the joint meeting of the House of Representatives' Commissions I, VI and VII and the State Budget Commission of the House on 25 June 1975.

17. Devaluation of the Rupiah (1978). Devaluation of the Rupiah took place in 1978. Devaluation is the official decreasing by a government of the value of a given country's currency against a foreign currency. Various explanations were given to the public about the policy. One way of conveying these explanations was through a television interview.

18. BBM Prices soar (1982). Oil-based fuel (BBM) prices soared in 1982. The price increase is closely linked to attempts to boost the State Budget of Income and Expenditure. Explanations about these two points were offered to the public. One way of conveying these explanations was through a television interview.

19. World's Oil-based Fuel Prices Dived (1986). In 1986 oil prices dropped sharply in a short time. The following was a forewarning to alert the public of its consequences. The drop in international oil prices resulted in a drop in foreign exchange and state earnings. To overcome the drop in state earnings the government deemed it important to devalue the currency. The public needed to be warned of the consequences.

IV. SETTLEMENT OF FOREIGN DEBT

20. Old and New Debts (1966–69). Old debts were those incurred by the previous government whose repayment has yet to be settled. Responsibility to repay old debts fell on the new government. It was the obligation of the new government to find a solution to old loans as best as it could and to avoid turning new debts into another burden.

21. A Once-And-For-All Settlement of Indonesia's Foreign Debt (1970). A once-for-all settlement was reached following an agreement between the Indonesian and creditor countries that are members of the Paris Club (France, Japan, the United States, the United Kingdom, Italy, West Germany, the Netherlands, Australia) in 1970 followed by agreements with other countries (Soviet Union, Poland, Hungary, East Germany, Romania and others).

A crucial role was played by Dr Hermann J. Abs from the Deutshe Bank and on the Indonesian side by Mr. Rachmat Saleh, who was at that time Deputy Senior Governor of Bank Indonesia, later on Governor of Bank Indonesia and then Minister of Trade, in the final settlement of Indonesia's foreign debt.

V. EQUITY AND DEVELOPMENT

22. Equitable Distribution Programme (1979). Equitable distribution of wealth is an important element in development and is one of its goals. Equity must become an integral part in a development programme; otherwise, it will be reduced into a mere slogan that will ruin development efforts.

23. Fostering Small Scale Enterprises (1977). The development of small scale enterprises is closely linked to the enforcement of social justice. Much has been done and yet challenges are massive and difficult. On the other hand, good regulations are in place, but they are little known and too underutilized to be of any benefit to small scale enterprises.

24. Food, Family Nutrition and Intersectoral Cooperation (1978). Improvement of family nutrition is closely related to food production and has a linkage to many other sectors. Therefore, working experiences in intersectoral cooperation and in other sectors can be of benefit in efforts toward improvement of family nutrition.

25. Poverty Reduction: The Indonesian Experience (1994). On the occasion of their 50th anniversary, the World Bank and the International Monetary Fund (IMF) asked me to give a presentation on poverty reduction in their conference in Madrid, Spain, on 29 September 1994. My presentation considered two things: (1) What lessons can be learned from Indonesia's experiences in achieving a rapid reduction of poverty. (2) What should the international community do to assist developing countries in achieving swift poverty reduction in their respective countries. On the first point, I described the Indonesian experience in development, on the second point I underlined the need for the international community to relieve developing countries of their burden of loans in a way similar to that through which Indonesia's loans were resolved.

VI. INDONESIA AND THE WORLD

26. In the Mutual Interest of Rich and Poor Nations (1982). Every year the European Economic Forum organizes the Davos Symposium at Davos, Switzerland, which is usually attended by many present and former cabinet members of developed and developing countries. I was invited to attend and address the Davos Symposium in 1982. While I highlighted cooperation opportunities in business and industry, I seized the opportunity to say that we in Indonesia agreed with the view that the current state of the world economy was freewheeling into stagnation. The persistent crises of the world economy are symptomatic of a structural malfunctioning of the international economic system and a basic imbalance in international economic relations. Therefore, I avowed that it is indeed in the mutual interest of rich and poor countries to take appropriate steps.

27. Indonesia Chaired the OPEC Conference in Bali at a Time When Iran and Iraq were at War. (1980). In 1980, when Professor Soebroto was still Indonesia's Minister of Energy, something happened that could never be forgotten by energy ministers of the other OPEC countries. In their meeting early that year, it was agreed that the OPEC session of 1980 would take place in Bali, Indonesia.

However, the Iraq-Iran war broke out in that same year. A decision was then required as to whether the session would remain slated or be put off. If the session were to be postponed, there would be no world oil price consensus and that could create chaos in the world crude oil market. If the OPEC session in Bali was to get underway as planned, the Iraq-Iran war would likely continue in Bali. The decision to proceed with or delay the OPEC session was left to the host presiding over it. What was Indonesia's decision and what happened?

28. Fifteen World Economic Phenomena that Stood Out During the Decade of the 1980s (1989). In 1985, the U.S. dollar depreciated sharply against the yen, mark and other currencies. This development, coupled with a sharp decline in oil prices in a short time, hit Indonesia's economy like a one-two punch.

29. Perception of Interdependence but Lack of Meaningful Action (1984). In 1984 the Yomiuri Shimbun, one of Japan's leading dailies, invited me to deliver a keynote address at the 1984 Yomiuri Symposium on the International Economy. In the address I referred to the increasing perception in the world of the growing interdependence of the world economy which, however, has not been translated into meaningful actions.

30. Advancing Mutual Understanding and Mutual Confidence (1996). In 1996 Nihon Keizai Shimbun, the leading economic daily in Japan, awarded me the Nikkei Asia Prize for Regional Growth. In my acceptance speech I said that I considered the honor conferred upon me "... as an expression of appreciation and confidence in my country, its people and its government ..." and that "My role has been limited to contributing in a small way to advancing mutual understanding and mutual confidence."

Widjojo Nitisastro
January 2010
Jakarta

PART I

PLANNING OF INDONESIA'S DEVELOPMENT

1

ECONOMIC ANALYSIS AND DEVELOPMENT PLANNING (1963)[1]

Introductory Note: *At the beginning of the 1960, the Indonesian economy was in a tragic state. The standards of living in society were very low and were undergoing setbacks from year to year. One of the main sources of this situation was the strong government opinion at the time that economic affairs were unimportant. There was also the firm notion in government circles at the time that economics was completely useless; it was even considered a cause of social degradation. There was a strong view among the public at that time that the science of economics was totally useless textbook thinking. Some even viewed this science as something that could harm the way of life of the people.*

In 1962, I was appointed professor of economics at the School of Economics, University of Indonesia. As normally practiced by colleges in Indonesia, a new professor is expected to deliver an inaugural speech in the relevant discipline. The core of my inaugural lecture in 1963 was that the economy was important to public welfare and had to be built through planning. For this development planning, economic analysis was required. This statement was a stark contrast to the prevailing and dominant view among government officials and a certain section of the society.

We are all aware of the reality that mankind is currently undergoing a process of enormous change as a result of the progress of science and its applications, which directly affect all aspects of life. The human race has succeeded in making rapid advancements in an effort to better understand its natural surroundings and to better formulate the prevailing laws of nature, which human beings consciously utilize to improve their own existence. The human capacity to grasp the essence of natural laws and apply them is so great that today mankind stands at a crossroads: one leading to the end of human existence as a consequence of the destructive forces created by science, and the other potentially bringing the entire human race toward higher standards of living more suited to the dignity of mankind.

The latter alternative is still only a potential reality because the astonishing capacity of men to conquer nature has yet to be coupled with a corresponding ability to manage and control themselves as human beings. Mankind has proven to be less than successful at shepherding relationships between men and between nations in such a way that the benefit derived from applied sciences can be enjoyed by the whole human race.

The sensitivity of the situation becomes evident as we examine the standards of living of world nations. Two facts come to the fore. The first is the presence of considerable disparity in average income. If the income levels were to be set out in a scale, the discrepancy between the lowest and highest average incomes would be around thirtyfold.

Secondly, the nations with high income levels also have a higher income increase rate than those with lower income levels. The result of both conditions is that the income difference is growing even larger with the passage of time instead of diminishing. In this way, the phenomenon of an ever-increasing gap arises between the high average income level and the low one. In terms of absolute difference, the gap will continue to widen as long as the rates of average income growth registered by the two groups remain identical. This is a natural consequence of the reality that a big difference in the initial levels of income cannot be neutralized by equal rates of growth in income. Obviously, there is the necessity for world nations with a low average income level to devote and muster all their attention and forces in carrying out large-scale development if the ever-growing discrepancy is to be halted.[2]

In the examination of this income disparity, the other noticeable fact is that the classification according to income levels, and thus the implications of their further growth, traverses the categories of economic and political systems. Those with high and low average incomes cover different economic and political systems. If the tendency of different growth rates persists, it is not impossible that in the future the economic powers arising from the disparity will have implications for the relationships among nations, with new patterns coming out of the shifts taking place today.

A comparison of standards of living and their rates of improvement among various nations is significant, not only for obtaining indications of future implications, but also because, as in all human relations, to a certain extent, a nation gains satisfaction with what it has achieved in relation to its productive activity and consumption patterns within the context of what other nations have achieved. The factors connected with this feeling of satisfaction with working activity and consumption also contribute to the achievement of even better standards of living by any given nation.

However, without reducing the significance of the comparison in terms of space, another possibly more relevant and more urgent comparison for nations engaged in development efforts is that of time, which is a comparison between their situation today and their state of affairs yesterday, as well as the perspective in store for them tomorrow. A reasonable improvement in their standards of living can boost confidence in their future and induce their willingness to make fairly big sacrifices at present for future interests.

Development, in fact, is a time based process, one of transformation as a breakthrough from a stagnant economic state to a cumulative growth of a continuous nature. Inherent in this process is the necessity for the given nation or people to make a choice between various alternatives. The choice covers various economic growth rate alternatives, which in themselves mean alternative rates of increase in the production of goods and services. Because the level of production of goods and services serves as an indicator of the level of investment, the choice basically involves alternative rates of investment. Since the investment is at present, and will cause a production increase at a later time, in essence, the act of investing bears implications to present consumption control, so that the choice concerns various alternative rates of consumption today to achieve production and consumption increases in the future. In other words, a community engaged in a development process cannot prevent itself from taking a decision on alternative choices linked to its readiness to control its level of consumption today to make production and consumption growth possible in the future. Besides these alternatives, there is also the necessity to choose patterns of investment, of income distribution, of institutional growth, and different other alternatives.

A nation engaged in development can make such decisions implicitly by leaving them to the various existing economic forces. But the people can also make a conscious and planned choice. In the latter case, there would be a planned development effort with strategic planning as its core. In principle, this planning involves two areas: the first is the conscious choice between the various concrete objectives to be achieved within a certain period of time on the basis of relevant social values, and the second is the choice between efficient and rational alternative methods to attain the goals. Both the determination of the aims to be reached over a given period and the selection of methods require certain standards or criteria, which also have to be selected in advance.

If we study the world communities currently engaged in the process of development, it is apparent that the undertaking for the greater part takes the form of planned development, although different meanings are assigned to the term planning and practices vary considerably. In this way, it is evident that the problem is no longer whether or not planning is a good system for the continuity of economic development, but rather, whether planning is regarded as an absolute requirement for achieving development. There is no question about whether or not planning should be adopted; the actual question concerns finding the appropriate planning methodology to ensure the achievement of development aims.

Development planning is meant to initiate and later guarantee a continuous process of development. This can only take place if the strategic factors of the development process are really under control within the planning effort. And this will only be guaranteed if the strategic factors of the development process in a given community or nation are clearly identified from the outset. In other words, a profound understanding of the essence of the development process is absolutely required before any approach is determined to ensure successful planning.

When we scrutinize the essence of the development process and its relation to planning methodology, it is apparent that this field is fertile ground for various disciplines of science, with economic analysis occupying a central position, supported on the one hand by social sciences and on the other by mathematics and inference statistics. In this context, it may be worthwhile to take a look at the analytical tools used and the method of approach to economic analysis in general, followed by a look at the economic analysis approach in relation to the development process, and finally at all of the resulting implications for the development planning methodology.

In approaching any problem in the economy, economic analysis involves the breaking down of or simplification of issues because economic life is very complex and the capacity of the human brain to encompass those complexities simultaneously is limited. Economic analysis does not seek to get a complete understanding of the entire matter at once, but rather seeks to identify the general relationships existing between certain economic phenomena. To this end, choices are consciously made between the diverse economic phenomena so that only a manageable number of them are selected as the determinants to be explicated, while the rest are considered irrelevant to the case at hand and, thus, set aside. The general relationships deemed existing between the comparatively relevant economic phenomena are then formulated into hypotheses. From the assumptions contained in the hypotheses, conclusions or implications are logically drawn, which can be combined to form specific predictions. If the predictions can endure empirical tests or verifications, the relevant hypotheses are regarded as tenable enough to explain the relationships present between the economic phenomena.

The relationships between the economic phenomena can be formulated as algebraic equations describing the relations between various variables and parameters. The latter have a constant value for a certain equation. Some variables are endogenous, namely those that affect other variables and conversely are also affected by these other variables. Other variables are exogenous, namely those that affect endogenous variables but conversely are not affected by these endogenous variables. In other words, the exogenous variable determinants are the variables that are not included in the framework of analysis.

Equations describing fairly simple economic relationships can be linear in nature, whereas for more complicated relationships non-linear equations can be used. Frequently an economic phenomenon is sufficiently represented by an equation, but several equations often also have to be used. A group of equations that as a whole describes a certain economic situation is called an economic model. There is the macroeconomic model, which covers the entire economy, and there is also the micro economic model.

In terms of mechanics, an economic model can be static in nature and can also be dynamic. In the former case the factor of time is ignored altogether, whereas in the latter time constitutes an explicit element. A dynamic model describes a process, while a static model is a "snapshot".

Then in a model, further simplification can be made by including the assumption that the actors who have to make decisions in this model are seemingly well-versed and in possession of perfect knowledge of the situation. If this simplification is not used, the element of uncertainty is explicitly observed by applying the calculation of probability.

The use of mathematical formulation in economic analysis has various advantages because it produces clear-cut definitions and relationships, presents explicit assumptions, enables tests on the logical consistency between assumptions and conclusions, and also because it can more easily indicate the interdependence between the economic phenomena being examined. Furthermore, as most economic phenomena are quantitative in nature, such as production volumes, levels of prices, consumption, savings, investment, national income and so forth, it enables statistical measurement based on empirical data.

Nonetheless, the application of mathematical formulation in economic analysis bears weaknesses that require proper attention, including too extreme simplification of complex realities, like the formulation of relationships presented in linear equations. For this reason, institutional studies and the formulation of relationships existing between qualitative concepts are also necessary. The use of mathematical formulation is often merely meant to obtain clear-cut descriptions.

The use of an economic model can be of highly significant assistance in economic decision making. Decision making concerning a policy is based on the choices between various available alternatives. In order to determine what alternatives are offered, there should first be some knowledge of the actual situation in the sense of identified values of relevant variables. Variables whose relationships are formulated in equations can be divided into two groups: the first consists of variables under the control of the decision maker, while the second comprises variables beyond the control of the decision maker.

The first type of variables is also called instruments or policy variables. An action in the form of an economic policy of the decision maker implies a change in the values of variables under his control. Based on equations describing the relationships between variables and existing in the economic model already determined, calculation can be made of the change that will occur in the values of variables beyond his control, as a result of the change effected on the values of variables under his control. The introduction of the alternative change to the values of variables under his control also results in an alternative change in the values of variables beyond his control, so that in this way calculation can be made of the consequences of the alternative actions of the decision maker. Based on a comparison of the consequences, the decision maker can choose from the alternative actions available to him.

In this manner, the use of an economic model can assist the decision maker in choosing the proper action rationally, in the sense that the decision maker has calculated and compared the consequences of various alternative actions that can be taken.

An economic model can also be used to analyze the progress of an economic development process. If the volume of production produced by the relevant community serves as the standard for the stage of economic growth, the equations or important relations used for this purpose are those connecting the volume of production on the one hand and the factors determining the rate of production on the other. Apart from traditional factors of production, namely capital, natural resources and labour, there are two other factors considerably affecting the rate of production, which are technology and the socio-political-cultural factor. The equations, therefore, indicate the relationships between the rate of production on the one side and the five other variables on the other, each constituting the determinant of production. The use of such equations explicitly shows that the rate of production growth, and thus the rate of economic growth, is not a mere economic phenomenon.

If we examine each of the variables affecting the rate of production, it is evident that each of them is also affected by the rate of production, so that mutual relationships occur between the rate of production and the various other variables. Then it is also apparent that each of the variables proves to be directly or indirectly affected by the various other variables in the equations. The rate of capital formation is considerably influenced by the levels of income and production, the custom of consumption, the situation of tax administration and other factors. The natural resources that can be effectively exploited greatly depend on technological advancement, investment input, population pressure and so forth. Labour productivity constitutes a function of health conditions, political equilibrium, the level of income and various other factors. Technological growth is directly influenced by the cultural factor, the level of investment and the situation of natural resources. And non-economic variables, too, constitute a function of the other variables.

This dynamic model composed of groups of equations or functions, each containing exogenous variables, clearly indicates that if a community is not yet successful in its effort to develop its economy, this cannot be attributed to merely one factor, like the low rate of capital formation, or a non-economic factor, or the rate of population growth. Such a phenomenon can only be understood if it is viewed as a resultant of the operation of a number of factors of wide diversity and at different rates of intensity, which in themselves are each a resultant of mutual influence with other factors. In this way one will only get an idea if the problem is seen within the entire framework of the complex interrelationships.

In studying an economy that has not yet developed, the other analytical tool applied in economic analysis is the concept of equilibrium. An undeveloped economy can be described as a state of dynamic equilibrium. It means that the economy moves and changes with time but the movement and change indicate no growth. The state of dynamic equilibrium can be stable and can also be unstable in nature. There is stable equilibrium if a moderate push creates another force that will restore the original state. Conversely, unstable equilibrium will just generate a force in line with the moderate push in the direction farther away from the original state of equilibrium.

A dynamic model analysis describing interrelationships in a community whose economy is undeveloped indicates the presence of stable dynamic equilibrium. A moderate push can lead the economy toward economic growth, but at the same time a negative force arises, which neutralizes the positive force so that the resultant of both forces is the reversal of the economy to its original state.

What implications can arise from the economic model describing the state of an as yet undeveloped economy and presented as a group of endogenous interrelationships, while indicating stable dynamic equilibrium? The presence of complex interrelationships shows that the condition that has to be fulfilled to make the relevant economy move toward growth is the existence of a simultaneous drive involving all the variables constituting production determinants. Any effort concentrated on only one of the determinants will just produce a local effect that will be nullified by the influence of various other variables over a short term. In other words, the economic development effort will only succeed if it is placed within the framework of an overall development undertaking that covers all relevant sectors. On the other hand, the economy represented as a state of stable dynamic equilibrium will only be induced toward sustainable growth if the push is really strong enough to undo the negative force that will bring back the state of equilibrium. It is thus obvious that the development effort will only succeed if it constitutes quite a huge enterprise and encompasses all sectors with a strategic role.

A development undertaking of such huge proportions implies the presence of a minimum level to be met while no upper limit is set. Within the framework of development planning, this is concretely defined as the amount of investment to be made. As no upper ceiling is fixed, there are also various alternative rates of investment. The alternatives have varying consequences in terms of the levels of production and income produced. On the other hand, the different rates of investment also have implications for the amounts of private savings required. The latter are closely related to the preparedness of the relevant community to sacrifice. Therefore, any level of production that can be achieved demands some extent of sacrifice. One of the planning activities in the initial phase is to clearly indicate the various alternatives each comprising the output desired and sacrifice made, along with their implications. Choices can then be made with the awareness that in order to achieve the outcome expected, there should be the sincerity to bear the burden of development.

The issue connected with output and sacrifice is one of the important aspects in economic analysis. In essence, this matter has to do with two things that are confronted with each other: what is desired and what is feasible. The former involves preference, while the latter concerns possibility or opportunity. The opportunity available is frequently limited, whereas our preference is to achieve as much as possible. In view of this, what we can do is to strive for a maximum value of what we want within the limits of possibility we are offered. In the context of determining the rate of investment, on the one hand the highest level of investment is expected, which will also turn out the highest level of production, while, on the other hand, the willingness of society to sacrifice is not unlimited. Consequently, what we can do is to strive for a maximum rate of investment within the limits of the preparedness of society to sacrifice.[3]

Another limitation of the rate of investment that can be reached is closely connected with the available methods for mobilizing the resources for investment. It is a matter of the relationship between the aims set and the methods applied to achieve them. It is frequently stated that when the aims have been determined, only the methods need to be chosen to attain the goals. It is true that besides the choice between alternative targets, alternative methods need to be chosen to reach certain aims. But the target choice also depends on the methods to achieve the goals set. It is unnecessary to choose certain targets that can only be realized by unfeasible methods. Therefore, the choice between targets of planning and the determination of methods to achieve the targets are two processes that cannot be strictly separated.

Determining the level of investment for an entire economy is the first step in planning. An economy is made up of various sectors and the entirety of all sectors is called the structure of the economy. As stated earlier, economic development will only succeed if (1) it is realized on a huge scale and (2) it encompasses all sectors. The latter by no means implies that the investment rates in relevant sectors are equal. Nor does it mean that investment funds should be allocated in such a way that the sectors reach the same growth rate. In economic development there is often a conscious reform of the existing structure, in the sense of changing the proportions between the sectors. This is because one of the causes of economic stagnation is frequently an economic structure containing weaknesses, such as too great role assumed by the export sector. This structural reform can be realized by creating different growth rates for the various sectors.

Although another economic structure is being organized, in the planned formation of the structure it remains necessary to guarantee consistency between the sectors. This is because an economy is a system or an organism, in which there are close relations between the existing parts. What happens in one sector both directly and indirectly creates repercussions for the other sectors. These strong interrelationships are present between the sectors of means of production and consumer goods, between the sectors of export and production for domestic purposes, and between the sectors of agriculture and industry.

In order to guarantee consistency in planning, various methods are applicable. One of them is based on the drafting of a multi-sector model, by using variables that represent targets and variables that represent methods to achieve targets as policy variables. A group of certain values for the policy variables constitutes a feasible program. By compiling various groups of values, alternative programmes can be obtained. The programme regarded as optimal is then chosen. The use of this method, which constitutes a multiple equation system, can guarantee the internal consistency required in planning.

Besides this method, which needs a lot of data, there is another simpler one using the approach of successive approximations, which starts with overall planning, followed by sector-wise planning, project planning and regional planning successively. Still another simpler method serves as an attempt to ensure consistency between supply of certain goods and the consumption of these goods by compiling a balance for the relevant goods.

The question of consistency plays an important role in economic analysis. An economy can only proceed smoothly as long as the internal consistency of the economy is guaranteed. Impaired consistency causes excesses and shortages. The situation has further cumulative consequences. It is, therefore, always necessary to strive for the avoidance of waste (in the sense of over production) and scarcity or bottlenecks.

The issue of consistency is closely related to prices, which receive great attention in economic analysis. A system of price formation based on the free convergence of supply and demand does indeed guarantee the avoidance of wastage and shortages. Moreover, a price system that fully accommodates these forces in the form of supply and demand can cause imbalances, which may just confuse planning. However, from the viewpoint of planning methodology, prices formed on the market are just something to be consciously affected so that the allocation of goods and other resources will be more suited to the goals of planning. Basically two ways can be taken: the first is to introduce administrative provisions, while the second is to affect the market through supply or demand.

The price problem in economic planning also arises in the framework of priority rating. Priority is rated on the basis of various economic and non-economic considerations, both founded on comparisons between the output gained and the sacrifice made. Economic considerations take the form of comparisons between cost and output. Broader economic considerations also cover positive and negative economic effects on other projects, as well as the circumstances around the projects. In the economic sense, cost is an alternative cost; meaning the actual cost if resources are used for other purposes. Prices formed on the market frequently are not suitable for use as the basis of decision making in planning. This is due to various reasons: the prices may not represent actual scarcity; the prices may not calculate the possibility of change in the scarcity as a result of the process of development. Such conditions cause inefficient allocation. Therefore, special prices called shadow prices can be compiled for planning purposes. In principle, the shadow prices describe equilibrium prices that will be formed in the case of efficient allocation of economic resources. At present the use of the shadow price concept in planning is growing.

Efficiency, rationality, consistency, and decision making based on alternative options are some basic points in economic analysis that play a central role in the methodology of planning. In addition, development planning still has a lot of other dimensions. One of them is the institutional aspect, which is closely connected with the role of the government and also has to do with the ownership of means of production. If the means of production in an economy is not entirely owned by the state, the role of the government in the development process covers the following: the first task is national development planning, including the formulation of aims to be achieved within a certain period, mobilization of development resources, and allocation of the resources for alternative uses that will guarantee the attainment of the goals already set. Then the government is obliged to carry out direct investment and later direct the production units resulting from the investment. Its further task is to develop people's potential and creativity toward investment and production in such a way that the targets already set by the government in its development plan are achieved.

The formulation of a plan is one of the main functions of the government. Yet, however complete and elegant the plan may be, it is the implementation of this plan that will finally affect the progress of the development process. As the plan is carried out by men (instead of robots), one of the important problems in planning is how to ensure that the men implementing the development plan do it in such a manner that the goals of the plan are achieved. The answer to this question depends on our idea of the motivation of the person executing the plan. In economic analysis, what is considered a main motivator is a material incentive. In fact, there are still other factors that receive very slight attention in economic analysis, namely the factors of awareness and coercion. The attempt to make the executors of the plan act according to the aims of the plan constitutes a combination of the three factors.

Another aspect of economic planning given very slim attention in economic planning circles is that of administration and politics. This is due to the abstract nature of economic analysis, which takes least heed of the institutional angle. One important aspect in the field of administration is supervision to guarantee the achievement of the targets of the development plan. Supervision is not an easy matter, and not infrequently the implementation of supervision simply prevents the attainment of the goals planned. In this context, the application of the concept of indirect supervision in economic analysis may better guarantee the achievement of targets.

In the administration of development planning the other matter receiving considerable attention (because it frequently causes problems) is the aspect connected with centralization-decentralization and coordination. With regard to the former, there is the phenomenon of alternate shifts: when centralization is excessive in decision making, a shift takes place toward decentralization, and when decentralization goes beyond limits so that consistency between the plan and its implementation is hard to achieve, a shift occurs toward centralization. In this context, there is the opportunity for economic analysis to compare the efficiency rates of the existing alternatives. As for coordination, there is the likelihood that it is often used as a substitute for an attempt to ensure consistency. Coordination also has direct influence on the method and speed of decision making. If consistency can be better guaranteed by more automatic methods, this will considerably minimize problems arising from actions of excessive coordination.

When we examine the description of the role of economic analysis in development planning, it is apparent that economic analysis indeed has an important role in planning methodology. But the weaknesses inherent in the analytical tools and methods of approach in economic analysis are also evident. The latter has to do with the conclusions already drawn based on economic model application, that "the rate of production growth, and thus the rate of economic growth, is not a mere economic phenomenon" and also the statement that "one will only get an idea if the problem is seen within the entire framework of the complex interrelationships". More systematic cooperation between economic analysis and other social sciences may give a deeper understanding of the problem, although it should always be kept in mind that cooperation between various sciences does not always produce satisfactory results and may bear disappointing elements.

The important role played by economic analysis in development planning methodology is connected with something that constitutes an essential matter for both, namely the logic of the process of rational decision making amid the alternative options available. This rationality manifests itself in the gist of efficiency and consistency, which are both central issues in development planning. It is obvious that for the effective realization of development planning, rational considerations assuming the form of efficiency and consistency criteria become something absolute.

It is also clear that for the growth of planning methodology, the growth of economic analysis is needed. Planning makes full use of the general relationships between economic phenomena developed in economic analysis. These relationships are sometimes referred to as economic laws, a term that does not seem fully suitable and can give rise to unnecessary misunderstandings. Apart from the question of terminology, the attention paid, especially to considerations of efficiency, rationality, consistency and what are called economic laws, will definitely expedite the growth of development planning. As once pointed out by Oskar Lange, a famous Polish economist, "... the economic laws can be made to operate in accordance with the human will, just like man, through modern technology, can utilize the laws of nature and make them operate in a way which conforms to his will" (Oskar Lange: *The Political Economy of Socialism*).

In the beginning of this review, it has been indicated how "The human race has succeeded in making rapid advancements in an effort to better understand its natural surroundings and better formulate the prevailing laws of nature, which are later consciously utilized to improve its own existence". It seems that on our way to an Indonesian socialist society, our effort to carry out planned development will be accelerated if we better understand the essence of the development process and make conscious use of economic laws for development purposes.

NOTES

[1] Inaugural speech as professor of economics at the School of Economics, University of Indonesia, Jakarta, delivered on 10 August 1963. This article is translated by Harry Bhaskara.

[2] If nation A has an average income level of 100 and nation B has 2,000, while the average income of each of them increases at the rate of two per cent a year, based on multiple interest at the end of the tenth year the average income of A becomes 121.9 and that of B becomes 2,438. The relative difference remains twenty times, but the absolute difference rises from 1,900 to 2,316.1. The relative difference would decrease from twenty to fifteen times if the average income of A increased by five per cent a year, meaning that the

income increase rate of A would be more than twice the income increase rate of B. In this case the absolute difference would rise from 1,900 to 2,275.1.

3   One should do away with the misunderstanding that sometimes occurs; that the principle to be adhered to is to strive for maximum output with minimum sacrifice. This is impossible to carry out. One of the two has to be considered a constant or at least seen as covering an area with certain limits. What can be strived for is to achieve maximum output with some sacrifice (or within certain limits of sacrifice) or with minimum sacrifice to gain some output (or to gain output within certain limits).

2

IMPRUDENT ECONOMIC AND FINANCIAL POLICIES (1966)[1]

Introductory Note: *Two important events took place in early January 1966: Huge student rallies to protest the government's attitude toward a recent coup known as the G30S/PKI and a week-long seminar organized by the Indonesian Students Action Front (KAMI) of the Faculty of Economics of the University of Indonesia (FEUI), a group that opposes the existing government's economic and financial policies. The packed seminar featured speakers from University of Indonesia (UI), as well as from outside the university. Among the UI speakers were Professor Sumantri Brodjonegoro (UI Rector), Professor Moh. Sadli, Professor Subroto, Professor Ali Wardhana, Professor Emil Salim and myself (all from FEUI). Proceedings from the seminar were published into a book titled "The Leader, the Man and the Gun" inspired by the title of the presentation made by Sri Sultan Hamengku Buwono IX in the seminar.*

P.A. Baran, a well-known Marxist, pointed out the difference between an "intellectual worker" and an "intellectual" in his article entitled: "The Commitment of the Intellectual". The first one employs his intellect and his brain in the way a "manual worker" utilizes his hands. In other words, an "intellectual worker" is a craftsman whose strength and skills lie in his brain power, not his muscle or the agility of his hands. The skill of a soldering worker, for example, is put to a test when he plugs holes in a pan or a cooking pot, for which he is paid for. He is not asking, nor does he care about, what the pan or the cooking pot is used for; closing the holes is all he cares about. Similarly, all an "intellectual worker" does is "sell his brain". He does not care about the impact of the use of his brain. An "intellectual worker", according to Baran — in C.P. Snow's words — has the attitude that:

> "... *we* produce the tools. *We* stop there. It is for *you*, the rest of the world, the politicians, to say how the tools are used. The tools may be used for purposes which most of us would regard as bad. If so, we are sorry. But, as scientists, this is no concern of ours."

On the contrary, according to Baran, an "intellectual" has a different attitude. "An intellectual is thus in essence a social critic, a person whose concern is to identify, to analyze, and in this way to help overcome the obstacles barring the way to the attainment of a better, more humane, and more rational social order. As such, he becomes the *conscience of society* and the spokesman of such progressive forces as it contains in any given period of history. And, as such, he is inevitably considered a 'troublemaker' and a 'nuisance' by the ruling class seeking to preserve the status quo..."

Thus, on one hand an "intellectual worker sells his brain", and has no concern of its consequences, on the other hand, an "intellectual" basically serves as a conscience of his society. And, everyone who regards him or herself as an intellectual (all but not exclusively university graduates and students) has to choose whether they want to become "intellectual workers" or to become the conscience for their society. Each of which has its own consequences.

The same goes with the academic world. Civitas academica may serve as "brain sellers" to a buyer who dares to pay the highest price, but they can opt to become civitas academica who serve as interpreters of what is in the conscience of the people and act as counselors of the people's inner voices, to show them what is going wrong, and warn them before something goes awry, as well as showing the right direction of development. The role of "counselors of the people's inner voices", perhaps, will gain due acceptance and appreciation, as well as a greater awareness of its usefulness.

We are grateful for this. However, an opposite reaction is also possible, in which universities or the people in those institutions are considered "troublemakers" or "nuisances". In this case, we will have to heave a sigh of relief and be dutiful, with the hope that their attitude will change one day. The social function as "counselors of the people's aspirations" should go on.

Responding to the current economic situation and in an effort to overcome its declining trend, the University of Indonesia has played its social role as "mentor of the people's conscience". UI Rector, Professor Sumantri, among others, has warned that the government's intention to sell office cars to high level officials at very low prices will have an adverse affect. In these past few days, we have heard a lecture from Professor Subroto who has scrutinized the government's export and import policies and concluded that the series of new policies do not reflect a serious intention on the part of the government to sustain the economy, and cited the concern that 1966 will not see the establishment of an appropriate internal and external balance.[2] We have also learned that Dr Ali Wardhana, who has done research on the 1966 Monetary Budget, has arrived at the conclusion that although the government's income and spending can be made to balance on paper, it is basically only "window dressing" in nature.[3] It is true that a piece of paper is docile and we can write anything on it. We also have heard from Professor Sadli, who has said loudly and clearly that the series of measures taken by the government at present would not meet expectations. He has also questioned why the government has made such a reckless move with such far reaching impact in the absence of economic, political and psychological preconditions. We all know the answers by now.[4] Lastly, we have also heard a lecture from Dr Emil Salim, who has added to our motto vocabulary, by stating that apart from our tasks to eliminate *exploitation de l'homme par l'homme and exploitation de nation par nation*, we have to thoroughly wipe out *exploitation de l'homme par nation and exploitation de nation par l'homme*.[5] On top of this, lectures from Professor Selo Sumardjan and Drs Fuad Hassan have shown us the roles that social and psychological factors are playing in our sinking economy.[6-7]

Hence, this series of lecture has fulfilled one of our social functions as a "social critic", which is to show what has gone wrong. The question might arise: "Why was this only criticism, shouldn't we have issued warnings prior to everything becoming irreversible?" This has actually been done and is, in fact, an inalienable part of "social criticism". For example, when rumors made their round in early December 1965 that a new economic measure was imminent, I did convey some thoughts on the impending measure in front of KESPEKRI (Indonesian Christian Workers Union) members; remarks that were reported by the press. It is, perhaps, sensible now to make a casual comparison between some of that thinking and thoughts arising later on.

In those thoughts, I underlined, among other things, the importance of the timing of the launching of the measure. I said that nobody should ever take a drastic measure during a famine. But look what happened? The government has steeply increased the prices of fuel, kerosene, and other important items precisely in the midst of a famine. On top of that, during Idul Fitri holiday, and like it or not, is exacerbating the grievances of the people. For civil servants, in particular, the price hikes have nullified the significance of the government's intention to raise their salaries. Prices have kept going up several times, while their salary levels have yet to rise.

I also warned the government against taking any spectacular measures stemming from a yearning for a quick, dramatic and impressive fix. In reality, the government has recently opted to take a very spectacular but hasty measure in devaluing the currency by cutting the value of the various banknotes. The purpose of this drastic devaluation of the currency was simply to increase the government's cash supply. But this has been overdone. It was as if attempting to kill a fly with a canon. The end result has been a living nightmare. It is also clear that technical preparation for the currency devaluation measure was less than adequate.

The government was also forewarned of the importance of the political and psychological aspects of the measure. When the government urges the people to make sacrifices following the raising of taxes, levies, prices, tariff's and others fees in order to boost its earnings, it is only natural for the people to see it as a moral duty for the government to set concrete examples by effectively slashing its spending first. What the government has done is exactly the opposite. It had raised prices and tariffs enormously, even before it attempted to prove that it could tone down its spending. The only thing the government could even come close to claiming was a prudent measure was the decision to sell state-owned cars to ministers and top government officials at very low prices. However, this is clearly not a cost-cutting measure; somehow, it appears to be more of a gift.

The government had also been forewarned that its apparatus needs to be put to task about the necessity of thoroughly ridding itself of all forms of dishonesty. They must be made to understand that nobody should ever use state companies as "cash cows" but must, rather, turn them into entities with a "leading and commanding position". There is, as yet, little indication that the government has taken any move in this direction.

I also pointed out in those statements of concern that the biggest danger of uncontrollable inflation was not the possible collapse and crumbling of our economy (since there is no such thing as a collapsed economy), but, rather, the real shifting of ethical values and norms in which dishonesty and social inequality would be taken for granted, leading to social and political conflicts that could be manipulated to worsen, and then engineered to trigger unrest that would culminate in an uprising. This was a very serious warning.

Foremost among that series of warnings was that the government should never make any move to overcome the economic woes that could possibly rupture the unity between the people and the Armed Forces (ABRI). This was especially true at a time when strong unity is called for. Most urgently needed are a high level of alertness and a highly tactful course of action.

Comparing the forewarnings and the measures taken by the government one can see that there has occurred a discrepancy in the assessment of the situation and in the evaluation of what moves should have been taken. One interesting thing is that the economic and financial measures taken by the government seem to have been shrouded by often repeated theories and terms that are seldom elaborated upon, thus making them to even more vague. Example of this confusing usage of theories and terms are: theory of balance at the highest level", "production approach", "non-conventional", and "minimum physical requirement".

There has always been a need for theories, but when they are used in policies, they should be linked to realities. The current reality shows that the theories brought forward by the government have been lacking in connectivity with our economic and political realities. Apart from this, is the fact that those theories are fallacies, with the terms being bandied about having no significance. Hence, listening to the series of lectures given by economic scholars in the seminar has prompted an awareness of something that seems quite odd. Defenders of the government's economic policies put an emphasis on theories, whereas lecturers on the economy underlined the living reality of the people. This is an upside down world.

The inadequate assessment of these realities has yielded inconsistent policies. For example, following the drastic devaluation of the Indonesian currency, the government threatened traders who raise the prices of their commodities with heavy punishment. On the other hand, the government has officially increased the prices of goods under its control as well as the prices of its companies. This has been done without revoking the earlier instruction. Crisis of confidence is the logical result. Without an authoritative bearing, no government can take effective economic measures. The absence of effective economic measures will downgrade the legitimacy of the government. This is not a vicious circle, but a downward moving spiral. Without care, this situation will lead to what is being said about some Latin American countries: "The economy grows at night. Why at night? Because at night the government sleeps". This type of economic downturn can be expected to lead to serious social and political upheavals, especially when the decline is accompanied by a widening social gap.

The widening social gap creates another downward spiral, linking the severe inflation with the shifting of ethical values and norms. Inflation has shifted those values and norms, and the acceptance as status quo of the social gap, which has been caused by inflation, drives even more bullish inflation. That is why it is necessary to consider the mental domain in any efforts at overcoming high inflation. This shift in values and norms must be curtailed by putting the tenets of the Pancasila (Five Principles) ideology into practice in terms of attitude, acts and daily lifestyles. China's leader Liu Shiao-Tji in his book: *How to be a Good Communist* says among other things that a good communist should be "the first to suffer hardship, and the last to enjoy comfort". In facing this fierce inflation spiral, it is not a bad idea to ask ourselves: "How to be a good Pancasilaist" and then try to put those principles into practice in our daily lives.

Closely linked to this issue are the role of the government, on the one hand, and the role of the people, on the other hand, in overcoming our economic downturn. The nature of the government's current economic and financial measures makes it seem as if inflation is solely a government issue, whereas — as pointed out by Sri Sultan Hamengku Buwono IX during the opening of the Week of Lectures and Seminars — the people are considered as mere objects in this matter.[8] An economic downturn cannot be overcome without the government and the people acting in concert. The people's enthusiasm is an absolute requirement. As stated in the Economic Declaration (DEKON), the people's potential development and creativity are musts in overcoming the current economic woes. It is interesting that the government has never touched on the Economic Declaration in its recent economic and financial measures.

Based on the responses and the examination and analysis set forth by the lecturing staff of the Faculty of Economics of the University of Indonesia, it can be concluded *that the series of economic and financial measures taken by the government recently are in principle an imprudent economic and financial policy, and that those measures would worsen the nation's current economic difficulties*. Hopefully, the conscience of the people, as expressed by the *civitas academica* of the University of Indonesia in response to the government's recent series of economic and financial policies will be able to counter the downward spiral of Indonesian economy.

NOTES

[1] My deliberation as Dean of the Faculty of Economics of the University of Indonesia, in a Seminar on Economics and Finance organized by KAMI (Indonesian Students Action Front of the Faculty of Economics of University of Indonesia), 10–20 January 1966. Published in *The Leader, The Man and The Gun*, PT Matoa, Jakarta, 1966, page 130–36. This article is translated by Harry Bhaskara.

[2] Subroto, "1966 Economic Policies in the International Trade Sector", pp. 54–60

[3] Ali Wardhana: "Notes on Government Measures in the Monetary Economic Sector", pp. 76–85

[4] Ir. Moh. Sadli, "Our Structural Monetary Economy Problems", pp. 87–96.

[5] Emil Salim, "Nurturing Pancasila Economy", pp. 98–109.

[6] Selo Soemardjan, "Sociological Impacts of Monetary Inflation", pp. 61–74.

[7] Fuad Hassan, "Some Psychological Aspects of Current Economic Problems", pp. 114–25.

[8] Sri Sultan Hamengkubuwono IX, "Leaders, Executors and Tools in Economic Development", pp. 28–39.

3

RESTRUCTURING INDONESIAN ECONOMIC FUNDAMENTALS WITH ECONOMIC PRINCIPLES (1966)[1]

Introductory Note: *Two big events took place at the University of Indonesia in 1966. The first one was the Seminar on Economics and Finance, on 10–20 January 1966 organized and held by KAMI-FEUI (Indonesian Students Action Front of the Faculty of Economics of the University of Indonesia). The second was a Symposium on the Awakening Spirit of '66: Exploring a New Path, organized and held by the University of Indonesia and KASI (Indonesian Scholars Action Front) on 6–9 May. The events of 11 March that led to changes in the governmental structure in Indonesia and the approach to its economic problems took place between these two important academic meetings. Professor Dr Ali Wardhana was the Symposium Chairman, while I acted as the moderator on economic issues.*

The section on the economic sector for the **Symposium on Awakening Spirit of '66: Exploring a New Path** was titled: Reorganizing the Fundamentals of the Indonesian Economy Based on Economic Principles.

First of all, it is important for us to know that improvements in the economy cannot be achieved solely by making speeches, or holding symposiums or seminars, or other such event; **concrete measures are also required for that**. Symposiums, seminars, and other discussions are merely a means for exchanging ideas to find a better road map or ways to overcome economic hardship. The outcome of such an exchange of ideas can further be defined into what is called a "concept". In fact, the number of concepts required to overcome the current economic difficulties has become large indeed. One of the most apt of these concepts came out of the Seminar on Economics and Finance Issues, which was organized by *KAMI FE-UI* (Indonesian Students Action Front of the Faculty of Economics of the University of Indonesia) on 10–20 January 1966). Thus, the question is how to implement those concepts or ideas that are alive in our society.

Another aspect is that, for most economic scholars especially those who are in universities, circumstances have significantly changed. Before 11 March 1966, the question was how to make top government officials aware that economic problems were important, could not be ignored and should be addressed in a rational and efficient manner. Today the government does not have to be told about the importance of economic problems. At the very least, the numerous public statements made recently have convinced us that there is now a profound recognition of the extent of economic hardship faced by the public among government circles, and that the nation's leaders are determined to address them. (This reality speaks for itself, but whether or not these apparent good intentions will yield concrete results remains open to question). Thus, in current reality, advising the government about the importance of the economy is "no longer an art", but rather a matter of course. There is no need for us to smash down open doors.

The question is how to transform the government's good intentions into reality. Clearly, introspection, followed by reorientation, on the state's economic policies is in order. This is reflected in the title of the symposium on the economic sector. The title implies two things: First, the economic fundamentals have to be restructured. This is so because a lot of our fundamentals have become confused or non-functional. We are all aware of this problem. Second, the restructuring process should be based on economic principles. This means that we have to be rational in addressing the current economic downturn. Being rational in looking into a problem and in finding its solution is a key basic economic principle.

The emphasis given to the importance of employing economic principles is because, basically, *Indonesia's economic decline is rooted in two things*:

1. It is a fact that our economy has been neglected for years, and it is still not getting the attention it deserves. It has continuously been pushed aside by other things, and often considered as a trifle or nothing at all.
2. In attacking economic problems, often, or even customarily, we have pushed economic principles aside. Economic principles which are based on rational thinking are deemed unnecessary or simply too conventional. This rejection of economic principles is often based on revolutionary sounding arguments, which are both remarkable and terrifying, but these are precisely the kind of things that have brought our economy down.

Overall, our economy has been neglected, and the way we have treated it has been irrational. Our management of the economy has far too often capitulated to the impact of catchphrases and slogans. This irrational attitude has been coupled with and exacerbated by a lack of control or adequate supervision. The logical consequence has been the fading away of objective evaluation of the outcome of endeavors or performance. The result is an ambiguity in evaluation that leads to distorted views of what is right and what is wrong. Something that is right at the outset can be far too easily said to be wrong down the line; the reverse is also true. Additionally, there is a lack of effective public input and civic control within an overly covert culture, especially as relates to disseminating statistical data. The absence of an effective control by the people is clearly contrary to the definition and spirit of the 1945 Constitution.

Therefore, it is very important that we begin paying attention to a number of economic principles that are valid at all times for managing any economy. Among these key economic principles are the balance between expenditure and revenue, between imports and exports, between the flow of goods and money, and between available employment opportunities and the growth of population in the working age bracket. The same goes with the law of efficiency in exploiting economic resources, the principle of impartiality in dividing the load and the pie, and the rule of the need for investment for economic growth.

We need to heed and employ these economic rules. To exploit natural resources effectively, we need to know the laws of nature and to apply them. The same goes with the economy. We must master economic principles in order to be able to employ them in propelling economic growth. One example is the economic principle that says expenditure should never exceed revenue. This principle is generally applied to the economy of a household. However, in principle, it applies to a state as well. For years the government expenditure has always exceeded its revenue. The gap has been plugged up by printing more money. Herein is the difference between the economy of a state and a household: unlike a state, a family cannot print money. Moreover, for years, the government's foreign exchange expenditure has far exceeded its export earnings. The gap has been closed by foreign debts. Denial of this simple economic principle will clearly have logical consequences. And we are currently suffering from those consequences.

Mismanagement of the economy can be likened to the poor preservation of our natural environment that eventually leads to flooding. If we recklessly cut down our forests, overlook the maintenance of our dams, and forget to excavate the silt accumulating on the bottom of our river estuaries, it is only logical that large-scale flooding will occur sooner or later. The same goes with economy. If we don't pay attention to our economy, if we let our expenditures swell without harmonizing it with comparable revenue, and if the flow of money gets bigger every day, but the flow of goods cannot cope with a corresponding speed, sooner or later the people will suffer. In this situation, the question is not "economic collapse" (which does not have a very clear meaning, particularly because Indonesia's economy has an agricultural base), but whether or not the social and political order can bear the impact of the rapidly declining economy.

It is clear that employing economic principles is imperative, because in the economy there is a thing called "inner logic". This is discernible by showing the relationship between the level of prices and the flow of money and goods. When we make such an evaluation of our economy, we should not be surprised to find a worrying condition. It is true that the flow of goods is greater than ever, but this simply cannot compete with the rapid buildup of the quantity of currency. For example, in 1965, when the production of rice rose by three per cent, it was still not possible to prevent price increases because the volume of money shot up by three hundred per cent during the same period.

Today, the government is paying a great deal of attention to economic problems. This is reflected in its numerous public statements on giving first priority to countering the current economic downturn. Now is the time to transform these intentions into actual remedies for the economy. To achieve this goal we need to intentionally employ economic principles. In other words, our economic problems should be solved by rational methods, irrespective of whether those methods are conventional or unconventional, or whether or not those methods are based on textbooks; what is important is that those methods should be rational, and are based on economic principles.

It is clear that this symposium on the economic sector is an invitation to the public to do some introspection on past economic policies and to reorient themselves to make way for future economic policies based entirely on economic principles.

NOTE

[1] My deliberations as moderator for the economic sector at the Symposium on the Awakening Spirit of '66: Exploring a New Path, at the University of Indonesia, 6–9 May 1966. This article is translated by Harry Bhaskara.

4

CONTRIBUTION OF IDEAS OF THE FACULTY OF ECONOMICS, UNIVERSITY OF INDONESIA TO THE SESSION OF THE PROVISIONAL PEOPLE'S CONSULTATIVE ASSEMBLY (MPRS) (1966)[1]

Introductory Note: *In 1966, the Provisional People's Consultative Assembly (MPRS) convened a session, which dealt with among other things an improved way of handling the Indonesian economy. [Note: At the time the People's Consultative Assembly (MPR) was not yet established. There was only the MPRS]. Some time before the session began, the Faculty of Economics, University of Indonesia (FEUI), prepared a contribution of ideas, which hopefully would help make the MPRS session a success. Inspired by a Symposium organized by the University of Indonesia and the Indonesian Scholars Action Front (KASI), which discussed* **"Exploring a New Path"**, *the contribution of ideas from FEUI was titled:* **The New Path in Economic, Financial and Development Policies**. *The contribution papers were distributed to different members of the MPRS at that time. Some portions were contained in articles published by newspapers. The Contribution of Ideas of the Faculty of Economics, University of Indonesia, was delivered to different members of the MPRS, which convened in 1966, and was prepared by Prof. Moh. Sadli, Prof. Ali Wardhana, Prof. Subroto, Prof. Emil Salim and myself, all of whom were professors in that department at that university.*

The Provisional People's Consultative Assembly of the Republic of Indonesia

Considering:

(a) that the deterioration of the Indonesian economy has reached such an extent that the sufferings of the Indonesian people are ever increasing;

(b) that the Indonesian people are determined to overcome the deterioration of the economy for the sake of executing the Message of the People's Sufferings;

(c) that the people are anxiously observing whether their aspirations for an improved economy and greater prosperity as reflected in the People's Three Demands will truly be fulfilled;

(d) that efforts to curtail and control the economic decline will only succeed if based on the good intent to conduct honest introspection within the framework of returning to the implementation of the 1945 Constitution in a genuine and consistent manner, as an objective guarantee to prevent the tendency toward the arbitrariness of a personality cult and toward the hostility of liberalist anarchism;

(e) that the first step leading to the improvement of the people's economy is a review of all the foundations of the existing economic, financial and development policies, with the aim of reaching an appropriate balance between efforts to be undertaken and objective to be achieved, which is an Indonesian Socialist society based on the Pancasila state philosophy;

(f) that a new path initiated by the younger generation, which adopts more equitable economic, financial and development policies and is imbued with the spirit of devotion to the upholding of justice, truth and promotion of welfare, will provide a breath of fresh air toward the relief of the people's sufferings.

In view of:

(a) The provisions and spirit of the 1945 Constitution in its entirety, and, in particular, articles 23, 27, 33 and 34;

(b) The Speech of the Deputy Prime Minister for Defense & Security Affairs/Minister and Commander of the Army on 17 June 1966 to welcome the Fourth General Session of the Provisional People's Consultative Assembly;

(c) The Economic Policy Statements by the Deputy Prime Minister for Economic, Financial and Development Affairs on 4 April and 12 April 1966;

(d) "Nawaksara", the Nine-Point Message of the President to the Provisional People's Consultative Assembly on 22 June 1966.

DECIDES:

To stipulate: THE DECREE ON THE NEW PATH IN ECONOMIC, FINANCIAL AND DEVELOPMENT POLICIES.

CHAPTER I
FOUNDATIONS OF ECONOMIC, FINANCIAL AND DEVELOPMENT POLICIES

Article 1

It is undeniable, based on current economic realities, such as the developments in prices, export decline, foreign exchange reserves, the conditions of roads and means of transportation, the rising costs of living, most notably for laborers and employees, the growing money supply, the mounting foreign debts, the downtrend in manpower performance, that the Indonesian economy has been undergoing a process of rapid deterioration, particularly over the last five years.

Article 2

Apart from severely damaging many of the core pillars of the economy, hyper inflation has also weakened the mental and spiritual bases of the nation. The disparity in standards of living between the people at large and a privileged group is growing wider. As a result, proper norms of living, such as diligence, modesty and honesty, are no longer appealing. Conversely, faith is weakening and the people have become easy prey for materialist and atheist teachings.

Article 3

The situation that makes the realization of a just and prosperous society based on Pancasila state philosophy even more of a distant dream has been brought about by two factors: (1) economic interests have always been overwhelmed by political interests, and (2) rational economic principles are always disregarded in dealing with economic problems.

Article 4

In fact, the main source of deterioration of the economy is the deviation from the genuine implementation of the 1945 Constitution. This is reflected in the absence of effective supervision by the people's representational and legislative organizations of the economic policies of the government. This immobilization of effective supervision has been coupled with the excessive cover-up of important economic information, including economic statistics.

Article 5

It is only proper to acknowledge that this situation, which is making the realization of the Message of People's Sufferings even more remote, has caused a major uprising in society as reflected in the declaration of the People's Three Demands. The Deputy Prime Minister for Defense & Security Affairs has very rightly stated that nobody knows better about the Message of People's Sufferings than the people themselves; certainly not the leaders who have made themselves impotent with myths.

Article 6

The awareness of the main causes of deterioration of the economy brings to mind the logical solution of returning to the genuine and consistent implementation of the 1945 Constitution, because the 1945 Constitution bears stipulations that enable and even mandate the effective supervision of government policies by the people through the people representational and legislative bodies.

Article 7

Effective supervision by the people, especially in the economic sector, must be done through the authority of the House of Representatives, which determines the state budget of income and expenditure, as well as approving the results of audits carried out by independent non-governmental agencies.

Article 8

With the restoration of the people's effective supervision over economic policies, in line with the essence of the People's Three Demands, the improvement of the people's economy will become the main priority, while the methods adopted to overcome this problem will be based on rational and realistic economic principles.

Article 9

In the meantime, for the sake of guaranteeing the continuity of efforts to surmount the deterioration of the economy and promote economic development, the meaning of "the revolution is not yet finished" must be clarified to alleviate political pressure on the economy and eliminate its influence as a pretext for economic waste.

Article 10

The Pancasila state ideology and the 1945 Constitution, particularly articles 23, 27, 33 and 34, must be consistently reflected in each and every economic policy as a basis for fostering the Indonesian economic system.

Article 11

The essence of this ideological basis will be the fostering of the Pancasila economic system that guarantees the progress of democratic economics and aims at creating a just and prosperous society with the blessing of Almighty God.

Article 12

Democratic economics will have these positive characteristics, namely:

(a) the economy is organized as a collective effort on a cooperative basis and therefore provides no room for class struggle;

(b) public resources and public funds are utilized through consultation with the people's representational and legislative institutions, which also supervise the disbursement and usage of the funds;

(c) all citizens are allowed the freedom to choose their own occupations and the right to employment, as well as to earn a decent living;

(d) property rights are based on the principle of public welfare and must not become a means of exploitation;

(e) the potential, initiative and creativity of all citizens can be fully developed within limits that pose no harm to public interests;

(f) any marginalized citizens must be guaranteed the right to social security.

Article 13

In democratic economics there will be no room for the following negative features:

(a) the system of free fight liberalism, which is conducive to the exploitation of human beings and other nations, and which, historically, has created and maintained the structural weaknesses in Indonesia's status in the world economy;

(b) the system of etatism, in which the state and its economic apparatus have full domination; dominating and eliminating the potential and creativity of economic units outside of the state sector;

(c) the phenomenon of monopolies, both private sector and state monopolies, which harm the public interest.

Article 14

The foundation for economic, financial and development policies in the operational sector will be the clear distinction between the program for stabilization and rehabilitation and the programme for development. At present, all endeavors will be devoted to the success of stabilization and rehabilitation, which means that the conscious putting off of the implementation of the development program.

CHAPTER II
NATIONAL PRIORITY SCALE

Article 15

The efforts to overcome the deterioration of the economy today, which will simultaneously enable large-scale economic development in the future, will occupy a top position in the entire national priority scale.

Article 16

On the national priority scale, domestic interests, particularly economic interests, will definitely receive priority over foreign policy interests.

Article 17

For long-term economic development, the priority scale will be as follows:

(a) agricultural sector,
(b) infrastructure sector, and
(c) industrial sector.

Article 18

The short-term programme will be composed of inflation control (economic stabilization) and production restoration (rehabilitation), with the following priority scale:

(a) the control of inflation,
(b) the fulfillment of food necessities,
(c) the rehabilitation of economic infrastructure,
(d) the promotion of export activities,
(e) the fulfillment of clothing necessities.

Article 19

With regard to economic projects, the main indicator on the priority scale will be projects that produce the goods and services most needed by the populace.

Article 20

The understanding of nation and character building will be brought back to a more appropriate meaning through efforts, such as successful economic development, that can give rise to national pride and in this way strengthen the sense of being a nation of character.

CHAPTER III
POTENTIAL ECONOMIC STRENGTHS

Article 21

Indonesia possesses potential economic strengths, which comprise:

(1) the potential and creativity of the people, and
(2) the availability of natural resources.

In order to turn the potential economic strengths into real economic strengths, natural resources will be exploited, processed and developed, while the people's creativity and capacity can be enhanced through education and training.

Article 22

Economic development will primarily mean the processing of potential economic strengths into real economic strengths through investment, application of technology, increased knowledge, enhancement of skills, and greater organizational and management capability. The main impediment in this case is the shortage of capital goods, the low level of technology and the lack of managerial and organizational personnel.

Article 23

The efforts to overcome the deterioration of the economy and the further development of economic potential will be based on the financial capacity of the Indonesian people themselves. However, this principle will not result in reluctance to utilize capital, technology and skills of foreign origin, as long as all the aid is truly dedicated to the economic interests of the people without causing dependence on other countries.

CHAPTER IV
ROLE OF GOVERNMENT

Article 24

The government will assume a positive role with the provisions and spirit of the 1945 Constitution as its orientation both in the period when efforts are undertaken to overcome the deterioration of the economy and in the period of economic development.

Article 25

Besides controlling and executing various economic activities itself, the government will be obliged to provide guidance for the private sector in carrying out maximum mobilization and development of the potential and creativity of the people.

Article 26

All the activities of the government, in controlling and executing undertakings in the public sector, as well as in providing guidance for the non-public or private sector, will constitute a harmonious whole covered and reflected in the short-term economic program (stabilization and rehabilitation) and the long-term program (development). From year to year these programmes will be reflected in the state budget of income and expenditure.

Article 27
The government will put greater emphasis on supervising the direction of economic activities rather than on controlling a maximum number of economic activities in the process of performing its role in the economic sector. Within this framework it is necessary to introduce the role of the bureaucracy in the system of supervision and to reduce the concentration of management in state owned enterprises.

Article 28
The principle of efficiency will serve as a guideline in the activities of the government in the economic sector, in the sense that any deviation from this principle will bring sanctions.

CHAPTER V
ROLE OF DOMESTIC PRIVATE SECTOR

Article 29
The definition of the domestic private sector will not be limited to large-scale or medium-scale enterprises only, but rather will also encompass the millions of small-scale producers engaged in agriculture, fishery, trade, and so forth, including farmers, fishermen, and small-scale traders. Cooperative organizations will also belong to the domestic private sector.

Article 30
Each of the groups in the domestic private sector will be obliged to develop the Indonesian economy. Pursuant to the government's duty to develop the potential and creativity of the people in the economic sector to the furthest extent possible, within the limits of the provisions and spirit of the 1945 Constitution, the domestic private sector will have the freedom to choose the business areas considered most relevant. The restriction of business activities in line with the 1945 Constitution will be separately stipulated.

Article 31

The growth of the private business sector will not ignore the principle of democratic economics as the core characteristic of the Pancasila economic system. Without ignoring the principle of efficiency, private business organizations will enable the growth of democratic economics and equity within their circles. For this purpose, supervision by the government apparatus is required. On the other hand, to ensure the steady expansion of its activities, the domestic private sector will be entitled to proper services and assistance from the government apparatus.

CHAPTER VI
ECONOMIC STABILIZATION AND REHABILITATION

Article 32

A consistent and truly operational programme for economic stabilization and rehabilitation will be promptly formulated and executed in order to surmount the problem of the deterioration of the economy.

Article 33

The main components of the operational programme for stabilization and rehabilitation will be:

(1) the physical plan, and
(2) the monetary plan.

Article 34

The programme for economic rehabilitation will be reflected in the physical plan, with the following main targets:

(1) the restoration and promotion of production capacity rates in the fields of food, exports and clothing,
(2) the restoration and promotion of economic infrastructure that supports the above fields.

Article 35

Minimum quantities of raw materials, spare parts, capital and so forth are required for the restoration of production capacity rates. These minimum requirements will be guaranteed in the Plan for Importation of Goods.

Article 36

Rehabilitation efforts will prioritize the restoration of production capacity rates in strategic or major sectors that can revive the potential and creativity of the people or can more speedily relieve the pressure of inflation.

Article 37

Bureaucratic impediments will be removed by eliminating the concentration of management in regions or production units without reducing the economic and political integrity of the nation in order to ensure the success of the rehabilitation efforts.

Article 38

The programme for economic stabilization will be reflected in the monetary plan, with the following main targets:

(1) the guarantee of rupiah and foreign exchange financing for the implementation of the physical plan,

(2) the control of inflation toward a price level and balance that are relatively stable and suited to the purchasing power of the people.

Article 39

In order to implement the programme for economic stabilization and rehabilitation, an integral policy will be introduced that encompasses the budgetary policy, the fiscal policy, the monetary policy, the price policy, the wage policy, the balance of payments policy, and so forth, along with institutional reform.

CHAPTER VII
STATE BUDGET OF INCOME AND EXPENDITURE

Article 40

In compiling the state budget of income and expenditure, attempts will be made to eliminate any existing deficit within a short period so that the main source of inflation can be removed.

Article 41

State income originating from direct and indirect taxes, as well as other sources of revenue, will be increased, and the collection and efficiency of utilization enhanced; all in accordance with the capacity of the people, and in line with a sense of equity and the state expenditure requirements.

Article 42
State expenditure will be directed toward (a) the fulfillment of the physical plan requirements, and (b) the control of inflation.

Article 43
Serious and effective economic measures will be promptly carried out through a drastic austerity programme to be applied consistently to civil, as well as military, expenditures.

Article 44
The monetary budget will be composed of:

  (a) the routine budget,
  (b) the development budget,
  (c) the foreign exchange budget, and
  (d) the credit budget.

In this way, the special budget will be abolished.

Article 45
The state budget of income and expenditure will be stipulated by law as required in the 1945 Constitution and its compilation will be finished before the year in which it comes into force.

Article 46
In auditing state assets, including state finances, the Financial Audit Agency will be obliged to intensify its measures according to its authority stipulated in the 1945 Constitution.

Article 47
Within the general framework of safeguarding state finances and supervision, as well as restructuring the currently confused banking system, a Banking Law and a Central Bank Law will be promptly introduced.

CHAPTER VIII
INTERNATIONAL ECONOMIC RELATIONS

Article 48
In managing international economic relations, the principle of national interests will always be prioritized. This means, among other things, that economic principles will be firmly adhered to in deciding on all foreign trade transactions.

Article 49
As exportation constitutes one of the main efforts to overcome the continued deterioration of the economy, promotion of exports from Indonesia will be a core focus. In the last several years, setbacks in exports have been due less to external factors than to domestic circumstances, including unbridled inflation, poor infrastructure, and increasingly muddled public administration. Therefore, the success in the promotion of exports depends on the successful adoption of appropriate measures domestically.

Article 50
The import policy will be directed toward the importation of goods that can directly promote production or that are in considerable need by the populace. In this context, the import policy will not be independent, but will become an integral part of the programme for economic stabilization and rehabilitation.

Article 51
The utilization of foreign exchange derived by the state from exports or from foreign loans will be done in a rational and honest manner. Measures will be taken to ensure that any wastage or deviations, as practiced in the past, will not recur, and that any relapse into such practices will be punished severely.

Article 52
The programme for stabilization and rehabilitation requires foreign loans. These loans will be justified only if they clearly constitute an integral part of the stabilization and rehabilitation plan as a whole.

Article 53

The amount of foreign loans that is considered acceptable will depend on the capacity for repayment in order to avoid increasing the already excessive burden of the public.

Article 54

In view of the limited capital domestically available compared with the need for national development, a foreign investment law will be promptly introduced.

Article 55

In spite of the fact that foreign loans and foreign capital can be utilized to surmount the deterioration of the economy and to implement economic development, the main focus will be overcoming all economic difficulties through the strengths of the nation in order to ensure that it will stand free from dependence on foreign financial resources.

Article 56

Efforts will be made promptly to enable Indonesia to reapply for membership of international economic institutions, such as the International Monetary Fund, the International Bank for Reconstruction and Development, the Asian Development Bank, and so forth.

CHAPTER IX
DEVELOPMENT PLANNING AND REGIONAL DEVELOPMENT

Article 57

As economic activities are today directed toward the realization of the stabilization and rehabilitation plan, the existing official plan for long-term development will be reviewed.

Article 58

In this context, all projects that lack economic feasibility or are not productive, along with all projects whose completion will exceed one year, will be promptly suspended.

Article 59

As long as the implementation of the stabilization and rehabilitation plan is not yet finished, the development of new projects that could disturb the implementation of the programme for stabilization and rehabilitation cannot and will not be justified.

Article 60

Economic development constitutes the development of economic potential (economic resources). Because the nation's prime economic potential can be found in the regions, national development will also mean regional development.

Article 61

High priority will be accorded to the rehabilitation and development of the nation's system of transportation for the sake of implementing regional development.

Article 62

Special attention will be given to the speedy introduction of provisions concerning:

- (a) the granting of extensive autonomy to regions,
- (b) the decentralization of the management of economic activities in the regions,
- (c) financial equilibrium between the central government and the regional administrations.

Article 63

In order to maintain harmony in national planning, regional development planning will be coordinated by the central government.

Article 64

In undertaking regional development, it will always be borne in mind that the economic growth in each region must eventually lead to national economic integration. This means, among other things, that all impediments disturbing the flow of goods between regions will be removed.

CHAPTER X
PREREQUISITE TO IMPLEMENTATION

Article 65
For the successful implementation of the various programmes, plans, policies and other things mentioned above, it is absolutely necessary to promptly establish and enforce a Cabinet for the Message of the People's Sufferings (AMPERA), which will be capable of realizing the programmes on which the people pin their faith and hope, and whose authority is based on the response of the people themselves, instead of the imposition of power by the ruling authorities.

Article 66
The AMPERA Cabinet is expected to constitute a harmonious team of experts, whose members are imbued with the spirit of Pancasila, and who will, as the guardians of AMPERA, work with the confidence of the people supporting them.

Article 67
The structure of the AMPERA Cabinet will be modest, efficient and effective, with clear descriptions of authority and responsibility, as well as rules of the game, that will be observed by all members.

Article 68
The ministers of the AMPERA Cabinet will be selected and appointed in line with the genuine essence of the 1945 Constitution, which means they must be capable of executing the government's authority without any protection from *"bapakisme"* (paternalism), and of assisting the president in determining executive policies without following the philosophy of *"nyumanggakaken bapak"* (unquestioning obedience), while closely cooperating with each other under the leadership of the president.

Article 69
In order to restore the people's confidence in the muddled economic apparatus, the entire state economic apparatus and the private business sector will be purged, in a consistent manner without discrimination, of the counter revolutionary elements of the Indonesian Communist Party (PKI)/September 30 Movement, along with their followers, and any

amoral and anti-social elements living in luxury at the expense of the people who have been made to suffer as a result of their actions.

CHAPTER XI
CONCLUSION

Article 70

All provisions, regulations and other stipulations that are incompatible with the provisions or essence and spirit of this decree will be declared null and void.

Stipulated in: Jakarta
On: 1966

LEADERSHIP
THE PROVISIONAL PEOPLE'S CONSULTATIVE ASSEMBLY
OF THE REPUBLIC OF INDONESIA

NOTE

[1] Contribution of Ideas of the Faculty of Economics, University of Indonesia, to the Session of the Provisional People's Consultative Assembly (MPRS), June–July 1966. This article is translated by Harry Bhaskara.

5

COMPARISON BETWEEN ARTICLES OF THE CONTRIBUTION OF IDEAS OF THE FACULTY OF ECONOMICS, UNIVERSITY OF INDONESIA TO THE DECISION OF THE PROVISIONAL CONSULTATIVE ASSEMBLY NO: XXIII/MPRS/1966 (1966)

Introductory Note: *The MPRS issued MPRS Decree No. XXIII/1966 on Economic, Financial and Development Policies. A comparison of the MPRS Decree and the Contribution of Thoughts from the Department of Economics, University of Indonesia (FEUI) shows that the various elements of those documents were in agreement. To assist the reader in contrasting the Decree and the FEUI Contribution, they have been placed side by side on the page with the Decree on the left hand side and the FEUI thoughts on the right.*

DECREE OF
THE PROVISIONAL PEOPLE'S CONSULTATIVE ASSEMBLY
OF THE REPUBLIC OF INDONESIA
No: XXIII/MPRS/1966
On
The Reform of the Foundations of Economic, Financial
and Development Policies

BY THE GRACE OF THE ALMIGHTY GOD
THE PROVISIONAL PEOPLE'S CONSULTATIVE ASSEMBLY
OF THE REPUBLIC OF INDONESIA

Considering:

(a) that in order to overcome the ever increasing sufferings of the people as a result of the deterioration of the Indonesian economy due to mismanagement, wastage, bureaucratic red tape, corruption and so forth, coupled with the counter-revolutionary rebellion of the September 30 movement by the Indonesian Communist Party and deviations from the 1945 Constitution, it is necessary to reform the policies in the economic, financial and development sectors;

(b) that the first step toward the improvement of the people's economy is a review of all the foundations of economic, financial and development policies for the purpose of creating the right balance between the efforts to be undertaken and the main target to be achieved; namely the Indonesian socialist society based on the Pancasila state philosophy;

(c) that with the awareness of the essence of the main source of deterioration of the economy, for the implementation of point b above, it is necessary to return to the genuine and consistent implementation of the 1945 Constitution, because the 1945 Constitution bears stipulations and objective guarantees that enable and even make mandatory the effective supervision by the people over government policies through the people's representational and legislative institutions.

In view of:

(a) The provisions and spirit of the 1945 Constitution, in its entirety, as well as articles 23, 27, 33 and 34 in particular;

(b) The President's "Nawaksara" (Nine-Point) Message to the Provisional People's Consultative Assembly on 22 June 1966, along with all its appendices;

(c) The contents and spirit of the segments of the Economic Declaration (Dekon) that are capable of addressing the People's Three Demands and the Message of People's Sufferings;

(d) The Memorandum of the Gotong Royong House of Representatives on Basic Thoughts toward the Solution of Difficulties in Economic, Financial and Development Sectors dated 9 June 1966;

(e) The function of the Provisional People's Consultative Assembly (MPRS) as contained in article 1 of the Internal Rule (MPRS Decree No. 1/MPRS/1966).

Taking into account:

Consultations in the meetings of the Provisional People's Consultative Assembly from 20 June to 5 July 1966.

DECIDES:

To stipulate: THE DECREE ON THE REFORM OF FOUNDATIONS OF ECONOMIC, FINANCIAL AND DEVELOPMENT POLICIES

CHAPTER I
FOUNDATIONS OF ECONOMIC, FINANCIAL AND DEVELOPMENT POLICIES

Article 1

With the awareness of the fact that the essence of the main source of rapid deterioration of the Indonesian economy in the last several years has been the deviation from the genuine implementation of the 1945 Constitution, as reflected in the absence of effective supervision by the people's representational and legislative institutions over

the economic policies of the government and the constant lack of harmony between political interests and economic interests, as well as the disregard for rational economic principles in dealing with economic problems, the solution will constitute a return to the implementation of the 1945 Constitution in a genuine and consistent manner.

Article 2[1]

Pursuant to the provisions in the 1945 Constitution, effective supervision by the people over the economic policies of the government will be conducted through the authority of the House of Representatives in determining the state budget of income and expenditure, as well as the authority of financial auditing by a non-governmental agency that reports all audit results to the House of Representatives.

Article 3[2]

With the restoration of the people's effective supervision over economic policies, in line with the essence of the People's Three Demands, while keeping in mind the importance of development in the spiritual

[1] Contribution of Ideas of the Faculty of Economics, University of Indonesia (FEUI), Article 7

Effective supervision by the people of the economic policies of the government, especially in the economic sector, is conducted through the authority of the House of Representatives with the determining of the state budget of income and expenditure, as well as through the authority of a non-governmental agency for financial auditing reports, which reports the results of all audits directly to the House of Representatives.

[2] Contribution of Ideas from FEUI, Article 8

With the restoration of the people's effective supervision over economic policies, in line with the essence of the People's Three Demands, the improvement of the people's economy should receive priority

and religious sector, the improvement of the people's economy will receive priority over other national issues, while the methods adopted to resolve the economic problems will be based on rational and realistic economic principles.

Article 4[3]

The ideological bases for fostering the Indonesian economic system, which must be reflected in any and all economic policies, will be Pancasila and the 1945 Constitution, particularly articles 23, 27, 33 and 34, along with their elucidation.

Article 5[4]

The essence of this ideological basis will be the fostering of the guided economic system based on Pancasila that guarantees the progress of democratic economics and aims at creating a just and prosperous society with the blessing of Almighty God.

Article 6[5]

Democratic economics will have the following positive characteristics:

(a) the economy is organized as a collective effort on the basis of cooperative principles and, therefore,

over national issues, while the methods adopted to resolve these issues should be based on rational and realistic economic principles.

[3] Contribution of Ideas from FEUI, Article 10

The ideological bases for fostering the Indonesian economic system that must be reflected in any and all economic policies are Pancasila and the 1945 Constitution, particularly articles 23, 27, 33 and 34, along with their elucidation

[4] Contribution of Ideas from FEUI, Article 11

The essence of these ideological bases is the fostering of the Pancasila economic system that guarantees the progress of equitable democratic economics and aims at creating a just and prosperous society with the blessing of the Almighty God.

[5] Contribution of Ideas from FEUI, Article 12

Democratic economics has the following positive characteristics:

(a) the economy is organized as a collective effort on a cooperative basis and therefore leaves no room for class struggle;

(b) public resources and public funds are utilized through consultation with the people's representational and legislative institutions,

will have no relation to the ideological structure of class struggle;

(b) public resources and public funds are utilized through consultation with the people's representational and legislative institutions, which also supervise the utilization of those resources and funds;

(c) branches of production that are important to the state and affect the livelihood of the majority of the populace are controlled by the state;

(d) all citizens are allowed the freedom to choose their occupations and the right to employment, as well as a decent living;

(e) the right to property is recognized for the sake of public welfare and, therefore, must not be used as a means of human exploitation;

(f) the potential, initiatives and creativity of all citizens can be fully developed within limits that pose no harm to public interests; and

(g) poor and neglected children have the right to social welfare security.

while the supervision over their utilization is also conducted by the people's representational and legislative institutions;

(c) all citizens are allowed the freedom to choose their occupations and the right to employment as well as a decent living;

(d) property rights are to be utilized for public welfare and must not become a means of human exploitation;

(e) the potential, initiatives and creativity of all citizens can be fully developed within limits that pose no harm to public interests;

(f) all citizens, particularly the marginalized, have the right to social security.

Article 7[6]

In democratic economics there will be no room for the following negative features:

(a) the system of free fight liberalism, which is conducive to the exploitation of human beings and other nations, and which, historically, has created and maintained the structural weaknesses in Indonesia's status in the world economy;

(b) the system of etatism, in which the state and its economic apparatus have full domination; dominating and eliminating the potential and creativity of economic units outside of the state sector;

(c) the phenomenon of monopolies, both private sector and state monopolies, which harm the public interest.

[6] Contribution of Ideas from FEUI, Article 13

In democratic economics there is no room for the following negative features:

(a) the system of free fight liberalism, which is conducive to the exploitation of human beings and other nations, and which, historically, has created and maintained the structural weaknesses in Indonesia's status in the world economy;

(b) the system of etatism, in which the state and its economic apparatus have full domination; dominating and eliminating the potential and creativity of economic units outside of the state sector;

(c) the phenomenon of monopolies, both private sector and state monopolies, which harm the public interests.

CHAPTER II
POTENTIAL ECONOMIC STRENGTHS

Article 8

Indonesia possesses potential economic strengths, which comprise:

(1) the potential and creativity of the people, and
(2) existing natural resources.

In order to turn these potential economic strengths into real economic strengths, natural resources will be exploited, processed and developed, while the people's creativity and capacity can be enhanced through education and training.

Article 9

Economic development will primarily mean the processing of potential economic strengths into real economic strengths through investment, the application of technology, increased knowledge, the enhancement of skills, and the facilitation of greater organizational and management capability.

Article 10

The efforts to overcome the deterioration of the economy and to further develop the nation's economic potential will be based on the financial and other capacities of the Indonesian people. However, this principle will not result in reluctance to utilize foreign capital, technology and skill, as long as all the aid is truly dedicated to the economic

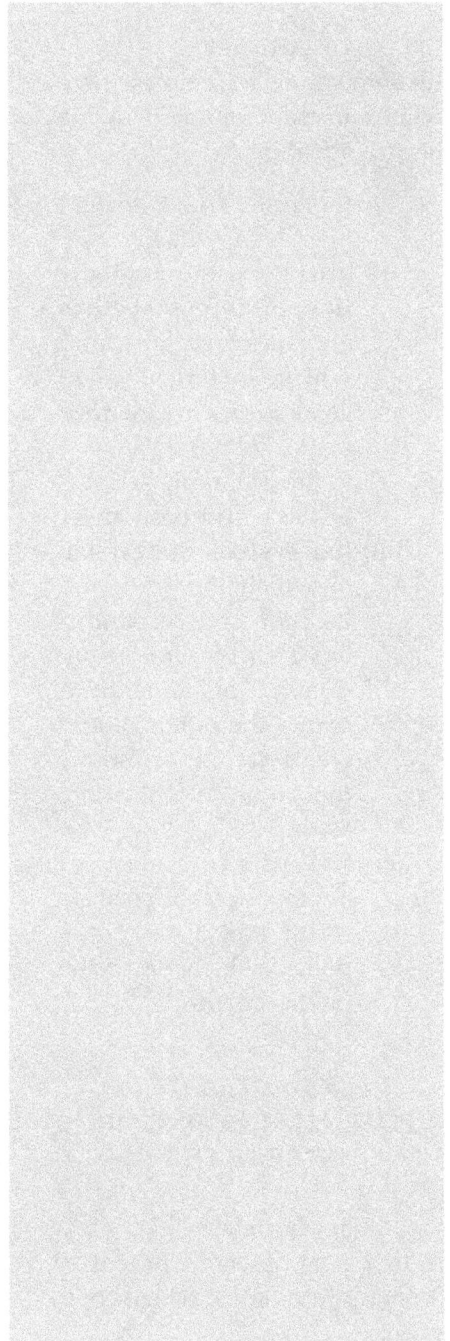

interests of the people without causing dependence on other countries.

CHAPTER III
NATIONAL PRIORITY SCALE

1. GENERAL

Article 11[7]

The efforts to overcome the deterioration of the economy today, which are expected to simultaneously enable large-scale economic development in the future, will occupy a top position in the overall national priority scale, so that domestic interests, particularly economic interests, will definitely receive priority over foreign policy interests.

Article 12

With regard to economic sector projects, the main indicator on the priority scale will be projects that produce the goods and services most needed by the populace.

2. SHORT-TERM DEVELOPMENT

Article 13[8]

In the operational sector, the foundation for economic, financial

[7] Contribution of Ideas from FEUI, Article 15

The efforts to overcome the deterioration of the economy today, which will at the same time enable large-scale economic development in the future, should occupy a top position on the entire national priority scale.

[8] Contribution of Ideas from FEUI, Article 14

In the sector of operations, the foundation for economic, financial and development policies is a clear distinction between the programme for stabilization and rehabilitation, and the programme for development. At present, all potential and endeavors must be devoted to the success of the stabilization and rehabilitation programmes, which means that the implementation of the development programme should be consciously put off.

and development policies will be a clear distinction between the programme for stabilization and rehabilitation and the programme for development. At present, all exiting potentials and concrete endeavors will be devoted entirely to the success of the stabilization and rehabilitation programme.

Article 14
Economic development will be synchronized effectively with the annual expansion of available manpower.

Article 15[9]
The short-term programme will be composed of inflation control (economic stabilization) and production restoration (rehabilitation), with the following priority scale:

(a) the control of inflation,
(b) the fulfillment of food necessities,
(c) the rehabilitation of economic infrastructure,
(d) the promotion of export activities,
(e) the fulfillment of clothing necessities.

Article 16
This short-term programme will be preceded by a rescue programme

[9] Contribution of Ideas from FEUI, Article 18

The short-term programme is composed of inflation control (economic stabilization) and production restoration (rehabilitation), with the following priority scale:

(a) the control of inflation,
(b) the fulfillment of food necessities,
(c) the rehabilitation of economic infrastructure,
(d) the promotion of export activities,
(e) the fulfillment of clothing necessities.

with the target of promptly surmounting the stagnation and disruption of food production, exports, clothing supply and economic infrastructure that supports the above fields by providing raw materials, spare parts and capital in minimum but adequate quantities.

Article 17

In order to surmount the deterioration of the economy, a consistent and solid operational programme for economic stabilization and rehabilitation will be promptly formulated and executed.

Article 18[10]

The main components of the operational programme for stabilization and rehabilitation will be:

(1) the physical plan, and
(2) the monetary plan.

Article 19[11]

The programme for economic rehabilitation will be reflected in the physical plan, with the following main targets:

(1) the restoration and promotion of production capacity rates in the fields of food, exportation and clothing,

[10] Contribution of Ideas from FEUI, Article 33

The main components of the operational programme for stabilization and rehabilitation are:

(1) the physical plan, and
(2) the monetary plan.

[11] Contribution of Ideas from FEUI, Article 34

The programme for economic rehabilitation is to be reflected in the physical plan, with the following main targets:

(1) the restoration and promotion of production capacity in the fields of food, export and clothing,

(2) the restoration and promotion of economic infrastructure that supports the above fields.

Article 20[12]

Minimum but adequate quantities of raw materials, spare parts, capital and so forth are required for the restoration of production capacity rates. The minimum requirements will be guaranteed in the import policy to function as an integral part of the programme for economic stabilization and rehabilitation.

Article 21[13]

Rehabilitation efforts will prioritize the restoration of production capacity rates in strategic or major sectors that can revive the potential and creativity of the people or can most speedily relieve the pressure of inflation.

Article 22[14]

In order to ensure the success of the rehabilitation efforts, all bureaucratic impediments will be eradicated through the decentralization of management of the regions, or production units, without diminishing the nation's economic and political integrity.

[12] Contribution of Ideas from FEUI, Article 35

Minimum quantities of raw materials, spare parts, capital and so forth are required for the restoration of the production capacity rates. The minimum requirements should be guaranteed in the Plan for the Importation of Goods.

[13] Contribution of Ideas from FEUI, Article 36

Rehabilitation efforts should prioritize the restoration of production capacity rates in major or strategic sectors that can revive the potential and creativity of the people, or can more speedily relieve the pressure of inflation.

[14] Contribution of Ideas from FEUI, Article 37

To ensure the success of rehabilitation efforts, bureaucratic impediments must be fully eradicated, through, among other things, the decentralization of management in regions, or production units, without reducing the nation's economic and political integrity.

Article 23[15]

The programme for economic stabilization will be reflected in the monetary plan, with the following main targets:

(1) the guarantee of rupiah and foreign exchange financing for the implementation of the physical plan,

(2) the control of inflation toward a price level and balance that are relatively stable and suited to the purchasing power of the people.

Article 24[16]

In order to implement the programme for economic stabilization and rehabilitation, an integral policy will be introduced, which encompasses budgetary policy, fiscal policy, monetary policy, price policy, wage policy, and the balance of payments policy, as well as institutional reform.

3. LONG-TERM DEVELOPMENT

Article 25[17]

The priority scale for long-term economic development will be arranged as follows:

(a) the sector of agriculture,

[15] Contribution of Ideas from FEUI, Article 38

The programme for economic stabilization is to be reflected in the monetary plan, with the following main targets:

(1) the guarantee of rupiah and foreign exchange financing for the implementation of the physical plan,

(2) the control of inflation toward a price level and balance that are relatively stable and suited to the purchasing power of the people.

[16] Contribution of Ideas from FEUI, Article 39

In order to implement the programme for economic stabilization and rehabilitation, an integral policy should be introduced, which encompasses the budgetary policy, the fiscal policy, the monetary policy, the price policy, the wage policy, the balance of payments policy, and so forth, along with institutional reform.

[17] Contribution of Ideas from FEUI, Article 17

For long-term economic development the priority scale is to be arranged as follows:

(a) the sector of agriculture,

(b) the sector of infrastructure,
(c) the sector of industry/ mining and oil.

(b) the sector of infrastructure,
(c) the sector of industry.

Article 26
Because economic activities are today directed toward the realization of the stabilization and rehabilitation plan, the remainder of the initial eight-year Plan for Overall National Development will be converted into the long-term plan as stipulated in Article 25.

Article 27
In this context, all wasteful or economically unfeasible or unproductive projects will be promptly suspended.

Article 28
Up to the completion of the stabilization and rehabilitation plan, the development of new projects that could disturb the implementation of this programme will not be justified.

4. REGIONAL DEVELOPMENT AND RURAL COMMUNITY DEVELOPMENT

Article 29
Economic development constitutes the development of

economic potential (economic resources). Because this economic potential can be found in the regions, national development will be considered identical with regional development.

Article 30
The rehabilitation and improvement of the communications system (including the construction of the Trans Sumatra Highway) and the development of rural communities will be prioritized for the sake of regional development.

Article 31
The implementation of the transmigration programme will be intensified and land reform will be expedited.

Article 32
Special attention will be given to the speedy implementation of provisions concerning:

(a) the granting of extensive autonomy to regions,
(b) the decentralization of the management of economic activities in the regions through coordination with regional administrations,
(c) the financial equilibrium between the central

government and the regional administration.

Article 33
In order to maintain harmony in national planning, regional development and rural community development planning will be coordinated by the central government.

Article 34
In undertaking regional development, it will always be borne in mind that economic growth in each region is required to achieve national economic integration. This means, among other things, that all impediments disturbing the flow of goods between regions must and will be removed.

Article 35
The implementation of the three-year development pattern in regions can be continued as long as it does not run counter to the provisions in this Decree.

5. DEVELOPMENT OF WEST IRIAN

Article 36
Special attention will be paid to the development of the West Irian region in all sectors in order to promote the standard of living

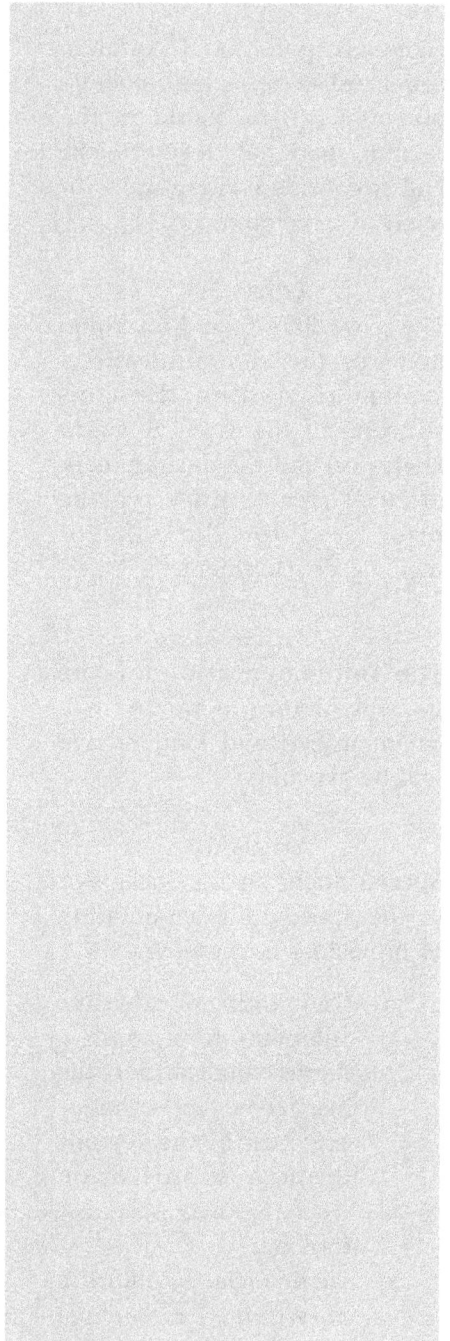

there and that region's harmony with the other regions.

CHAPTER IV
ROLE OF GOVERNMENT

Article 37[18]

The government will assume a positive role in line with the provisions and spirit of the 1945 Constitution both in the period when efforts are undertaken to overcome the deterioration of the economy and in the period of economic development.

Article 38[19]

Besides controlling and executing various economic activities itself, the government will be obliged to provide guidance for the non-government sector and facilitate the maximum mobilization and development of the potential and creativity of the people.

Article 39[20]

All the activities of the government for the control and execution of undertakings in the public sector, as well as in providing guidance for the non-public sector, will constitute a harmonious whole covered and reflected in the short-term economic programme (stabilization and rehabilitation) and the long-term programme

[18]   Contribution of Ideas from FEUI, Article 24

The government will assume a positive role with the provisions and spirit of the 1945 Constitution as its orientation both in the period when efforts are undertaken to overcome the deterioration of the economy and in the period of economic development.

[19]   Contribution of Ideas from FEUI, Article 25

Besides controlling and executing various economic activities itself, the government is obliged to provide guidance for the non-governmental sector and to facilitate the maximum mobilization and development of the potential and creativity of the people.

[20]   Contribution of Ideas from FEUI, Article 26

All the activities of the government, in controlling and executing undertakings in the public sector, as well as in providing guidance for the non-public or private sector, will constitute a harmonious whole covered and reflected in the short-term economic programme (stabilization and rehabilitation)

(development). From year to year these programmes will be reflected in the state budget of income and expenditure.

Article 40[21]

In performing its role in the economic sector, the government will put greater emphasis on supervising the direction of economic activities rather than on controlling the maximum number of economic activities. Within this framework it is necessary to streamline the supervision system of the bureaucracy and to decentralize the management of state owned enterprises.

Article 41[22]

The principle of efficiency will serve as a guideline in the activities of the government in the economic sector, in the sense that any deviation from this principle will be subjected to punitive measures.

CHAPTER V
ROLE OF COOPERATIVES

Article 42

Cooperatives constitute an important and appropriate apparatus in the organizational structure of the Indonesian economy set up on a cooperative

and the long-term programme (development). From year to year these programmes will be reflected in the state budget of income and expenditure.

[21] Contribution of Ideas from FEUI, Article 27

The government will put greater emphasis on supervising the direction of economic activities rather than on controlling a maximum number of economic activities in the process of performing its role in the economic sector. Within this framework it is necessary to introduce the role of the bureaucracy in the system of supervision and to reduce the concentration of management in state owned enterprises.

[22] Contribution of Ideas from FEUI, Article 28

The principle of efficiency should serve as a guideline in the activities of the government in the economic sector, in the sense that any deviation from this principle will result in punitive measures.

basis, and will function as forums of struggle and protection, particularly for the interests of the common people.

Article 43

Cooperatives execute the duties of providing services and engagement in production, as well involvement in other economic sectors, and will be empowered through the implementation of Article 33 of the 1945 Constitution. The government will be obliged to provide guidance for and conduct supervision over, as well as providing facilities and protection, to cooperatives. For this purpose it is necessary to formulate provisions stipulated by law, in the form of laws governing Cooperatives and Domestic Private and State-owned Enterprises.

CHAPTER VI
ROLE OF THE DOMESTIC PRIVATE SECTOR

Article 44

Pursuant to the government's duty to develop the potential and creativity of the people in the economic sector to the farthest extent possible, within limits of the provisions and spirit of the 1945 Constitution, the domestic private sector will have the freedom to determine relevant business areas, as long as that does not affect the livelihood of the majority of the people, and is not strategic in nature.

Article 45[23]

Each of the groups in the domestic private sector, with the definitions and fields of activities of the groups being stipulated by law, will be obliged to develop the Indonesian economy.

Article 46[24]

The growth of the private business sector will not deviate from the principle of equitable democratic economics as the core characteristic of the guided economic system based on Pancasila. Without denying the principles of efficiency, private business organizations will enable the expansion of democratic economic practices within their circles. For this purpose, supervision by the government apparatus is required. On the other hand, the domestic private sector, for the sake of the expansion of its activities, will be entitled to proper service, protection and

[23] Contribution of Ideas from FEUI, Article 30

Each of the groups in the domestic private sector is obliged to develop the Indonesian economy. Pursuant to the government's duty to develop the potential and creativity of the people in the economic sector to the farthest extent possible, within limits of the provisions and spirit of the 1945 Constitution, the domestic private sector should have the freedom to determine relevant business areas. Any restriction of business activities on the basis of the 1945 Constitution should be separately stipulated.

[24] Contribution of Ideas from FEUI, Article 31

The growth of the private business sector must not run counter to the principle of democratic economics as the core characteristic of the Pancasila economic system. Without denying the principle of efficiency, private business organizations should enable the

assistance from the government apparatus. In this context, the existence of a private sector business forum is necessary.

CHAPTER VII
FINANCIAL POLICY

Article 47[25]
In the compiling of the state budget of income and expenditure, attempts will be made to eliminate the deficit within a short period so that the main source of inflation can be removed.

Article 48
A sound balance between material, spiritual and political expenses will be reflected in the formulation of the budget of expenditure.

Article 49[26]
State income originating from direct and indirect taxes, as well as other sources of revenue (particularly from state owned enterprises), will be increased and their collection intensified efficiently, in line with the capacity of the people, within a sense of justice and in accordance with the need for state expenditure.

expansion democratic economics practices within their circles. For this purpose, supervision by the government apparatus is required. On the other hand, to ensure the growth of its activities, the domestic private sector should be entitled to proper service and assistance from the government apparatus.

[25] Contribution of Ideas from FEUI, Article 40
In compiling the state budget of income and expenditure, attempts should be made to eradicate any deficit within a short period so that the main source of inflation can be removed.

[26] Contribution of Ideas from FEUI, Article 41
State income originating from direct and indirect taxes, as well as other sources of revenue, will be increased, and the collection and efficiency of utilization enhanced; all in accordance with the capacity of the people, and in line with a sense of equity and the state expenditure requirements.

Article 50[27]

State expenditure will be directed toward:

(a) the fulfillment of physical plan requirements, and
(b) the control of inflation.

Article 51[28]

Serious and effective economic measures will be promptly carried out through a drastic austerity program applied consistently to civil as well as military expenses.

Article 52[29]

The monetary budget will be composed of only:

(a) the routine budget,
(b) the development budget,
(c) the foreign exchange budget,
(d) the credit budget.

In this way, the special budget will be abolished and the projects thus far financed with that budget will be integrated into the routine, development and foreign exchange budgets.

Article 53[30]

The state budget of income and expenditure will be stipulated by law as required in the 1945 Constitution and its compilation

[27] Contribution of Ideas from FEUI, Article 42

State expenditure is to be directed toward:

(a) the fulfillment of physical plan requirements, and
(b) the control of inflation.

[28] Contribution of Ideas from FEUI, Article 43

Serious and effective economic measures will be promptly carried out through a drastic austerity programme to be applied consistently to civil, as well as military, expenditures.

[29] Contribution of Ideas from FEUI, Article 44

The monetary budget is to be composed of only:

(a) the routine budget,
(b) the development budget,
(c) the foreign exchange budget,
(d) the credit budget

In this way, the special budget will be abolished.

[30] Contribution of Ideas from FEUI, Article 45

The state budget of income and expenditure is to be stipulated by law as required in the 1945 Constitution, and its compilation will be finished before the year in which it is to come into force.

Article 54[31]

In auditing state assets, including state finances, the Financial Audit Agency will be obliged to intensify its measures according to the authority as stipulated in the 1945 Constitution.

Article 55

A Banking Law and a Central Bank Law will be promptly introduced within the framework of safeguarding state finances in general, and of supervising, as well as restructuring, the banking system in particular.

CHAPTER VIII
INTERNATIONAL
ECONOMIC RELATIONS

Article 56[32]

Domestic interests will always receive priority in the management of international economic relations in line with a free and active foreign policy. This means, among other things, that economic principles will be firmly adhered to in deciding on foreign trade transactions.

should be finished before the year in which it is to come into force.

[31] Contribution of Ideas from FEUI, Article 46

In auditing state assets, including state finances, the Financial Audit Agency will be obliged to intensify its measures according to the authority as stipulated in the 1945 Constitution.

[32] Contribution of Ideas from FEUI, Article 48

In managing international economic relations, the principle of national interests will always be prioritized. This means, among other things, that economic principles will be firmly adhered to in deciding on all foreign trade transactions.

Article 57[33]

As exportation of goods and services constitutes one of the main efforts to overcome the deterioration of the economy, all attempts will be sought to promote Indonesian exports.

Article 58[34]

The import policy will be directed toward the importation of goods that can directly promote production or that are required by the public in line with the plan for imports.

Article 59

The utilization of state foreign exchange derived from exports or from foreign loans will be done in a rational and honest manner.

Article 60[35]

The programme for stabilization and rehabilitation requires foreign loans. These loans will only be justified if they really constitute an integral part of the stabilization and rehabilitation plan as a whole.

[33] Contribution of Ideas from FEUI, Article 49

As exportation constitutes one of the main efforts to overcome the continued deterioration of the economy, promotion of exports from Indonesia will be a core focus. In the last several years, setbacks in exports have been due less to external factors than to domestic circumstances, including unbridled inflation, poor infrastructure, and increasingly muddled public administration. Therefore, the success in the promotion of exports depends on the successful adoption of appropriate measures domestically.

[34] Contribution of Ideas from FEUI, Article 50

The import policy will be directed toward the importation of goods that can directly promote production or that are in considerable need by the populace. In this context, the import policy will not be independent, but will become an integral part of the programme for economic stabilization and rehabilitation.

[35] Contribution of Ideas from FEUI, Article 52

The programme for stabilization and rehabilitation requires foreign loans. These loans should only be justified if they constitute an integral part of the stabilization and rehabilitation plan as a whole.

Article 61[36]

The acceptable total of foreign loans that can be received will depend on the capacity for repayment in the future in line with not increasing the already excessive burden of the people.

Article 62[37]

In view of the limited capital domestically available compared with the need for national development, a foreign investment law, including coverage of resident foreign capital, will be promptly introduced.

Article 63

Government Regulation No.10/1959 will be renewed and elevated to the status of law.

Article 64[38]

Although foreign loans and foreign capital (including production sharing) can be utilized to surmount deterioration of the economy and implement economic development, the priority will be to leverage the nation's determination to overcome economic difficulties to free itself from foreign dependence through its own inherent strengths.

[36] Contribution of Ideas from FEUI, Article 53

The amount of foreign loans that is considered acceptable will depend on the capacity for repayment in order to avoid increasing the already excessive burden of the public.

[37] Contribution of Ideas from FEUI, Article 54

In view of the limited capital domestically available compared with the need for national development, a foreign investment law should be promptly introduced.

[38] Contribution of Ideas from FEUI, Article 55

In spite of the fact that foreign loans and foreign capital can be utilized to surmount deterioration of the economy and implement economic development, there should be the determination to overcome economic difficulties with the strengths of the nation and to free the nation from foreign dependence.

Article 65[39]

Efforts will be promptly made to enable Indonesia to reapply for membership of international economic institutions, such as the International Monetary Fund, the International Bank for Reconstruction and Development, and so forth.

CHAPTER IX
PREREQUISITE TO IMPLEMENTATION

Article 66[40]

For the successful implementation of the various programmes, plans, policies and other things mentioned above, it is necessary to improve the structure of the government, whose authority is based on the mandate of the people and their aspirations, so that it will be more capable of realizing the programmes on which the people pin their faith and hopes.

Article 67[41]

The governmental structure mentioned above will constitute a harmonious whole made up of teams, whose members are experts imbued with the spirit of Pancasila and functioning as guardians of the Message of

[39]   Contribution of Ideas from FEUI, Article 56

Efforts should be promptly made to enable Indonesia to reapply for membership of international economic institutions, such as the International Monetary Fund, the International Bank for Reconstruction and Development, the Asian Development Bank, and so forth.

[40]   Contribution of Ideas from FEUI, Article 65

For the successful implementation of the various programmes, plans, policies and other things mentioned above, it is absolutely necessary to promptly establish and enforce a Cabinet for the Message of the People's Sufferings (AMPERA), which will be capable of realizing the programmes on which the people pin their faith and hope, and whose authority is based on the response of the people themselves, instead of the imposition of power by the ruling authorities.

[41]   Contribution of Ideas from FEUI, Article 66

The AMPERA Cabinet is expected to constitute a harmonious team of experts, whose members are imbued with the spirit of Pancasila,

People's Sufferings (Ampera) on the basis of the trust and support of the people.

Article 68[42]

The said governmental structure will be modest, efficient and effective, with clear descriptions of authority and responsibility.

Article 69[43]

Under this governmental structure, all ministers will be appointed and placed in line with the genuine essence of the 1945 Constitution.

CHAPTER X
CONCLUSION

Article 70[44]

All provisions, regulations and other stipulations that are incompatible with the provisions or essence and spirit of this decree will be declared null and void.

Article 71

The Gotong Royong House of Representatives and the government will execute the provisions in this Decree.

and who will, as the guardians of AMPERA, work with the confidence of the people supporting them.

[42] Contribution of Ideas from FEUI, Article 67

The structure of the AMPERA Cabinet should be modest, efficient and effective, with clear descriptions of authority and responsibility, as well as rules of the game to be observed by all members.

[43] Contribution of Ideas from FEUI, Article 68

The ministers of the AMPERA Cabinet will be selected and appointed in line with the genuine essence of the 1945 Constitution, which means they must be capable of executing the government's authority without any protection from "bapakisme" (paternalism), and of assisting the president in determining executive policies without following the philosophy of "nyumanggakaken bapak" (unquestioning obedience), while closely cooperating with each other under the leadership of the president.

[44] Contribution of Ideas from FEUI, Article 70

All provisions, regulations and other stipulations that are incompatible with the provisions or essence and spirit of this decree are to be declared null and void.

Stipulated in: Jakarta
On: 5 July 1966

THE PROVISIONAL PEOPLE'S CONSULTATIVE ASSEMBLY
OF THE REPUBLIC OF INDONESIA

Chairman,
signature
(Dr. A.H. Nasution)
General

Deputy Chairman,   Deputy Chairman,
signature   signature
(Osa Maliki)   (H.M. Subchan Z.E.)

Deputy Chairman,   Deputy Chairman,
signature   signature
(M. Siregar)   (Mashudi D.)
Brigadier   General

Copied in accordance with the original
Administrator, MPRS General Assembly IV
signature
(Wiluyo Puspo Yudo)
Major General

6

THE ESSENCE AND CONSEQUENCES OF MPRS DECREE NO. XXIII, YEAR 1966, ON ECONOMIC, FINANCIAL AND DEVELOPMENT MATTERS (1966)[1]

Introductory Note: *One of the major events of 1966 was the Session of the Provisional People's Consultative Assembly (MPRS), which has come up with a decision for the sector of the economy titled MPRS Decree No. XXIII: "Policy Foundations for the Reform of Economic, Financial and Development Fundamentals." Every MPR or MPRS (Provisional/Interim MPR) Decree is of great significance and must be fully understood by the entire society, especially MPRS Decree No. XXIII, which, essentially, is a correction of the way the economy had been handled in the previous period that has been causing suffering for the community for years. This 10 July 1966 article is an attempt to explain the "Essence and Consequences" of MPRS Decree No. XXII as announced on 5 July 1966.*

The description below is aimed at examining the essence and consequences of **MPRS Decree No. XXII, dated 5 July 1966** in the areas of economics, finance and development. To examine the essence of a decree means to put the main matters in it under a spotlight. To discuss the consequence of a decree, meanwhile, is to describe in detail the steps that must be taken to implement it.

A proper understanding of the essence and consequences of this MPRS decree is needed for the implementation of the decree itself. However, this understanding is especially needed to ensure effective supervision and control by the People over the implementation of the decree.

No matter how good a decree may be, it will be meaningless unless its implementation becomes a reality. Lack of proper implementation would lead to greater disappointment. On the other hand, not infrequently, steps toward implementation are taken that are actually not compatible with the substance and spirit of the decree itself. It may even happen that these steps, justified by various pretexts, turn out to be deviations from the decree.

It is now the obligation of the Indonesian People to sharply oversee the application and implementation of the MPRS decree in the field of economics so that its implementation will really conform to the essence of the decree itself.

Content and Systematic Organization

The Fourth General Assembly of the MPRS in July 1966 has produced a comprehensive decree in the encompassing field of economics and the economy: MPRS Decree No. XXIII/MPRS/1966: "POLICY FOUNDATIONS FOR THE REFORM OF ECONOMIC, FINANCIAL AND DEVELOPMENT FUNDAMENTALS".

This Decree comprises 71 articles and is divided into 10 chapters as follows: I. Fundamentals and Principles of Economic, Financial and Development Policies; II. Potential Economic Power; III. National Priority Scale (made up of: 1. General; 2 Short-Term Development; 3. Long-Term Development; 4. Development of Regions and Rural Communities; 5. Development of West Irian); IV. Role of the Government; V. Role of Cooperatives; VI. Role of National Private Circles; VII. Policies on Financing; VIII. International Economic Relations; IX. Pre-conditions for Implementation; X. Conclusion.

In principle, this decree covers two major things: the ideal fundamentals and operational matters. The ideal fundamentals cover the main things that must always be strongly upheld in determining economic policies. This decree emphasizes the need to strongly abide by the principle of a democratic economy or democratic economy within the context of returning to the implementation of the 1945 Constitution in its pure form and in a consequential manner. As a matter of fact, democratic economy is the principle constituting the essence of the provisions on the economy in the 1945 Constitution, as already explained in the Elucidation of the Constitution. However, for several years this principle has, deliberately or otherwise, been pushed back and replaced by other ideological fundamentals, so that it has practically become forgotten.

The return to the upholding of the principle of a democratic economy will bring a number of consequences, among others, the necessity for the people to monitor, supervise and control the utilization of the state's assets and finance; the guarantee of the right for citizens to choose their own occupations; acknowledgement of individual proprietary rights and their application; a governmental role focusing more on economic activities than on the control of the entire economy; the obligation of civil servants to serve the people (and not to be served), particularly as relates to economic activities.

Operational matters are related to the practical problems existing in the economy today. The increasing degradation of the people's economic situation requires immediate handling. The most prominent issue in this MPRS Decree is the emphasis that the economic decline must be handled rationally and realistically. This is seen among other things in various stipulations about short-term programmes, the state budget, international economic relations and so forth.

Therefore, the essence of this MPRS Decree can be formulated as an attempt to overcome the decline of the economy in a pragmatic way by returning to the appropriate fundamentals and foundations.

Main Sources and Solutions

Today the Indonesian people, hovering between fear and hope, are watching whether the alleviation of their economic burden can really become a reality. It is no exaggeration that what is expected today is not economic progress but just alleviation of this heavy burden.

This expectation can only be fulfilled if our leaders openly exhibit thoughtfulness and good intentions.

This MPRS decree begins with a stance on the introspection in relation to past actions impacting the current situation. The preamble says among other things for consideration: "that to overcome the increasing sufferings of the people as a result of Indonesia's economic decline ... it is necessary to reform the policies existing in the areas of economics, financial matters and development"; and also: "that the first step towards the improvement of the People's economy is the reassessment of all fundamentals utilized in the formulation of economic, financial and development policies".

This reassessment has led the MPRS to the main conclusion formulated in Article 1 as follows: "The only solution is to return to the implementation of the 1945 Constitution in an appropriate and consequential manner, because it has been realized that the main cause of Indonesia's rapid economic decline over the last few years has been the manipulation in the implementation of the original 1945 Constitution, as reflected in the absence of effective control from the people's representational institutions over the government's economic policies, and the consistent lack of harmony among political and economic interests, as well as the disregard for rational economic principles in facing economic problems."

A Brief Breakdown of the Matter

The above lengthy sentence of Article 1 from the MPRS decree contains profound introspection and can be broken down into several parts as follows:

(1) it is admitted that there has been rapid economic decline in the last few years;

(2) it is realized that the main source of this economic decline has been the manipulation of the pure implementation of the 1945 Constitution, as reflected in the following:

    (a) the absence of effective control from the people's representational institutions over the government's economic policies;

    (b) the consistent lack of harmony among economic and political interests; meaning that economic interests always give way to political interests; and

(c) disregard for rational economic principles in facing economic problems;

(d) it is stated that the solution to this economic decline is to return to the implementation of the 1945 Constitution in an appropriate and consequential manner.

This brief break down of the issues introduces a different way to view the problem than has been employed in the past. For example, an open attitude toward admitting that there has been rapid economic decline is quite the opposite of the past habit of attempting to cover up the difficult economic conditions with various pretexts. This is also the case with efforts to seek out the main source of economic decline in our own actions; specifically the manipulations occurring in the implementation of the principles set out in 1945 Constitution. This attitude is quite different from the past habit of always blaming other people (particularly the neo-colonialists and the imperialists) for our economic difficulties.

Manipulation

Acknowledgement of the absence of effective control by people's representational institutions indicates apt and thoughtful recourse to introspection about our current problems. In the past, the high-sounding motto of "social control" was often heard. However, in reality the DPR-GR and MPRS have failed to exercise meaningful control over the government, particularly in the field of the economy. It is logical, then, that without control, arbitrary acts would become rampant.

Also interesting is the acknowledgement that economic interests have always been required to give way to political interests. This condition is the result of the assumption that the economy is trivial in comparison to politics. Automatically, what is trivial must not be dedicated or involved with what is considered major; namely political issues, particularly foreign policy. Certainly, anything considered unimportant will not be given much attention and will, as a result, be neglected.

Furthermore, regarding the neglect of rational economic principles, it is a fact that this attitude took on cult proportions in the past. Economic principles, such as the need for a sound state budget, were considered a conventional idea and textbook thinking that had to be thrown away. The economy was addressed with nothing more than with heroic and revolutionary sounding slogans. In fact, however, these slogans were intended only to cover up a lack of capability, and failure and manipulation. Automatically, this approach to the economy accelerated the decline of Indonesia's economy.

The solution to this economic decline as set forth in Article 1 above is something highly logical. The main source of economic decline has now been identified as the manipulation in the appropriate implementation of the 1945 Constitution. Therefore, a logical solution is to return to the proper and consequential implementation of the 1945 Constitution.

Concrete Significance in the Field of the Economy

The question has also arisen as to: What is the concrete meaning of returning to the proper and consequential implementation of the 1945 Constitution in the field of economy?

The answer to this question can be found in Article 2 and Article 3 of the MPRS decree, which, in essence, states that:

(1) effective control by a people's representational institution over the government's economic policies must be upheld again, and will be applied through the following channels:
   (a) the authority of the House of Representatives (Dewan Perwakilan Rakyat) in determining the state budget of revenues and expenditures;
   (b) the power of the Supreme Audit Agency, which is outside the government and reports the results of all audits to the House of Representatives;
(2) while, of all the nation's problems, the matter of improving the economic situation must be given chief priority;
(3) with the best way to face these economic problems being a solid basis in rational and realistic economic principles.

The State Budget and the 1945 Constitution

The 1945 Constitution firmly requires effective control from the people's representational institutions; especially regarding the state budget of revenues and expenditures. As stated in Sub-article (1) of Article 23 of the 1945 Constitution: "The state budget of revenues and expenditures shall be determined every year by law." While the Elucidation of the

Constitution states that "... in the case of determining the level of revenues and expenditures, the position of the House of Representatives is stronger than that of the government. This shows people's sovereignty."

This means that it is the obligation of the Government and the House of Representatives to eliminate the negative practices of the past, such as, for example, asking the House of Representatives to ratify the state budget long after the budget has been implemented so that the ratification was only formalistic in nature. Or the practice of drawing up an additional budget that far exceeds the master budget already ratified, as well as the practice of establishing as many special accounts as desired.

The Supreme Audit Agency and the 1945 Constitution

Regarding the Supreme Audit Agency (BPK), the 1945 Constitution stipulates in Sub-article (5) of Article 23: "A Supreme Audit Agency is to be set up, whose regulation will be stipulated by the law, to audit the state budget for the purpose of establishing accountability. The outcome of this audit will be reported to the House of Representatives." Pertaining to this matter, the Elucidation of the Constitution states that: "The way the government spends the expenditure fund already approved by the House of Representatives must conform that decision. In order to monitor and check on the fulfillment of this responsibility by the government, there must be an agency that is free from the influence and authority of the government; any agency that is accountable only to the government cannot perform such a heavy obligation. On the other hand, neither does this agency stand above the government. That's why the authority and obligations of this agency will be stipulated by the law."

At present the position of the Supreme Audit Agency (BPK) is inseparable from the influence and authority of the government, while the House of Representatives cannot exercise effective control to see whether the government has actually spent the people's money in conformity to the stipulated budget. That's why it is obvious that one of the concrete steps expected from the government and the House of Representatives in implementing this MPRS Decree is to restore the position and working methods of the Supreme Audit Agency (BPK) to the status stipulated in the provisions set out in the Constitution.

The Economy is the Main Priority

Of all of the nation's problems, the problem of improving the economic conditions of the people must be given the main priority. This decree is a correction to the manipulations of the past, in which economic interests were always forced to give way to political interests.

Each and every nation is always bound to face a number of nationwide problems and each must determine which problem must be prioritized for resolution at any given time. To this end, a national priority scale has been drawn up. This is a list of national problems that must be prioritized. In the past, political problems were prioritized, while today the MPRS has stipulated that it is the economic problems that must be made the top priority.

At this point, it is best to briefly examine the relationship between politics and economics. It is true enough that politics and economics cannot be separated. This is something that has finally been fully realized. The result of the inter-twining of politics and economic matters has been felt by the Indonesian people. The political atmosphere in the past has led to economic disorder, while the decline of the economy has increased political tension. So, first of all, because this has come to be understood, it should no longer have to be necessary to emphasize that these two things are actually inseparable.

However, in the context of a discussion on priorities, other aspects of politics and economics also have to be taken into consideration. Every time a priority is determined, this means making a decision. And every time a national priority is determined by a people's representational institution or by the government, this means making a political decision. Political decisions may vary. There are political decisions that place political interests above economic interests (for example a political decision to establish a close cooperative relationship with the People's Republic of China without heeding its consequences on the Indonesian economy). On the other hand, there are also political decisions that prioritize the economic interests of the people above political interests (for example, a decision to stop confrontation, which has used up a lot of public funds).

MPRS Decree No. XXIII is a political decision that, among other things, requires prioritizing the improvement of the economy above resolving all other national problems, including political matters. The consequence of this political decision is, among other things, that the government's domestic and foreign policies must be modified in such a way that they will really support the effort toward improving the overall economy.

Application of Economic Principles

Furthermore it has also been stipulated that the best way to face economic problems is the strict application of rational and realistic economic principles. This is a correction to the manipulation of the past, when all core economic principles were set aside. The consequence of this decree is that every economic policy of the government must be based on sound economic principles and no longer on high-sounding slogans. This means that every act in the field of economy must be truth tested and evaluated on the basis of economic principles, regardless of whether or not this act is conventional or otherwise. An act conforming to textbook wisdom is not always wrong and what runs counters the textbook may not be correct.

A concrete example is that the government's spending can no longer be based on the capacity of the treasury to print money. This wisdom can be found in any economics textbook. It is a sound and logical principle. That's why it must be strongly upheld. On the other hand, there is no textbook that recommends that foreign exchange reserves should be "used up" arbitrarily and that "no thought should be used" in burdening the next generation with foreign debts. Because the ways of the past are so unconventional, they must be employed no longer in today's rational economy.

All this means that the government is obligated by the people to remain standing with both feet on the ground, no matter how high in the sky are the stars that we are reaching for.

The Pancasila Five Point Ideology and the 1945 Constitution

The solution to economic decline is the return to the implementation of the 1945 Constitution in a proper and consequential manner. This is what the MPRS has stipulated. The concrete meaning of this solution in the area of economic policies has just been described above. Now, what will be the consequences of this solution in relation to the development of Indonesia's economic system?

Article 4 stipulates that the ideal foundations for the development of Indonesia's economic system are Pancasila and the 1945 Constitution, particularly Articles 23, 27, 33 and 34, along with their elucidation; there are no other appropriate foundations. This is in conformity with the nation's return to the implementation of the 1945 Constitution in an appropriate and consequential manner.

Regarding the 1945 Constitution, attention must be paid particularly to articles 23, 27, 33 and 24, as these articles contain provisions about economy. Article 23 regulates the state budget of revenues and expenditures; taxes; currency; and the responsibility, as well as accountability, for the state finances. Sub-article (2) of Article 27 stipulates a citizen's right to a decent job and living. Article 33 is a quite famous, important article, but has been very rarely mentioned in the last few years. As for Article 34, it stipulates that poor people and neglected children will be taken care of by the state.

The Elucidation of the 1945 Constitution documents also plays an important role, particularly for the field of economy. The elucidation of Article 23, for example, shows the way that the state budget of revenues and expenditures should be determined as the manifestation of the people's sovereignty principle. Furthermore, the position of the Supreme Audit Agency is also elucidated. Likewise, the elucidation of Article 33 has significance because, among other things, it refers to the principle of a democratic economy.

As for the essence of the ideal foundations for the economy, this is formulated in Article 5 of the MPRS decree as follows: "The essence of the ideal foundations for the economy is the development of a guided economic system on the basis of Pancasila that guarantees the practice of a democratic economy and is aimed at creating a just and prosperous society blessed by the One Supreme God".

A Democratic Economy, Liberalism and Etatism

According to Article 5, the practice of democratic economy must be guaranteed in Indonesia's economic system. What is democratic economy? This is not a new term. The elucidation of the 1945 Constitution states: "The fundamentals and foundations of a democratic economy are set forth in Article 33. Production is carried out by all under the leadership or supervision of community members. The prosperity of society is prioritized, not the prosperity of individuals". And also:

"The economy is based on the democratic principle of prosperity for everyone".

Article 6 of the MPRS decree refers to the positive characteristics of a democratic economy. Among other things, it is stated that the management of the economy constitutes a joint effort on the basis of a familial principle (Sub-article (1) of Article 33 of the 1945 Constitution), and therefore does not recognize the structure of class struggle. Individual property rights are recognized and will be applied for the benefit of the entire society, and, as such, may not be used as a tool to exploit our fellow human beings. Citizens are also allowed the freedom to choose their own occupations, while the potential, initiative and creativeness of every citizen must be fully developed within limits that won't harm public's interest. In the meantime, pursuant to Sub-article (2) of Article 33 of the 1945 Constitution, the branches of production important to the state, and which affect the livelihoods and lives of many people will be controlled by the state.

From the point of view of negatives, according to this MPRS decree, a democratic economy is opposed to "free fight liberalism" as well as "etatism" (statism), and does not desire monopoly, which is disadvantageous to society. The evil of "free fight liberalism" has often been described and heard. On the other hand, the term "etatism" is rarely heard, although actually this system, also known as statism, has become a reality in Indonesia lately. In the system of "etatism" the state and the state's economic apparatuses are fully dominant and push back, as well as kill, the potential and the creativity of the economic units beyond the state sector. Nearly everything has been made state property, or nationalized, and the state (or more appropriately the people holding power in a state) has attempted to regulate the entire economy in an exaggerated manner. The consequence of "etatism" is not much different from that of "free fight liberalism"; namely the rampancy of arbitrary acts. In "free fight liberalism" arbitrary acts are carried out under an individual's own name and for individual interests. In the system of "etatism", arbitrary acts are done in the name of the state and most of the times they are actually intended to support an individual's own interests.

These principles of democracy are clearly reflected in the MPRS decree. Among other things, this is seen in the emphasis put on the significance of the public's control over the state's economic policies, the significance of the practice of de-bureaucratization, or the revamping of the civil service and governmental administrative systems, as well as the development of regional economic activities, etc.

What about the Economic Declaration (Dekon)?

This MPRS decree only refers to Pancasila and the 1945 Constitution as the ideal foundations for the economy. So, what about the Economic Declaration (Dekon), and the MPRS decree on "Policy Reversals toward Self-Reliance" ("Banting Stir untuk Berdikari"), among others?

In the entire MPRS Decree No. XXIII the term "Dekon" or "Economic Declaration" has been referred to only once; in the preamble. It is stated: "Considering: ... the content and spirit of parts of the Economic Declaration (Dekon) that can fulfill the Three Demands of the People (Tritura) and the Message of People's Suffering (Ampera)".

The parts of the Economic Declaration considered as fulfilling the Tritura and Ampera can indeed be found in various articles of this MPRS decree. For example, the stipulation about the potential and creativeness of the People as a potential economic force that must be aroused. Likewise, the stipulation about the reform or de-concentration of management, particularly in the context of regional development.

So, this decree does not consider Economic Declaration in its entirety as the ideal foundation for the democratic economy, but borrows only certain parts of it. In the context of returning to the implementation of the 1945 Constitution in an appropriate manner, this is correct. The Economic Declaration indeed contains good provisions, but it also contains things that can be used as material for political guerrillas. Among other things, the Economic Declaration generalizes foreign capital (particularly capital from the PRC) and domestic capital. Also, it states that to overcome economic difficulties, it is necessary to achieve "mutual assistance" with the nationalist, religious and communist forces ideology (Nasakom) as the pillar.

The same thing is true of the berdikari (self-reliance) motto. In this MPRS decree there is no mention of this word "berdikari". However, the essence of the sense of this word can be clearly seen in various articles; among others, Article 64, which states: "Although offshore loans and foreign capital can be made use of (for example, production sharing) in overcoming economic decline and in economic development, there must, however, be a determination to overcome economic difficulties by relying on our own power and a determination to free ourselves from dependence on foreign countries."

Therefore, this MPRS decree does not examine one by one the previous decrees or mottos stipulated in the past, but it has started fresh by using only Pancasila and the 1945 Constitution as the foundations for a democratic economy. Regarding what has been stipulated in the past, Article 70 stipulates that: "All decrees, regulations, provisions and other documents that do not conform to the content or spirit of this decree are declared null and void."

Therefore, all economic policies in the future must have, as the point of departure MPRS Decree No. XXIII. Regarding the Economic Declaration, Banting Stir untuk Berdikari and other declarations or documents, only the segments that conform to the content and spirit of MPRS Decree No. XXIII will remain applicable.

The Roles of Government and De-bureaucratization

The sustainability of the principle of democratic economy must be guaranteed, according to the MPRS decree. This principle is clearly reflected in various articles; among others an article regarding the role of government.

The 1945 Constitution grants a positive role to the government in the field of the economy. Article 33 states that production branches important to the state and controlling the livings of many people will be controlled by the state. In the last few years, the state sector has indeed been increasingly expanded with the greater number and variety of state enterprises.

Due to its preoccupation with taking care of these state enterprises, the government has often forgotten its other task of providing appropriate guidance to sectors outside of the state sector. Likewise, developing the potential and creativeness of the people has also been neglected. As a result, the non-state sector has not enjoyed guidance, but has instead experienced constraints. As for the potential and creativeness of the people, instead of developing, they have been weakened as a result of many conflicting regulations.

Article 38 of the MPRS decree emphasizes the need for balance between these two tasks of the government; initiating and implementing certain economic activities, and providing guidance for economic activities beyond the state sector. In this context, it is stated in Article 40 that

"... the government must put a greater emphasis on supervision of the direction of economic activities rather than just trying to control as many economic activities as possible." In other words: The government's obligation is not to establish as many state enterprises or state-owned limited liability companies as possible, but to pay more attention to providing guidance for and undertaking supervision of the people's economic activities, so that they will develop toward a sound direction. This is a segment of this decree that needs underlining.

To provide guidance and undertake supervision are not easy. Currently, the most popular practice to undertake supervision is through licensing. So, various regulations (including the regulation to regulate regulations) have emerged and efforts have been made to exploit obsolete regulations from the Dutch East Indies era. Those who wish to develop their economic undertakings will end up expending their time and energy to process permits and licenses. Finally, "short-cut" practices have emerged along with the usual consequences. This "guided economy" has become the economy of regulations and finally an anarchic economy.

It is in this context that Article 40 emphasizes: "... it is absolutely necessary to introduce de-bureaucratization of the administrative system ..." What matters is not whether or not control and leadership are necessary, but the way in which control and leadership are exercised. The implementation of de-bureaucratization means revamping or reforming the current ways of exercising control and regulation practices. The consequence will be the scrapping of many agencies or institutions that are not needed and the revocation of various regulations that will only add to our difficulties.

Of course, the implementation of the de-bureaucratization process in a consequential manner will not be easy as many parties have an interest in maintaining various agencies and regulations. It is here, among other things, that it is possible to measure the extent a government is really courageous enough to undertake an economic clean-up without discrimination.

The government will also need this courage to consequently implement Article 41, which reads: "The principle of efficiency must become a guideline in the activities of the government in the field of the economy, in the sense that deviations from this principle must be subjected to punitive measures."

This, among other things, means that whether or not a state enterprise is viable and appropriate must be measured against this principle of efficiency. The same is true of the success or failure of the leaders of a state enterprise in performing their duties. If this decree is to be seriously implemented (this must still be proven), the function of some state enterprises as half-way houses and as milk cows will come to an end.

Cooperatives and the Domestic Private Sector

The elucidation for Article 33 of the 1945 Constitution states, among other things, that the corporate structure most suitable to the provisions in this article is that of a cooperative. The MPRS decree underlines this matter by stating that a cooperative is an organization through which the interests of the common people, in particular, will be fought for and protected.

It is said in Article 43 that the Government is obliged to provide guidance, supervision and so forth to cooperatives. To this end, it is necessary to have decrees in the form of laws on cooperatives, the domestic private sector, and state enterprises.

The principle of democratic economy is visible not only in the role given to cooperatives, but also in the provisions regarding the role of the domestic private sector. Among other things, it is stipulated that domestic private circles enjoy freedom to choose their respective business areas within the limits set by the existing decrees and the spirit of the 1945 Constitution, while the definition and stipulation of the areas of activities will be regulated by the law.

This decree conforms to one of the characteristics of democratic economy, namely the obligation of the government to develop, as far as possible, the potential and creativeness of the people. At present, there have been too many limitations and constraints suppressing the initiatives and activities of the people.

In the meantime, the freedom for the domestic private sector must automatically disallow any kind of manipulation or deviation from the essence of the principle of democratic economy itself. To this end, Article 46 emphasizes the need for supervision and control by the government's apparatuses to ensure that the principles of the democratic economy will continue to develop within private business organizations themselves.

On the other hand, Article 46 also stipulates that: "... for the sake of the development of their activities, the domestic private circles will be entitled to obtain proper services, protection and assistance from the state administration. "In fact, this is quite natural and should actually be that way. The state apparatus is there to serve and guide and not to be served. However, it is also seemingly deemed necessary to emphasize this because in reality this is not the case today. In the past few years the civil service has become larger and each segment of the bureaucracy feels obligated to regulate or put things in order. Eventually there has developed a trend toward over-organization with all of the logical consequences, especially stagnation and arbitrary acts.

In connection with the implementation of this MPRS decree, it should be realized that what matters for the state apparatus is not that it ensures that everything is orderly and properly regulated, but that under its supervision and guidance, economic activities can be encouraged and further developed. We must keep in mind that things can be made so orderly and properly regulated that the result is stagnation.

The Problems of Stabilization and Development

In the operational area, MPRS Decree No. XXIII stipulates that economic problems must be given the chief priority. This has been firmly stated in Article 11: "… domestic interests, particularly economic interests, must explicitly be prioritized rather than the interests of foreign politics." I think that this need not be and cannot be formulated in a clearer way.

Particularly in the field of the economy, priority will be given to projects that will turn out goods and services that the people need directly. Article 27 stipulates that: "…all projects that are not economical or are not productive must be immediately postponed." Also, this, I think, cannot be any clearer.

One thing that must be paid attention to is the stipulation in Article 13, which emphasizes the need for a clear distinction between the programme of stabilization and rehabilitation on the one hand and the programme of development, on the other. This distinction is important as it will affect policies. Economic development is related with economic growth. To this end, large-scale investments will be needed. However, this is possible only after the economic situation and the economy have become quite stable; namely when prices no longer continue to soar. To make this possible, stabilization in the monetary area and the rehabilitation of production will be needed.

Regarding this, it is stated in Article 17 that: "… a consistent and solidly operational programme of economic stabilization and rehabilitation must be immediately stipulated and implemented." While Article 13 states:

"At present all potentials and efforts must be devoted to the success of stabilization and rehabilitation."

This means that economic development at present has to give way to economic stabilization and rehabilitation efforts. Among others, it is stated in Article 28 that during this period "... any new projects that may disturb the implementation of the stabilization and rehabilitation programmes are to be abandoned."

Operational Programme

At present there is no operational programme for economic stabilization and rehabilitation in place. That's why the above-mentioned decree is quite appropriate. An operational programme is defined as a systemic programme that is ready for implementation. One of its characteristics is that it is quantitative in nature and that there is a clear timeframe for it. In addition, an economic programme must also be consistent. This means that its elements must conform to, instead of conflicting with, one another.

The drawing up of a programme of stabilization and rehabilitation that is sufficiently operational will take time. In the meantime, economic problems must not be left unattended. That's why it is necessary to precede the operational programme with a rescue programme (Article 16). A rescue programme differs from the programme of stabilization and rehabilitation in that a rescue programme is not comprehensive, but rather, ad hoc in nature. This means that it deals only with certain problems in a specific manner.

Therefore, viewed from the aspect of time, there are three kinds of programmes:

(a) a rescue programme;
(b) a programme of stabilization and rehabilitation; and
(c) a development programme.

Particularly regarding the programme of stabilization and rehabilitation, pursuant to Article 15, the priority scale is as follows:

(a) inflation control;
(b) sufficiency in food;
(c) rehabilitation of economic infrastructure;
(d) boosting of export activities;
(e) sufficiency in clothing.

As for long-term economic development, the priority scale is as follows (Article 25):

(a) agricultural sector;
(b) infrastructure; and
(c) the industrial, mining and oil sectors.

Physical Plan and Monetary Plan

An operational programme of economic stabilization and rehabilitation comprises two components: (a) a Physical Plan, and (b) a Monetary Plan. The Physical Plan reflects the programme of rehabilitation. Its main goal must conform to the short-term priority scale already stipulated, namely: food, exports, infrastructure, and clothing. For example, the application of the Physical Plan in the foodstuffs sector covers not only a food production plan, but also a plan for the importation of rice, the importation of fertilizer, as well as the repair of roads important for food distribution, and so forth.

As for the Monetary Plan, its main goals are: (a) guaranteeing the coverage of both the rupiah and foreign exchange expenses for the implementation of the Physical Plan, and (b) controlling the rate of inflation. These are aspects of stabilization.

The two plans are closely related to one another. On the one hand a plan is drawn up that is limited only to certain targets and to this end the funds necessary to covering the related expenses must be available. On the other hand, this physical plan must be feasible, and capable of being implemented. To this end, attention must be paid to the scope of the expenses so that an appropriate amount of funds can be made available. The amount of funds available will be highly dependent on the other aspect of the Monetary Plan: inflation control. This last mentioned element is aimed at achieving a relatively stable level and balance in prices conforming to the purchasing power of the people.

The implementation of this operational programme requires various consistent policies. These, among other things, will encompass: budget policies, fiscal policies, monetary policies, price policies, wage policies, foreign balance of payment policies, and so forth. As well, all of this will have to be coupled with institutional revamping.

Specially regarding the revamping of institutions, Article 22 emphasizes the need to break through all bureaucratic constraints by means of de-concentrating and de-centralizing management in the regions or production units without harming economic unity and domestic political unity.

Each of these policies must be an integral part of a programme of economic stabilization and rehabilitation. For example, to restore the capacity of production, raw materials, spare parts and so forth will be needed in, at least, minimum quantities. This minimum need must be guaranteed in an importation policy, which cannot stand alone, but must be an integral part of a comprehensive plan.

All this has consequences on implementation, either in terms of structure or working method. The structure of government must be such that it will actually guarantee the implementation of the physical and production plans. As for the working method of each, it must be kept in mind by all that none of this is being done in the interest of a specific region, but for the sake of the achievement of the goals already stipulated in the overall national-in-scope plan. In other words, a working method must have as its point of departure the fundamental understanding that the success of the plan for the entire nation is the responsibility of all. To this end, a new and different working climate from that still in place today will be needed.

Taxes and Austerity

Of all the economic policies that constitute elements of the programme of economic stabilization and rehabilitation, two policies have been paid special attention in this MPRS decree. The first is the policy on the state budget of revenues and expenditures, and the other is the policy on foreign economic relations.

Regarding the first, Article 47 stipulates that: "… efforts must be made so that the deficit can be abolished in a short time…" To make this possible, on the one hand the state's revenues must be increased and on the other hand the state's expenditures must be cut drastically.

In this connection, Article 49 stipulates that: "State revenues originating from direct and indirect taxes, together with other revenues (particularly from State Enterprises), must be increased while efficiency and intensification of levies must be enhanced." It is also stated that increases in revenues must be compatible with the capacity of the people, the existing sense of justice and the actual real need for state spending. The stipulation in this article is very important. Today, the state's revenues are very limited. It is not possible to stop inflation without increasing the state's revenues.

On the other hand, Article 51 stipulates that: "Earnest and effective austerity must be immediately introduced through a drastic austerity programme that applies to both civilian and military spending." This is a stipulation that nevertheless must be implemented for the sake of reducing the deficit and therefore curbing the rate of inflation. It should be remembered that what is required is drastic and that this policy of austerity covers both the civilian and military sectors.

The Special Budget is Abolished

Furthermore, in the context of ensuring the soundness of the state budget it has been stipulated that the special budget must be abolished, so that the monetary budget will consist of only the routine budget, the development budget, the foreign exchange budget and the credit budget. This is an important stipulation, because, up to now, the amount of the special budget has never been determined (always based on memory) so that it has become an uncertain factor in the entire monetary budget. It is stated in Article 52 that all budgets for projects funded by this special budget up to now must be integrated into the routine, development and foreign exchange budgets. Therefore, better supervision can be done.

In this context, another important stipulation is that the budget must be written into a law and that the drawing up of the budget must be completed before the year in which it is to go into effect. This is logical. However, for many years, this was not the case, so that a budget had become of little significance. This stipulation has the consequence that the budget for 1967 must be quickly prepared right now.

Another article pertaining to financial matters emphasizes the need for a Decree on the Basic Law on Banking and the Law on the Central Bank. The first is related to the fact that banking conditions today are far from sound, while the second is required urgently to return the Central Bank to its proper function.

National Interests in Foreign Economic Relations

Regarding the policy on foreign economic relations, Article 56 emphasizes: "In establishing international economic relations pursuant to free and active foreign policy, the principle of national interests must always be prioritized. This, among other things, means that in determining foreign trade transactions, strong economic fundamentals and principles must be strongly adhered to." In the past, foreign trade was indeed frequently based on the interests of political relations. A trade relationship like that would automatically lose its usefulness, at some point even becomes disadvantageous to Indonesia's economy.

Particularly concerning offshore loans, it is stated that these loans can be justified only if they are really an integral part of the stabilization and rehabilitation plan as a whole. This means that any loan falling outside of the stabilization and rehabilitation plan will not be justified. Another important stipulation is: "The size of an offshore loan that can be taken will depend on the capacity to repay it in the future without increasing the people's burden, which is now already very heavy." (Article 61) This stipulation means that the taking out of and use of an offshore loan must really be prudent. Otherwise, it will only increase the burden in future.

Potential Power, Real Power and Foreign Capital

In the past the entrenched illusion that Indonesia's natural riches were so abundant that nobody should worry about the nation's economic condition held sway. In a more realistic tone, this most recent MPRS decree does not refer to "abundant natural riches", but it refers to "natural resources" that are "potentially available". It is emphasized that potential economic wealth must still be transformed into real economic power. This means that before the outcome of the exploitation of these resources can be enjoyed by the people, this natural wealth must still be excavated, processed and developed. To this end, capital increase, the use of technology, improved skills, enhanced management, and so forth, will be needed.

In this context, Article 10 states that the development of economic potential must be based on self-reliance, but this must not lead to the unwillingness to make use of capital, technology and skills available from abroad. Of course, the condition will be that these foreign resources must be dedicated to the economic interests of the people of Indonesia and will not lead to our nation's dependence on foreign countries. To implement all of this, the need to immediately stipulate a law on foreign capital, including domestic capital originating from foreign sources, has been stipulated clearly in Article 62.

A matter that is also related to domestic capital of foreign origins is the stipulation in Article 63 to the effect that "Government Regulation No. 10/1959 should be renewed and promoted into a law".

National Development is Identical with Regional Development

Up to now, there has been a predominant misconception that regional development is something different and separate from national development. Article 29 of MPRS Decree No. XXIII puts this idea to rest by stating that: "Economic development is the development of economic resources. As these economic resources are found in the regions, national development is identical with regional development."

It is also stated that for the sake of the implementation of regional development, priority must be given to the rehabilitation and improvement of a communication and transportation system, as well as the development of rural communities. Transmigration must be intensified, while the implementation of land reform must be accelerated.

Article 32 stipulates the immediate implementation of:

(a) the granting of broad autonomy to the regions;
(b) de-concentration of the management of economic activities under the coordination of regional administrations; and
(c) the financial balance between the central government and regional administrations.

These three things are of great significance to the improvement of regional economic activities. Therefore, it is very important to ensure their immediate implementation.

In the context of bringing about harmony, we must keep in mind that, at the end of the day, the economic growth of each region must be geared towards national economic integration. To this end, all constraints hampering the traffic of goods between regions must be abolished (Article 34). It is also in this context that the planning of the development of regions and rural communities must be coordinated by the central government.

Follow-up in the Executive and Legislative Fields

The description made at great length above shows just how widespread and extensive the problems are in the economic, financial and development fields covered by the MPRS decree. The task now is to implement, in detail, the provisions in this decree. In this context, the steps toward implementation must strictly conform to the essence of this decree.

Specifically regarding implementation, Article 71 stipulates that: "The Gotong-Royong House of Representatives and the government are assigned to implement this decree." This special assignment shows that the implementation of this decree is rooted not only in the legislative branch (among others, in legal products such as the Law on the Central Bank, the promotion in the status of Government Regulation No. 10/1959 to law, and the Basic Law on Banking) but also in the executive branch (among others things, in the drawing up and implementation of a Physical Plan and a Monetary Plan).

In the case of implementation in the executive sector, Articles 66–69 stipulate pre-conditions. It is emphasized in these articles that, for the success of various programmes, and policies, it will be necessary to reform and improve the state bureaucracy so that civil servants will work as a harmonious team within a simple, efficient and effective structure.

Thus are the main points in this MPRS decree, along with the steps that must be taken to implement it. The Indonesian people, through the MPRS, have, thus, laid down the "POLICY FOUNDATIONS FOR THE REFORM OF ECONOMIC, FINANCIAL AND DEVELOPMENT FUNDAMENTALS" This decree contains the expectation of alleviating the economic burden of the people. The problem now is how to turn this expectation into reality. It will be proven in the future whether this MPRS Decree No. XXIII/1966 is only a document that is nice to read, or whether it can really be the foundation for a turning point for the economic situation of the Indonesian people.

NOTE

[1]   An article written as Dean of the Faculty of Economics of the University of Indonesia, regarding MPRS Decree No. XXIII/MPRS/1966 on *"Policy Foundations for the Reform of Economic, Financial and Development Fundamentals"*, Jakarta, 10 July 1966. Various parts of this article have been published in various dailies. This article is translated by Harry Bhaskara.

7

CHALLENGES IN INCREASING FOOD PRODUCTION IN INDONESIA (1968)[1]

Introductory Note: *In 1968 the Indonesian economy was in a state of transition which was of great significance for the period to come. In coping with the economic chaos inherited from the past, the government embarked on a course to stabilize and rehabilitate the economy. The major cornerstones of the stabilization and rehabilitation programme were: (1) to put order in our own house through fiscal and monetary measures, (2) to rely more on sound economic principles by providing greater freedom and more incentives; and (3) to re-establish sound economic relations with the rest of the world.*

In implementing the stabilization and rehabilitation programme, we needed to know more about the demand and supply of rice in the Indonesian economy. With huge imports of rice, slow progress in food production, and rising food prices, the government and the general public have taken an increased interest in the food problems of the country. This workshop was a reflection of that interest.

At the initiative of the chairman of the Lembaga Ilmu Pengetahuan Indonesia (LIPI or the Indonesian Istitute of Sciences), Professor Sarwono Prawirohardjo, a Workshop on Food was organized. He invited the National Academy of Sciences of the USA to participate at the workshop and asked me to deliver the keynote address in the workshop, which took place in Jakarta in May 1968.

Increased food supply from domestic production is a prerequisite for long-term economic growth. Unless there is a substantial increase in food production, there will be a continued drain on foreign exchange to import food and a continued threat of inflation led by upward pressures of food prices. Major increases in food production is the top priority in the Five Year Plan which is currently under preparation.

The food production strategy as presently envisaged consists of a number of elements: Foremost is the creation of an economic climate which will make it profitable for farmers to use increased quantities of modern inputs. Also, to make sure that these new inputs — fertilizers, pesticides, and improved seeds — will be available at the farm level at the right time and right prices. Within this longer-run framework, it is important to choose the short-run courses of action.

In the short run, emphasis is placed on the availability of improved seeds — particularly the new rice varieties — chemical fertilizers, pesticides, and irrigation water. The potentialities of the new varieties are so high that they give us more hope to achieve our objective of rapid increase in rice production in a shorter time than otherwise. However, there are some doubts as to how this introduction could be achieved on a widespread basis. How fast can the seed multiplication proceed without endangering their purity? In addition to the difficult process of distributing the new seeds, there are also the problems of assuring the presence of complementary inputs such as fertilizers and insecticides, and of providing the extension support required to inform farmers of the necessary cultivation practices. Given both the uncertainty and the importance of the seed programme, what will be the best way to ensure success in the multiplication and distribution of the new rice varieties.

Given the uncertainty of the seed programme, we realize that the major short-run impact on food production will come through increased fertilizer use on older varieties. In other words, we are considering a fertilizer saturation for all parts of the rice economy. To achieve this rapid increase in fertilizer use, several questions come up. First, what active role should be played by the private sector in fertilizer distribution? We would like to see an expansion of the private sector, but what are the actions to encourage this sector? What should be the scale of the fertilizer import programme, when compared to the effective demand for fertilizer in the countryside, and to the problems of distribution?

With regard to insecticides, the problem seems to be rather different. There are indications that insecticide usage has been falling below recommendations for some time. This may be caused by the difficulty for the farmer to see a 10 to 30 per cent increase in production through the use of insecticides than to recognize the 50 per cent or more increase in production through the use of fertilizers. This problem might be more severe with the newer varieties due to a lack of inbred resistance. In addition, maintenance of sprayers seems to be a big problem. As a result, sprayers break down faster than the normal life expectancy.

We realize the potential and need for a rehabilitated and expanded irrigation system in many parts of Indonesia, especially in Java. This is especially true when one considers that the new rice varieties need much more controlled water supplies.

At present a higher priority is put on rehabilitation rather than expansion of the irrigation system. The question is how fast this work can be completed. We need a plan indicating the areas to be rehabilitated, and the concomitant dredging and erosion control necessary in the catchment areas to prevent immediate re-siltation with the consequent damage to the irrigation system. Another aspect to be studied is whether a system must be designed in which the farmer must pay for the regulated water supply to enable the local authorities to maintain the just-rehabilitated irrigated areas. On top of it, a unitary control of water management is probably a necessary condition for an efficient water supply and development. We do hope that this workshop can give us some specific suggestions with regard to the above problems and to the directions of the water resources development programme.

Irrigation, fertilization, disease control, and the use of improved seed varieties have only a limited effect on the productivity of land if not accompanied by improved methods of cultivation. In the past, the majority of inventions and innovations which led to improvement in methods of cultivation came from the farmers themselves. Even now, self-discovery is still important in contributing to improvements in methods of cultivation. However, given the level of education of the farmers, the scale of operation, their limited resources, and their attitude toward risk, improvement of methods of cultivation will undoubtedly be a slow process. To increase the speed at which new techniques of production are developed, an effective agriculture research programme must be conducted. Again, here, a plan for agricultural research is needed indicating the timing and research areas which should be explored, consistent with the national needs.

The emergence of commercial agriculture accompanied by an increasing use of off-farm inputs raise the working capital requirements of the farmers. The characteristics of food farming in Indonesia in terms of scale of operation and marketable surplus, require the farmer to rely heavily on credit for his financial expenditures. As such credit provides the basis for increased production efficiency. To meet this demand, an efficient rural credit system is needed to provide credit timely with a convenient repayment programme suited to the money flow from the cropping cycle, and based on a reasonably simple procedure. Within this long-run strategy what are the short-run tactics to meet the growing demand for credit in the rural areas?

Increased agricultural production requires incentives to farmers by decision makers, and a positive response of farmers to those incentives. In this regard, the Indonesian government has adopted the policy that the price relationships should be such that the use of fertilizer and other modern inputs will be profitable to farmers. However, the problem we would like to suggest for deliberation is whether the price relationship, as adopted by the government, reflects the appropriate level of the terms of trade for agriculture, and what are the specific policy techniques that should be used to assure the profitability of the new inputs? In other words, there seems to be a conflict of interest in implementing this policy. Increasing the terms of trade for agriculture might stimulate agricultural production. However, such an increase, assuming that it were possible to achieve, would add to the production cost dilemma in the industrial and the estate sectors of the economy.

Another related aspect of farmer's incentives is the uncertainty he is facing at the time he has to make the decision. The difference between the expected value of the increased output and the cost of the use of new inputs is crucial in the decision making of the farmer. To a large extent gain determines the farmers incentive to use the new inputs. Considering the scale of operation of Indonesian food production, the cash expenditure for the purchase of new inputs is relatively large, especially when the farmers have to pay it in advance. It is true that under certain conditions the profit of such an investment will be large. But the great uncertainties which the farmer faces make the use of the new inputs a risky business. At the time he must make the decision he knows for certain only the price of the new inputs. Other factors such as weather, soil response, and price of output, which determine the pay-off, are uncertain. Two steps which the government can take to reduce this risk has been suggested and indeed have major attractions. First, guaranteed prices of the output eliminate one major uncertainty with regard to the monetary pay-offs. Second, subsidized input prices to reduce the cost of implementing the new inputs. Both raise the question of administrative feasibility. And put in the proper economic context, both suggestions have wide repercussions on the country's development effort. The second suggestion has certainly less an impact (via cost) on the estate sector and hence on exports. This question is at present one of the important issues. We would appreciate if the food workshop can give us some clue with regard to the direction of finding a solution.

The increased use of new inputs and the expected increases in output will require improved marketing facilities and procedures. In fact the more efficient the marketing institutions perform their function, the more feasible will be the programme of increasing production through introduction of new inputs. Our food marketing mechanism is far from efficient. This is mainly due to poor conditions of the existing infrastructure, the lack of standardization and grading, poor storage and transportation facilities, and imperfections in the market. Under such conditions the marketing systems could not reflect changes in retail and wholesale prices at the retail level. The adverse consequences of this type of inefficiency is known and need not be elaborated. The question we have in mind is what is the best marketing policy to be pursued by the government to ensure efficiency in this sector?

So far I have discussed only the supply side of the food problem. It is also of the utmost importance to look at the food problem from the point of view of demand. One of the causes of the problem of the food economy of Indonesia is the differences which exist between the production and consumption patterns. The policy implications of this problem are either to change the consumption pattern to conform to the production pattern, or vice versa.

There seem to be advantages to change the existing consumption pattern. First, it would lessen the overwhelming dependence of the population on rice. Second, it would reduce the consumer's resistance to alternative foods in times of rice shortages. Finally, if the substitutes are available in the world market at prices much lower than rice, it would conserve foreign exchange. An attempt to substitute rice by corn during the previous regime ended up in failure mainly because it did not take into account consumer preferences. Recently, however, there is some evidence which indicates that consumers would indeed accept wheat grains if and when there are sizable price differentials in their favor. Since wheat flour can be obtained at much lower prices than rice, there is a possibility of importing it in sufficient quantities in order to keep their prices low. We would appreciate the views of the participants of the workshop on this subject and would invite information on this matter as has been experienced elsewhere.

NOTE

[1] Keynote Address in Workshop on Food held by Lembaga Ilmu Pengetahuan Indonesia (LIPI or the Indonesian Institute of Sciences) and the National Academy of Sciences of the USA, Jakarta, May 1968.

8

THE BASIC FRAMEWORK OF THE FIVE-YEAR DEVELOPMENT PLAN (REPELITA) (1968)[1]

Introductory Note: *The compilation of the First Five-Year Development Plan (Repelita I) began in 1967 and continued in 1968. The implementation of Repelita I began in the fiscal year of 1969–70. At the time, the fiscal year started on 1 April and ended on 31 March of the following year. When Repelita I was being drafted, exchanges of views were held with various circles concerning the basic guidelines of the entire five-year plan programme. Because Repelita I was already under preparation, its basic framework was utilized as material for the exchanges of views on the basic ideas of the overall five-year plan program.*

At present (1968) the compilation and specifications for Repelita are underway. The Basic Framework for Repelita still requires further detailing because at this time it contains only basic guidelines. Input, in the form of thoughts and opinions, would therefore, be very much appreciated toward the improvement of the Basic Framework for the Five-Year Development Plan Programme.

The starting point for formulating the Basic Framework is the long period of time that will be required for the completion of the development process. This period has to be divided into phases that are reflected in the various five-year development plans. Therefore, the first Repelita should be seen as the beginning of a series of five-year development plans. These five-year plans may emphasize different sectors in line with economic growth rates. So if the development of agriculture as the primary concern in the first five-year plan turns out to be really successful, the main priority in the second Repelita will shift toward other sectors.

The five-year development plans will later be segmented into more detailed annual plans. These annual plans will cover: the physical plan, the financing plan and the plan for development policies. All of these plans, as a whole, should be reflected in the State Budget of Income and Expenditure (APBN). In this way the targets to be annually achieved will be clear and the priority of the state budget will be the implementation of the five-year development plan. With the situation ever changing as development proceeds, and with more information becoming available, adjustments and improvements of the five-year development plan can be introduced annually. In this way, the Repelita programme will be flexible in nature.

The Basic Framework of the present five-year development has three dimensions:

(1) Details according to sectors;
(2) Details according to periods; and
(3) Details according to regions.

Development details have been set out for around twenty sectors, including agriculture and plantations; industry and mining; infrastructure; regional development; rural development; cooperatives and transmigration; tourism; education; health; and family planning.

The details, set out according to periods, constitute the description of the Basic Framework in concrete annual plans. Meanwhile, the details set out according to regions involve the geographic distribution of activities being planned. In this connection, the projects to be developed in each of the regions must be selected on the basis of the maximum promotion of economic growth. In other words, all development activities should have a leveraging effect.

As we are aware, the agricultural sector will play a central role in the first Repelita, with primary attention being paid to food production.

Within the next five years, breakthroughs must be accomplished in the agricultural sector so that it can provide a basis for encouraging growth in other sectors during the implementation of the following five-year plans.

The designation of the agricultural sector to occupy the central position is apparently understood. However, it is worthwhile to spell out the reasons for role it has been selected to play:

(1) Indonesia's production is for the greater part agricultural production, so that the promotion of this sector will greatly contribute to an increase in overall production nationally;

(2) the majority of the Indonesian people work in the agricultural sector, so that the improvement of this sector will promote the livelihood of most of the population;

(3) any increase in agricultural production also constitutes one of the important sources of export promotion;

(4) agriculture constitutes a source of raw materials for industrial development;

(5) the agricultural sector, as it increases its income, will serve as a market for industrial products and in this way promote the growth of the industrial sector;

(6) the agricultural sector is expected to resolve food issues related to the high price of rice on the world market;

(7) development experiences in other countries have taught us that prioritizing industry — as in India and the People's Republic of China (when they undertook their first five-year plans) — does not live up to expectations, whereas the prioritization of agriculture — as in Pakistan and other countries — has been fruitful.

In the agricultural sector, which assumes a central role in the whole of national development, some of the efforts under planning are:

(1) overall improvement of the existing irrigation systems, completion of irrigation projects already started, as well as the evaluation of surveys, planning and commencement of new irrigation projects — in this context, labor-intensive projects utilize available manpower;

(2) effective erosion control, which is to be carried out along with irrigation development;

(3) widespread utilization of high-yielding seedlings, as well as experimentation toward developing new prime seedlings through research activities;

(4) more extensive utilization of fertilizers and pesticides by accurately planning their procurement and striving to increase their production domestically;

(5) the promotion of quality agricultural equipment of domestic origin;

(6) expansion of crop planting areas, such as tidal paddy fields and others through, among other things, manpower movement within the framework of transmigration;

(7) counseling and guidance by the relevant state apparatus for the promotion of agricultural efficiency.

Apart from the efforts involving physical production, there are institutional aspects to the development effort, such as:

(1) a price policy that better stimulates food production by taking into account the proper balance between the price of fertilizers purchased by farmers and the price of unhusked rice purchased by the government;

(2) loans for farmers through rural banks, village granaries, village cooperatives and so forth;

(3) in order to ensure the smooth flow of marketing, attempts will be made for the development and repair of infrastructure connecting production and consumer areas, the removal of barriers to marketing routes and the creation of shortcuts between farmers and consumers in order to increase the income of farmers;

4) problem solving in connection with land affairs within the framework of completing land reform and the planning of land use, besides efforts to guarantee a fair share for farm workers.

Within the framework of increasing food production as a source of protein, fishery and animal-based production will be promoted through counseling and improvement in marketing and storage systems, as well as in animal disease control.

Because all efforts are being focused on the expansion of food, especially rice, production, in order that food stocks can be supplied domestically rather than through imports, government policy requires the seeking out of alternative staple foods, which can be produced locally or, if necessary, imported.

For the production of export crops, improvements will be made in the management and marketing systems in the plantation sector. Counseling and guidance will be provided for smallholder plantations by the government apparatus to help increase more efficient production.

Research will be conducted to ascertain the feasibility and continuity of the production of alternative food products and the possibility of replacing them with other export crops. This is especially true for estate products that show signs of falling into decline on the international market.

Efforts in the forestry sector are to be directed toward:

(1) utilizing forestry products for domestic production activities, such as materials for people's housing, paper plants and so forth;
(2) increasing exports, if possible in the form of manufactured materials;
(3) reforestation within the framework of soil fertility maintenance, erosion prevention, and flood control.

Even if agriculture receives top priority in the first Five-Year Development Plan, over the long term the intention is to gradually create a balanced economic structure.

Industrial development planning has the following priorities:

(1) industries producing materials that directly support agricultural development, particularly food production, such as fertilizer, pesticide, agricultural equipment industries and so forth;
(2) industries processing agricultural products, such as rubber and timber, for both domestic consumption and exports;
(3) industries, particularly the textile industry, producing import substitution products; over the long term, a proper balance between the various operations of the textile industry will be strived for;
(4) industries, such as light manufacturing and handicrafts, with the capacity of absorbing a great deal of manpower without reducing efficiency levels;
(5) abandoned industrial projects resulting from past foreign loans should be revived and utilized to the furthest extent possible so far that their operations can be brought into better harmony with current development planning priorities.

In the mining sector, more emphasis must be focused on mining products with good prospects on the international market, including fossil oil. Mining operations will gradually also cover the domestic processing of raw materials from mining.

The national policy on fuel and energy will strive to facilitate harmony among the various sources of fuel and energy within the framework of developing the mining sector.

Although the development of industrial and mining operations will by no means to be fully undertaken by the government, it will be responsible for the creation of a climate conducive to the development of these industries by the private sector.

The creation of a climate conducive to production applies not only to private companies but also to state owned enterprises, and covers measures to ensure smooth marketing, provide electricity and other production facilities, a selective credit policy, management counseling and education. All of these actions have to be consistent with one another and form an integral whole for industrial development planning.

Within the framework of fostering Indonesia as a single political and economic entity, the improvement of infrastructure receives high priority and covers the following activities:

(1) the improvement and upgrading of roads, particularly those linking food and export commodity producing areas with food consumption areas and export ports. Preparations are being made for possible road network development. In line with this, facilities are to be built for road and vehicle maintenance;

(2) improvement of railway transportation so as to increase the utilization of available capacity;

(3) improvement and expansion of sea communication facilities, including lighthouses, beacons, ports, and so forth;

(4) improvement of air communication facilities, such as airports important to economic routes, terminals, telecommunication connections, and landing lights, in order to increase flight frequency. The next phase in the field of air communication is to expand domestic communication networks, especially to cover the regions needing;

(5) improvement and expansion of telecommunication connections between major cities and major ports, and between land transport and sailing vessels, and so forth;

(6) in the field of electricity, harmony between the distribution and transmission networks and the development of generating plants is to be more efficiently strived for. Power generating plants are being built and are near completion. With the national policy on fuel and energy as the starting point, electricity development has to promptly take into account the choice between various sources of electrical energy.

In planning the improvement and development of infrastructure, efforts are made to create harmonious relations between land communication, sea communication and air communication, by observing regional conditions and needs.

These are a number of issues involving various economic sectors, the planning for which will be further detailed.

In addition to physical planning, the planning of various development policies has also been specified. In this case, attention is being paid particularly to policies aimed at creating a climate that guarantees the effective mobilization of economic resources and production capacity in the public/state sector, as well as in the private sector. In this context, the role of the government and private sector entities is complementary. The measures to be taken in the government sector have specifically determined and stipulated in development planning, while planning for the private sector is primarily implemented through policy direction.

The government is prioritizing investment in the fields of infrastructure and public welfare, such as education, health and so forth, whereas the majority of investment in other sectors is expected to come from the private sector. If investment in any private sector development in any important sector does not reach a level considered conducive to facility growth, the government will invest in that sector.

Efforts are being made to mobilize funding for the financing of planned development activities by expanding government, private sector and external resources.

Government resources are to be increased by raising state revenue to the maximum, while routine expenditure is seriously controlled, so that the portion for development expenditure can be raised. The increase in state revenue, from direct taxes, indirect taxes and other receipts, is to be adjusted to the needs of state expenditure, the people's capacity to support such polices, and the public's sense of social justice, while the efficiency and intensification of their collection will be enhanced so that the portion of national income utilized for development investment grows bigger. Besides that, a selective, well directed policy will be implemented so as to provide an incentive for economic activities.

The State Budget of Income and Expenditure, which must be utilized within the year for which it is effective year, is to reflect the priorities and policies of the Five-Year Development Plan (Repelita) and take account of the principles of balance between the amount of state income and that of expenditure.

State expenditure is to be selective so as to achieve the most appropriate and healthy division between routine expenditure and development expenditure. Serious and effective economic policy has to be promptly carried out, particularly in relation to routine expenditure, through a strict austerity plan.

The private resources are to be enhanced in various ways, among others by:

(a) improving financial and banking institutions, as well as differentiating the structures and rates of interest that stimulate the use of the banking system;

(b) introducing monetary and credit policies that are designed to achieve and maintain financial stability, as well as being aimed at developing the banking system, increasing deposits and directing loans for development in line with five-year plan priorities;

(c) realizing the facilities available pursuant to the Law on National Capital, the Law on Cooperatives and so forth;

(d) activating mutual assistance efforts in villages, such as those involving village granaries, cooperatives and so forth.

The development financing requirement in the form of foreign exchange is to be derived from export promotion, as well as import substitution and the utilization of external capital through loans and through direct investment.

Export promotion to increase the foreign exchange reserves for development financing must be strived for by various means, including the removal of physical and administrative impediments. The pattern of exports must be improved in the sense of diversifying export items, particularly mining products, so as not to merely rely on a limited number of items.

Importation has to be directed in such a way that the pattern of imports accurately reflects the needs of development and the needs of the people at large. Within the framework of saving foreign exchange, operations that produce import substitution products are to be promoted, especially those using large quantities of domestic materials.

External loans of a long-term nature at a low lending rate and with a fairly long grace period for development implementation are to be strived for, so that their repayment in the future will not impose an excessive burden. Direct investment from foreign capital is to be directed toward sectors in line with the priorities of the five-year plan. The utilization of external capital for development is also to be increased within the framework of cooperation with international economic institutions.

The business and investment climate for development will be improved through various policies, such as the fiscal policy, the monetary policy, and the balance of payments policy, all of which have to form a harmonious whole that promotes national development without endangering the level of stability already achieved. The series of policies should further strengthen the level of stability already achieved and in this way stimulate the process of development.

The five-year plan specifications, set out according to sectors, determines the targets to be achieved and realized through investment in certain projects, as well as through various policies that are in harmony and consistent with each other. In this context, in the first phase the operations that continue rehabilitation efforts are to be described.

The targets, investments and policies of the five-year development plan have to be reflected in the State Budget of Income and Expenditure from year to year, along with the planning and improvement of stipulated targets, investments and policies in line with latest developments.

Policies on research and other scientific activities must be consciously adopted in accordance with development needs, with surveys, designs and feasibility studies preceding any sectoral or project planning as basic elements in preparation for more complete plans.

The financing of development projects, as well as purchases, must be really prudent so that extensive operations can be undertaken with limited funds. For this purpose, financing and purchasing systems that guarantee an effective economy must be introduced. For the maximum utilization of funds, a comprehensive and effective system of financial supervision is required.

Thus are some of the basic guidelines involving the planning of various development policies. The planning of these policies is no less important than the planning of investment meant for the development projects. For this reason, consistency among the various policies and between the policies on one side and the investments on the other, is very important. For example, development of the textile industry requires not only investments in textile projects, but also an import policy, a credit policy and other policies that stimulate the growth of the industry.

The other aspect requiring attention within the framework of the various policies has to do with the fact that there is always a relationship between planning and implementation. In this connection, and also because planning is a continuous process, the adjustment and improvement of plans is a necessity.

Within the framework of the ongoing development planning activities, various questions have arisen. Among them is: Has the time now come to plan our development efforts, especially as we are at present still in the process of carrying out stabilization and rehabilitation efforts?

On this matter, it should be noticed that stabilization and rehabilitation on the one hand and development on the other are indeed different, but they are not in opposition.

The difference between the two is not black-and-white, but rather the process of growth from one into the other is a myriad shades of gray. In this context, as already described above, the development efforts of the initial years of the five-year plans are being directed toward operations that continue rehabilitation efforts, besides preparing for the development of new projects for the coming years. Likewise, with regard to the relationship of development to stabilization efforts, it has been affirmed that development policies have to be planned in such a way that they pose no danger to stabilization efforts, but rather they just further strengthen the level of stability already achieved, and in this way further stimulate the process of development. Then, with regard to the necessity to undertake development planning efforts, it should be noted that the Provisional People's Consultative Assembly (MPRS) has stipulated the requirements for the formulation and implementation of the five-year development plans.

The other question asked is whether what is now available is not a development plan because it is general in nature rather than quantitative, and certainly not yet concrete. Furthermore, the matters under planning are logical ones.

In this context, we must note that only the Basic Framework of the Repelita fiver-year plan has been set into place, and contains little more than basic guidelines that indicate the directions to be taken and a number of measures to embark upon.

Further specifications can and will be made on the basis of the directions determined. And, as already indicated, the further details of the Basic Framework are currently being worked out, covering the details according to sectors, details according to periods and details according to regions.

With regard to the statement that the matters being planned are logical ones, it is only natural that planning should take a logical course, instead of speculative stances. In this connection it should also be noted that logic cannot always be consistently adhered to.

As for the quantitative details of the Basic Framework, their preparation is now underway, involving the various sectors, as well as overall figures. For example, based on very provisional calculations, estimates can be made of additional capital needs from external sources, in the form of both direct investment and loans.

In the coming years we will continue to be obliged to repay the debts taken out in the past. Even if we manage to reschedule repayment, the amount of new capital needed from abroad within a period of five years is estimated at around $2 billion to 2.5 billion. However, if the debt repayment cannot be rescheduled, a bigger sum will be needed, possibly reaching $3.5 billion. These figures are based on very provisional calculations, but they provide an inkling idea that the development of Indonesia is going to be harder due to the debt repayment burden. Therefore, it is absolutely necessary for us to be very careful in securing any new loans, in particular in relation to their amounts and conditions, as well as their utilization.

NOTE

[1] The description of the five-year plan programme by the Chairman of the National Development Planning Agency (BAPPENAS) containing basic ideas for the Repelita programme material for exchanges of views with various circles in the course of 1968. This article is translated by Harry Bhaskara.

PART **II**

IMPLEMENTATION OF INDONESIA'S DEVELOPMENT

9

PROGRESS AND CHALLENGES OF INDONESIA'S DEVELOPMENT (1990)[1]

Introductory Note: *The University of California at Berkeley invited me to give a presentation at The Walter and Phyllis Shorenstein Symposium on Economic Challenges in the Pacific-Asian Region in San Francisco on 28 March 1990. In my presentation I reviewed a number of critical challenges to Indonesia's development: the rapid-albeit declining-population growth on a relatively small island; the immense challenge of debt management to keep away from a debt crisis in the face of exchange rate volatility of major world currencies; continuous and consistent economic reforms, policy adjustments and restructuring; sustained progress in poverty alleviation; and preventing further environmental degradation. I also mentioned a number of other challenges: maintaining food self-sufficiency; human resource development; securing employment opportunities for a labor force growing at 2.3 million annually; reconciling the rapid growth of large enterprises with the country's ideals of equity and social justice; a purposeful government able to provide a sense of direction to the development process but also able to discard outdated regulatory functions and to encourage participatory development at the grassroot level.*

Let me start with an update of some statistics on Indonesia, most of which are certainly quite familiar. The total population of Indonesia in 1990 is about 182 million, out of which 110 million live on Java. Indonesia has the third largest population in Asia and the fifth largest in the world, after China, India, the United States and the Soviet Union.

The vigorous implementation of the family planning programme has brought about a demographic transition: Total fertility rate declined from 5.6 children in 1970 to 3.4 children at present, while the crude birth rate came down from 43 in 1970 to 28 births per 1000 persons. Meanwhile mortality rates have also declined substantially: Infant mortality rate decreased from 124 in 1970 to 58 infants per 1000 live births, while the crude death rate came down from 19 in 1970 to 8 deaths per 1000 persons.

As a result of the demographic transition the rate of population growth has decreased from 2.5 per cent in 1970 to just below 2 per cent per year. For Java the growth rate is about 1.5 per cent and for the other Indonesian islands 2.4 per cent. A significant feature of the decrease in population growth is the fact that it was achieved during a period of very rapid declining mortality. Even with the lower growth rate of 2.0 per cent the current increase of total population of Indonesia is at least 3.5 million persons each year. Had the growth rate remained at 2.5 per cent, the annual population increase would have been even more higher: 4.5 million persons each year. Looking into the future and assuming a continued reduction in fertility, the total number of population is expected to be around 213 million by the turn of the century.

Clearly, one obvious and serious challenge for Indonesia's development is its rapid — albeit declining — population growth with its concentrated geographical distribution on a relatively small island. The decline in population growth is due to the rapid decrease in fertility and in spite of the very rapid decline in mortality. The systematic implementation of Indonesia's family planning programme based on voluntary participation together with the substantial expansion of education of women are major factors inducing the decline in fertility.

However, further declines in fertility and in the rate of population growth will be much more difficult. Contraceptive use increased substantially from less than 10 per cent in 1970 to more than 45 per cent of eligible couples at present. Further increases require considerably more effort to reach and motivate larger numbers of contraceptive acceptors.

Moreover, there is the serious problem of resource availability. The Indonesian family planning programme has been supported by the government's budget and by international assistance for population. While the expanded programme continues to receive very high priority in the government's budgetary allocation — even in times of severe budgetary constraints — there is currently a distinct decrease in the availability of international assistance for population. A critical decline in the availability of international resources for family planning will jeopardize the required programme expansion with serious implications for further decreases in fertility and population growth. In turn the latter will have a considerable impact in the future on unemployment among the younger working age population as well as on environmental degradation. Confronted with severe limitations on the availability of international resources, a careful reexamination of the existing programme is currently being conducted, among others to explore carefully the possibility of partially shifting family planning by stages from a free program to a fee-for-service programme.

Let me now move to another challenge faced by Indonesia's development — a completely different type of challenge, which illustrates the diversity of challenges faced by a developing country. It has to do with Indonesia's foreign debts. Let me again start with some statistics. During the three years period from 1985 to 1987 Indonesia's stock of total outstanding debt increased from US$31.2 billion to US$50.2 billion, an increase of US$19 billion or 60 per cent. Its annual debt service payment increased from US$4.2 billion in 1984 to US$6.9 billion in 1987, an increase of US$2.7 billion or 64 per cent. The very sharp increase in total outstanding debt as well as in annual debt servicing is primarily due to the substantial realignment of major world currencies, in particular the massive depreciation of the US dollar against the Japanese yen. A large portion of Indonesia's debts were denominated in yen and in currencies other than the US dollar. It has been estimated by the International Monetary Fund that more than 80 per cent of the increase in Indonesia's stock of total outstanding debt and about two-third of the increase in its debt service payments were attributable to the effects of the depreciation of the US dollar.

The impact of the massive depreciation of the US dollar on Indonesia's development was even worse because of its timing. It coincided with the sharp decline in the international price of oil in 1986. At that time around 70 per cent of Indonesia's export earnings came from oil and liquefied natural gas. Indonesia's development thus received a double blow: the steep fall in oil prices — from US$25 per barrel at the beginning of 1986 to less than US$10 during the middle of the year — and at the same time the enormous depreciation of the US dollar — from US$1 = Yen 285 in 1985 to US$1 = Yen 125 in 1987.

Of course, the two major Pacific countries did not realligned their currencies in order to intentionally hurt a developing country in the Pacific. The reallignment of currencies was considered necessary to hopefully reduce deficits and surpluses in the current account of their respective balance of payments. But in arriving at such a crucial decision they certainly ignore completely the grave effects of their actions on the balance of payments of Indonesia and other countries in similar circumstances. The fact remains that in deciding on matters with global ramifications the major industrial countries do not — or at least do not adequately — take into account the probable effects of their decisions on developing countries. For members of the G-7, or for that matter the G-2, most developing countries seem to continue to be on the periphery, far away from the center of their major attention.

The recent appreciation of the US dollar to around U$$1 = Yen 158 actually implies some form of limited debt relief for Indonesia. But again, such relief is not the result of a deliberate policy action on the part of the economic superpowers. It is rather the unforeseen consequence of their inability to contain their exchange rate movements within certain boundaries they consider most desirable. At present a concerted effort is being mounted by the major industrialized countries to move their exchange rates back into those boundaries. If they succeed, the present limited relief for Indonesia's foreign debts will turn out to be only temporary and short-lived.

It is well known that Indonesia is straddled with a heavy burden of foreign debt. But it is probably not widely recognized that Indonesia's stock of total outstanding debt is exceeded by a few developing countries only. Its debt service ratio is of the same order of magnitude as most of the World Bank's category of "the seventeen highly indebted developing countries" — Argentina, Bolivia, Brazil, Chile, Colombia, Costa Rica, Cote d'Ivoire, Equador, Jamaica, Mexico, Morocco, Nigeria, Peru, Philippines, Uruguay, Venezuela and Yugoslavia. Nevertheless, Indonesia is not included in this category of countries. These seventeen developing countries are not only heavily indebted, but are also in a debt crisis.

Unlike these seventeen countries, Indonesia is not in a debt crisis, in spite of its heavy burden of foreign debt. Despite very tight foreign exchange constraints, Indonesia continues to service its external debt fully and timely. It does not universally announce a limit on payments of interest or repayment of principal. It does not look for rescheduling of its debt with foreign governments. Nor does it invite international banks to renegotiate the terms and conditions of its outstanding debt. It also does not have any standby arrangement with the IMF. Adjustment loans from the World Bank and the Asian Development Bank are agreed upon not on the basis of certain conditionalities which are to be implemented, but rather based on economic reforms and policy adjustments already carried out by Indonesia on its own.

Some may raise the question as to why Indonesia does not join the group of countries renouncing or renegotiating its debts. The answer is simple: of all feasible options thoroughly considered, the one that has been chosen is the least bad alternative. Of course it does not consist of timely and fully servicing of debts only. It implies the postponement of major capital intensive projects, devaluations, flexible exchange rate management, prudent fiscal and monetary policies, tax reforms, financial sector reforms, waves of deregulation of foreign trade and industry, rollback of non-tariff barriers, tariff reform, improving the climate for investment, developing the stock exchange, and an all-out effort to capture foreign markets for non-oil exports. All these measures, implemented in a consistent manner, result in a substantial growth of non-oil exports, investment and employment. Instead of capital flight, the country is at present enjoying a robust capital inflow, ranging from official development assistance, financing from multilateral financial institutions, financing from export-import banks, commercial bank credits, and direct investment.

Another issue which attracts wide ranging interest is the question whether all those economic reforms, policy adjustments and restructuring do not result in an ever-increasing burden for the poor. A number of studies have been carried out to measure the incidence of poverty and its trends. One of these studies is contained in a World Bank report, which concluded that there was a decline in the incidence of poverty from 33 per cent in 1984 to about 22 per cent in 1987, implying an absolute decline in the number of poor Indonesians from about 53 million to around 37 million in 1987.

The report of the World Bank further elaborated that the success in reducing poverty during the adjustment period was due to two factors. First, the development efforts before the adjustment period — before the substantial decline in oil prices — was directed at establishing a strong rural economy and put into place an extensive network of social and physical infrastructure, such as the rapid expansion of primary schools throughout the archipelago leading to universal primary education, integrated rural centers for health, nutrition and family planning, extensive networks of rural roads, irrigation and flood control. The second factor is related to the fact that the economic reforms and policy adjustments contained elements geared toward sustaining progress on poverty alleviation. Budgetary expenditures in "poverty-related" sectors — such as agriculture, human resource development and transfers to regional and local governments — were protected relative to other sectors. Moreover, the combination of trade and industrial deregulation as well as real exchange rate adjustments led to a rapid recovery and growth in investment and employment in manufacturing and agriculture.

A reduction in poverty, as stated in the World Bank report, is indeed clearly noticeable. But the fact remains that 37 million Indonesians still belong to the absolutely poor. This is certainly a major challenge for Indonesia's development, particularly since in carrying out its development programmes the country is committed to the triple objectives of equity, growth and stability.

Perhaps I should conclude my remarks with a short discussion on another major challenge for Indonesia's development: the issue of environment. It is at present fully recognized in Indonesia that development not properly prepared and implemented will damage the environment. On the other hand, it is also widely perceived that poverty and lack of development are major causes of environmental degradation. Therefore, it is strongly felt that the pattern of development to be pursued by Indonesia should be sustainable and at the same time also participatory in nature. Nevertheless, it is also realized that sustainable development requires more rather than less resources. That it is decidedly more rather than less costly.

There is also a growing awareness in Indonesia that developing countries should not be required by the developed countries to carry out sustainable development while at the same time these industrial countries themselves continue with their established patterns of production and consumption which is already enormously damaging to the world environment. An example is the energy dilemma. On a per capita basis Indonesia's energy consumption is very low, even lower than most countries in Asia. The country's resources include oil, coal, and hydropower. If industrial countries discourage the use of such resources for Indonesia's development without presenting viable alternatives, while they themselves continue with their existing pattern of lifestyle based on a huge consumption level of oil and coal, it will be logically construed as a deliberate effort on their part to prevent the country from ever getting developed. Therefore, there should be more effort on the part of industrial nations to effectively prevent further enviromental damage in their own countries, while at the same time be much more forthcoming in sharing the burden of the higher cost of sustainable development of developing countries.

To summarize: while Indonesia has achieved substantial progress in many fields, the country's development still faces many critical challenges. In my remarks I have touched upon a few major challenges: the rapid population growth and its concentration on a relatively small island; the urgent requirement to further expand the family planning programme at a time of deteriorating international support; the immense challenge of debt management to keep the country away from a debt crisis in the face of volatile exchange rate movements of the major world currencies; the challenge of broadening and strengthening the national economy through continuous and consistent economic reforms, policy adjustments and restructuring; the uncompromising challenge of sustaining progress in poverty alleviation; the major challenge of preventing further environmental degradation through sustainable development.

There are of course still *many other challenges* of at least the same urgency and seriousness, such as: the challenge of maintaining food self-sufficiency in the face of rapid population growth and increased income; the growing challenge of human resource development; the huge challenge of securing employment opportunities for a labour force growing at a rate of 2.3 million annually; the challenge of reconciling the rapid growth of large business enterprises with the country's ideals of equity and social justice; the challenge of nurturing a purposeful government able in providing a strategic sense of direction to the process of development, but also able to discard outdated regulatory functions and to encourage participatory development at the grassroot level.

NOTE

[1]   Presentation at the University of California at Berkeley Symposium in San Francisco, 28 March 1990.

10

SOME FEATURES OF INDONESIA'S ECONOMIC DEVELOPMENT DURING THE LAST TWENTY-FIVE YEARS (1993)[1]

Introductory Note: *In 1993 the Government of Japan took the initiative to organize The Tokyo International Conference on African Development (TICAD) and I was invited as a guest speaker, in particular on the agenda item "Asian Experience and African Development". I was very encouraged that Japan, one of the richest countries in the world, gave special attention to the suffering of millions of people in Africa. In my presentation I emphasized the many similarities of the challenges faced by Indonesia and the countries in Africa, including the diversity of its population and the many challenges to be faced. During that occasion, my colleagues who also attended the Conference (professors Sadli, Emil Salim and my other colleagues) had occasions to interact with delegates from different countries in Africa, which later on was followed up with many visits by Sadli and Emil Salim to those countries. The intensive interactions with the actual problems they saw in Africa strengthened their convictions in arguing for the relief of the debt-ridden countries in their* *meetings with officials of the multilateral agencies (the World Bank and the IMF) as well as in their meetings with representatives of the highly developed countries. It was encouraging news for all of us when the multilateral agencies finally introduce the HIPC (Heavily Indebted Poor Countries) debt relief for the highly indebted developing countries, although the pace of relief was unfortunately slow.*

It is a great honour for me to be invited as a guest speaker to the Tokyo International Conference on African Development. The theme of the second agenda of the Conference is "Asian Experience and African Development". Since my knowledge on development is limited to the experience of one country only — Indonesia — perhaps the best contribution I can provide to the Conference is to present some features of the economic development of Indonesia during the last twenty five years.

In order to provide the necessary setting, let me start with some statistics and a little bit of history. Indonesia is the largest archipelago in the world, consisting of more than 17,000 islands. Its length from west to east is about the distance from Accra to Mogadishu, or from London to Kuwait, or from San Francisco to somewhere in the Atlantic Ocean east of New York.

Indonesia's total population in 1993 is around 185 million. In terms of population size, Indonesia is the fourth largest country in the world after China, India and the United States of America. More than 100 million people live on the relatively smaller island of Java, which has a population density of about 800 persons per square kilometre — probably one of the most densely populated areas in the world.

In terms of diversity, Indonesia's population consists of some 300 ethnic groups, each with its own cultural heritage. Apart from the national language — the Indonesian language — there are about 365 languages and dialects spoken in the different regions. Most Indonesians are Moslems, while the rest are Christians, Catholics, Hindus, and Buddhists.

As to the country's recent history, Indonesia proclaimed its independence in 1945 right after the end of the Second World War in the Pacific. It was soon followed by Indonesia's War of Independence, which lasted until the end of 1949. The Second World War and the War of Independence, which took most of the decade of the 1940s, exacted a huge toll, not-only in terms of human suffering but also in the destruction of productive assets and the country's infrastructure.

During the first twenty years of independence the country was preoccupied with problems of nation building and national unity. It was a daunting challenge in view of the size of the country, its highly complicated geography, its large population, its diversity in terms of cultural heritage, ethnic groups, languages and dialects. For years the country had its share of internal conflict, civil strife, uprising and insurrection.

As a consequence, the general economic conditions deteriorated rapidly, particularly during the first half of the 1960s. The nation faced a myriad of problems, including widespread food scarcity, hyperinflation, stagnant industries, substantial unemployment, rapidly deteriorating infrastructure, balance of payments crisis, dwindling international reserves, and rapidly mounting foreign debt arrears. The country was in such desperate condition that many international analysts and observers held out little hope for Indonesia's future.

The turning point came in 1966, more than two decades after independence. The new government of President Suharto adopted a pragmatic economic stabilization and rehabilitation programme. Its major objectives were a reduction in the rate of inflation, the provision of food and clothing to the population, rehabilitation of the infrastructure, and increased exports. With the achievement of the objectives, the country then embarked on the implementation of a five year development plan within the framework of a twenty-five year long-term development programme.

The fundamental objectives of the plan were growth, stability and equity. These three objectives turned out to complement each other rather than compete against each other. Economic and political stability was a prerequisite for growth. Rapid growth helped alleviate poverty as one of the objective's of equity. Without equity the objective of stability could not be achieved.

To achieve all these goals a number of policies was pursued. One was the principle of a balanced budget. The second was a fully convertible currency and an open capital account. Third, a competitive exchange rate. Fourth, a programme to deregulate domestic production, foreign trade, and the financial sector. Furthermore, high priority was given to agricultural and rural development. Investment in infrastructure, human resource development, including health and education, were also high on the priority list.

Twenty-five years ago Indonesia was one of the poorest countries in the world, with a per capita income of only US$50. At present per capita income is US$650, while average GDP growth is almost 7 per cent. In 1970, 60 per cent of the population or 70 million people lived in absolute poverty, while in 1990 the percentage was 15 per cent or 27 million people. While the country used to be the biggest rice importer in the world (with imports of 2 million tons of rice), since 1984 Indonesia is self-sufficient in rice. Moreover, the family planning programme which started in 1968 has been very successful.

A Once-and-for-All Settlement of Foreign Debt

In 1966 Indonesia was confronted with a severe foreign debt crisis. Debt payments due, including arrears, exceeded exports earnings. A settlement was reached with the Paris Club countries for the rearrangement of debt service payments. The 1966 settlement provided for relief from payments of principal and interest due in 1967. The amounts were to be repaid over 8 years following a 3-year grace period. Interest was charged on the rescheduled amounts.

Since the agreement of 1966 covered only the payments due in 1967, another meeting was held in 1967 for the rescheduling of payments due in 1968. Similarly, in 1968 another meeting was held for the rescheduling of payments due in the following year. Thus, it was necessary to have negotiations every year on debt rescheduling of payments falling due in the following year.

Furthermore, every year after an agreement was reached at the Paris Club, further bilateral negotiations had to be conducted with individual creditors based on the agreement with the Paris Club. There were at that time twenty-two creditor countries, of which seven were participants of the Paris Club while the remaining were not. The latter had to be persuaded to agree on the rescheduling of Indonesia's debt based on the terms of agreement with the Paris Club.

While the year after year rearrangement of debt provided some degree of relief, it was obvious that it could not become the basis of a viable long-term settlement of Indonesia's debt crisis. Not only were the grace period and the repayment period too short, but the amount rescheduled was limited to payments due in the following year only. Such an arrangement implied that rescheduling agreements had to be negotiated every year and that, soon, the rescheduled amounts would have to be rescheduled again. The continuing debt negotiations, year after year, created a never-ending climate of uncertainty, both for the government in working out its annual budget and its monetary policy as well as for the private sector which as a consequence kept postponing its investment decisions.

Not less serious was the fact that such an arrangement also had an impact of a different nature. At that time, during the late 1960s, Indonesia had a very limited number of people who had the capability to work out programmes for economic recovery and growth. But they were totally preoccupied with the never-ending process of debt negotiation as a result of the year after year rearrangement of the country's debt.

It was fortunate for Indonesia that its Paris Club creditors also realized the serious shortcomings of such an arrangement. It was recognized that the year after year rescheduling could not become the basis for a viable long-term settlement of Indonesia's debt crisis. Without further postponement of rescheduled maturities the payments burden of new loans extended to Indonesia would create another payments crisis in the early 1970s.

If another debt crisis was to be prevented, a more durable settlement had to be negotiated and agreed on. Such a durable settlement would enable Indonesia to have access to the necessary financial resources and to embark on a process of sustained growth. For that purpose there was a need for an assessment of Indonesia's debt problem, to be followed by proposals for a final settlement. It was strongly felt by the Paris Club creditors as well as Indonesia that such an assessment and proposals for settlement should not be requested from a creditor nor from the debtor, since both were parties to the debt problem. Instead it should be requested from a third party.

The Paris Club and Indonesia decided then to invite a third party to make an assessment of Indonesia's debt problem and to come up with proposals for a final settlement of the debts. The third party invited was Dr Herman J. Abs, the highly respected banker and authority on finance from Germany.

In preparing his assessment and in working out his proposals Dr Abs was assisted by a joint working group of staff members of the

World Bank and the IMF. The joint working group provided assistance in working out short range and longer-range balance of payments projections and in calculating the prospective effects of alternative debt rescheduling formulae on Indonesia's balance of payments and prospects for economic growth. A simulation model was prepared with alternative assumptions regarding aid levels and terms, debt rescheduling formulae and export growth rates. An assessment was made on the implications of the alternative assumptions on the balance of payments, including the capacity to service new external debt, and on the domestic economy including the prospective rate of economic growth.

Dr Abs submitted his assessment of Indonesia's debt problem and proposals for a final settlement based on the following considerations:

(1) There should be a "once-for-all" long-term debt settlement, not subject to periodic re-negotiations.
(2) The debt settlement should ensure the restoration of the creditworthiness of Indonesia.
(3) The debt settlement should be based on a strict application of the principle of non-discrimination.

As to the specific proposals, Dr Abs suggested the following:

(1) The principal sums owed by Indonesia were to be repaid in full over a period of thirty years in equal installments and with no grace period.
(2) Interest on old debts together with interest agreed upon in earlier rescheduling negotiations was to be cancelled.
(3) The new loan would be free of interest.
(4) No distinction was to be made between the different types of creditors as well as between the different purposes for which the loans had been extended.

A number of creditor countries had serious problems with some aspects of the Abs proposal. After further deliberations a number of amendments were introduced. The final settlement agreed upon in April 1970 between Indonesia and the Paris Club countries were as follows:

(1) Repayment of principal in thirty years beginning in 1970 to 1999.
(2) Repayment of contractual interest in fifteen years beginning in 1985 to 1999.

(3) No further interest would be charged on the amounts deferred.
(4) Indonesia had the option to defer part of the payments of principal
     due during the first eight years to the last eight years, which was
     the period 1992–99, with payments of an interest of 4 per cent.

Since 1970 no other rescheduling of Indonesia's foreign debts was
necessary. Through careful debt management and timely implementation
of economic reforms and structural adjustments Indonesia had been
able to prevent another foreign debt crisis throughout the twenty-two
years period.

The final settlement of Indonesia's debts twenty-two years ago could
only be achieved because both sides, the creditors and the debtor, were
determined to arrive at a once-for-all settlement by both sides doing
their utmost. Thus, the debtor put its own house in order by carrying
out effectively a comprehensive programme of economic stabilization.
On the other hand, the creditors made an all-out effort to explore and
to work out a debt settlement which was truly a final settlement.

The following may illustrate the determination of the creditors. The
final settlement of Indonesia's debt crisis as worked out in the Paris
Club did initially not received the support of the Government of Japan
since it was contrary to provisions in the existing laws of Japan. Had
the Government of Japan at that time continuously opposed such a
settlement in the Paris Club, no agreement could have been reached and
the objective of finding a final settlement would not have been achieved.
Instead, the Government of Japan made a determined effort to overcome
such legal impediments by successfully introducing an amendment to
the existing law. In today's language of development cooperation, it
was an act reflecting a true spirit of cooperation between partners in
development.

The settlement of Indonesia's debt in 1970 was a final settlement
which enabled the country to have access to financial resources and to
move forward to a process of sustained growth. It is very unfortunate
that the Paris Club creditors since then continued stressing their view
that the final settlement of Indonesia's foreign debt was a unique case,
which should not become a precedent for the debt settlement of other
developing countries.

Perhaps today, twenty-two years after the final settlement of
Indonesia's debt problem and in view of the still large number of
developing countries with heavy debt burden, the Paris Club creditor

countries and the international financial institutions may agree to apply the main features of Indonesia's debt settlement to relevant cases. The main difference is probably the fact that for most developing countries with a heavy debt burden today the rescheduling of debt is far from sufficient. A substantial reduction of both the stock of debt and debt service is a necessary condition for reviving the development process.

Repeated reduction of debt service payments or the provision of new loans instead of debt reduction create uncertainties which may become counterproductive for the investment climate. What is required for most severely indebted developing countries at present is a substantial debt and debt service reduction in a single operation, instead of in stages in order to arrive at a final settlement of the debt problem. Moreover, in order to achieve a reasonable rate of economic growth, the final debt settlement and new flows of financial resources are to be worked out as integral components of a comprehensive external financing package.

Weathering External Shocks

Let me now move to another challenge faced by Indonesia's development. It is a completely different type of challenge. It also illustrates the divergence in potential challenges faced by a developing country. During the three years period from 1984 to 1987 Indonesia's total outstanding debt increased from US$31.2 billion to US$50.2 billion, an increase of US$19 billion or 60 per cent. Its annual debt service payment increased from US$4.2 billion in 1984 to US$6.9 billion in 1987, an increase of US$2.7 billion or 64 per cent.

The very sharp increase in total debt outstanding as well as in annual debt servicing is mainly due to the realignment of world currencies, in particular the rapid depreciation of the US dollar against the Japanese yen and other major currencies, while a substantial proportion of Indonesia's debts was denominated in yen and other currencies than the US dollar. It has been estimated by the International Monetary Fund that more than 80 per cent of the increase in the stock of outstanding debt and about two-thirds of the increase in debt service payments were attributable to the valuation effects of the depreciation of the US dollar.

The impact of the sharp depreciation or the US dollar on Indonesia's development was even worse because of its timing. It coincided with the sharp decline in the international price of oil in 1986. Indonesia's development was thus receiving a double blow: the sharp fall of oil prices and at the same time the sharp depreciation of the US dollar.

Of course, the two major Pacific powers did not realigned their currencies in order to intentionally hurt a developing country in the Pacific. The realignment of currencies was considered necessary in the hope to reduce deficits and surpluses in the current account of their respective balance of payments. But they certainly ignore completely the effects of their actions on the balance of payments of Indonesia and other countries in similar circumstances. The fact remains that in deciding on matters with global ramifications the major industrial countries do not, or at least do not adequately, take into account the probable effect of their decisions on developing countries.

As a consequence of major currency realignments Indonesia is saddled with a heavy burden of foreign debt. Its stock of outstanding debt is among the largest of all developing nations in Asia and compared to all developing countries in the world it **is** only exceeded by a few countries. In terms of debt service ratio it is of the same order of magnitude as most of the highly indebtedly developing countries.

However, Indonesia is not included in the category of the highly indebted developing countries. These countries are considered not only heavily indebted, but are also in a debt crisis. In spite of its heavy debt, Indonesia is not in a debt crisis. Despite of tight foreign exchange constraints, Indonesia continue to service its external debt orderly and timely. It does not unilaterally announce a limit on payments of interest or repayment of principal. It does not look for rescheduling of its debt with foreign governments. Nor does it invite international banks to renegotiate the terms and conditions of its outstanding debt. It also does not have any standby arrangement with the IMF since 1970. Adjustment loans from the World Bank and the Asian Development Bank are agreed upon not on the basis of certain conditionalities which are to be implemented, but rather based on reforms and policy adjustments that Indonesia has already carried out on its own.

Some may raise the question as to why Indonesia does not join the group of countries renouncing or renegotiating its debts. The answer is simple: of all feasible options that have been thoroughly considered, the one that has been chosen is the least bad alternative.

Of course it does not consist of timely and orderly servicing of debts only. It also means embarking on a comprehensive set of economic

reforms, policy adjustments and restructuring. It implies the postponement of major capital intensive projects, devaluations, flexible exchange
rate management, prudent fiscal and monetary policies, tax reforms,
financial sector reforms, waves of deregulation of foreign trade and
industry, rollback of non-tariff barriers, tariff reform, improving the
climate for investment, developing the stock exchange and an all-out
effort to capture foreign markets for non-oil exports.

All these measures, which had to be implemented in a consistent
manner, resulted in a substantial growth of exports, employment and
investments. Instead of capital flight, the country is enjoying robust
capital inflow, ranging from official development assistance, financing
from multilateral financial institutions, financing from export-import
banks, commercial bank credits, and direct investment.

Poverty Alleviation

Another issue which attracts wide ranging interest is the question
whether all those economic reforms, policy adjustments and restructuring
did not result in an ever-increasing burden for the poor. A number
of studies carried out to measure the incidence of poverty and its
trend concluded that there was a decline in the incidence of poverty
from 60 per cent in the 1970s to about 15 per cent in 1990, implying
an absolute decline in the number of poor Indonesians from around
70 million to about 27 million in 1990. The success in reducing poverty
during the difficult adjustment period in the 1980s was due to two
factors

First, the development efforts before the adjustment period was
directed at establishing a strong rural economy and put into place an
extensive network of social and physical infrastructure, such as primary
schools leading to universal primary education, integrated centres for
health, nutrition and family planning, rural road networks, irrigation
and flood control.

The second factor is related to the fact that the economic reforms
and policy adjustments contained elements geared toward sustaining
progress on poverty reduction. Budgetary expenditures in "poverty-
related" sectors — such as agriculture, human resource development
and transfers to regional governments — were protected relative to
other sectors.

Moreover, the combination of trade and industrial deregulation and real exchange rate adjustments led to a rapid recovery in investment and employment in manufacturing and agriculture.

While a reduction in poverty is noticeable, the fact remains that 27 million Indonesians still belong to the absolutely poor. This is another challenge for Indonesia's development, particularly since in carrying out development the country is committed to the triple objectives of equity, growth and stability.

NOTE

[1]   Address at the Tokyo International Conference on African Development (TICAD), Tokyo, 6 October 1993.

11

OIL AND THE INDONESIAN ECONOMY (1985)[1]

Introductory Note: *The Indonesian Petroleum Association invited me to give an address at its convention commemorating the centennial of the oil industry in Indonesia on 8 October 1985. In the address I pointed out that: "Compared to many countries in the world Indonesia is indeed blessed with an abundance of natural resources. Rich natural resource endowments, however, are no guarantee for rapid economic growth.... Only with the proper policy mix will the availability of abundant natural resources provide a strong base for a strong growth of a country's economy." I then referred to the sharp increases of oil prices in the seventies which led to rapid expansion in investment in the public as well as private sectors. I also highlighted a set of adverse conditions in the oil market that had forced the government to take the following measures: a steep devaluation of the currency coupled with a flexible exchange rate management policy to maintain our external competitive edge; reassessment of government expenditure that resulted in a US$10 billion rescue; extensive reform of the banking sector resulting in rapid growth of domestic savings; major reform of the tax system to mobilize domestic non-oil resources; sweeping reforms in customs, shipping, and harbour management to strengthen the non-oil export drive.*

The present convention of the Indonesian Petroleum Association is of special importance since *today we commemorate the centennial of the oil industry in Indonesia.* Permit me on this memorable occasion to express my congratulations to all of you for your participation in the successful development of the country's natural resources into an industry of utmost importance for furthering the nation's development goals.

Compared to many countries in the world Indonesia is indeed blessed with an abundance of natural resources. Rich natural resource endowments, however, are no guarantee for rapid economic growth. Moreover, a number of countries with limited natural resources have been very successful in their development efforts. Only with the proper policy mix will the availability of abundant natural resources provide a strong base for a sustained growth of a country's economy. In this respect Indonesia is a case in point. At present oil and gas in Indonesia play a crucial role in bringing about a broad based pattern of sustained economic development. Annually about 60 to 70 per cent of total foreign exchange earnings as well as budgetary revenues originate from oil and gas.

About fifteen years ago, around 1970, the proportion of foreign exchange earnings originating from oil was around 35 per cent, while 25 per cent of budgetary revenues came from oil. Sharp increases in oil revenues together with other sources of budgetary revenues enabled a rapid expansion in investment expenditures in the public sector. In turn, this expansion of the public sector, such as rapidly-growing expenditures in irrigation system, road network, education and training, health and nutrition, power and telecommunication, created an environment conducive to investment and production in the private sector. Since then the Indonesian economy experienced sustained economic growth throughout the seventies. Real gross domestic product grew at an annual average rate of 7 per cent over 1974–78, while during 1979–81 the average rate of growth was 6.5 per cent annually.

A significant breakthrough took place in the agricultural sector, particularly in rice production. A concerted effort in investments, research, agricultural extension and a set of price policies resulted in a spectacular growth in rice production during the past six years. A few years ago Indonesia imported around two millions of rice. At present the absence of Indonesia as a buyer in the world market of rice contributes significantly to a very substantial decline in world prices of rice. Success in rapidly increasing rice production, however, presents new problems.

Gone are the problems of scarcity. Enter the problems of oversupply, of shortages in warehousing, of deteriorating stocks, of rapidly growing financial requirements. The success in increasing rice production and the availability of sufficient rice stocks enables the country to embark upon a wide-ranging programme of food diversification.

Meanwhile, new problems and challenges came up during the early years of the eighties. During fiscal years 1979–80 and 1980–81 the balance of payments registered a surplus in its current account of almost US$3.0 billion. However, the weakening of the international oil market resulted in a complete reversal: the current account of the balance of payments showed a deficit of US$2.7 billion in 1981–82 and ultimately became US$6.8 billion in 1982–83. These adverse developments led to a swift implementation of a number of far-reaching measures: a substantial currency devaluation together with flexible exchange rate management to maintain external competitiveness, rephasing of the public sector investment programme resulting in a US$10.0 billion reduction in expenditures, an extensive reform of the banking system resulting in a rapid growth of domestic savings, a major reform of the tax system with a view to mobilize domestic non-oil resources, and more recently sweeping reforms in customs, shipping and harbour administration in order to substantially strengthening the non-oil export drive.

In the meantime, a number of developments took place in the oil sector. Indonesia became the largest producer of LNG in the world, while the completion of the three oil refineries enables Indonesia to meet domestic demand as well as providing the option to export oil products. Furthermore, Pertamina is to be highly commended for achieving accountability and auditability in its finances, as well as for its success in substantially reducing government subsidies on the domestic sale of oil products. Production and exports of oil, however, remained constrained by the weakening world market of oil.

A review of the world economy indicates that the economic recovery in the industrialized countries turns out to be uneven and accompanied by relatively high levels of real interest rates and unemployment, and a moderate level of inflation. There has been a deceleration of economic growth and a further slowing down of the industrial economies seems to be expected.

These developments already had a negative impact on non-oil exports of developing countries, including Indonesia. Commodity prices are generally at low levels, both for agricultural products as well as minerals.

Manufactured exports from developing countries are facing even more streneous tariffs as well as non-tariff barriers.

Recently a realignment of the exchange rates of the major currencies had been carried out through a coordinated intervention of the exchange markets by the major industrialized countries. It remains to be seen whether these coordinated efforts are the beginning of joint efforts of larger ramifications or whether it will be of a passing nature. A lasting realignment of the exchange rates of major currencies, however, seems to require more fundamental changes in fiscal and monetary policies in these countries.

All these developments in the world economy — the slowing down of the economies of the industrialized countries, the high real rates of interest, the possible realignment of the exchange rates of major currencies — together with shifts in the structure of the oil industry will have their impact on the world oil market. This implies that the challenge of marketing in the world oil market will be even more demanding. In the meantime, steady and continuous oil and gas exploration activities remain to be very important for the Indonesian economy.

NOTE

[1]   Address at the Convention of the Indonesian Petroleum Association in Jakarta on 8 October 1985.

12

MAKING TOUGH AND PAINFUL
DECISIONS (1991)[1]

Introductory Note: *The disorder in the world economy has been going on for years, affecting virtually all countries. But it is mostly the developing countries that have borne the brunt of it. Hence, it is an absolute necessity for leaders of developing countries to be persistently vigilant and to avoid any doubt in making the necessary decisions, however difficult or painful they may be.*

President Soeharto has never shown the slightest hesitation in making well-thought over decisions in leading the country, no matter how difficult and painful they would be. Two of his many decisions will be described below, the first was made in 1968 and the second in 1986. The first decision was related to the increase of fuel prices (BBM), while the second one was linked to the devaluation of the rupiah in September 1986, although he had said in January of that year that the rupiah would not be devaluated. Said he during the devaluation: "I consider it to be the upper ground morally, and that it is more responsible to tell it like it is to the people, while consciously making this painful decision for the sake of long-term development planning, than refraining from making the painful decision merely for the sake of saving my face because of the statement I had made earlier."

Twenty-five years ago, the prosperity level of the Indonesian people was quite low; the economy was in a mess; the people were engaged in dissonant relations — verging on war — with neighbouring countries. Now, Indonesia, together with Singapore, Thailand, Malaysia, South Korea and Hong Kong, is among a small group of developing countries considered successful in their development. However, Indonesia still has a long way to go. There are many goals still to be reached. Many weaknesses are still to be rectified. There is no place for complacency.

Yet, it is clear that Indonesia has done well in its economic development. During the twenty-five years of development under the leadership of Pak Harto (President Soeharto), the living standard, the level of intelligence, and the welfare of the people have gradually increased. At the same time, a sound foundation has been laid down during every phase of development for the next stage of development.

There are many among us who did not experience the time when development had yet to kick-off in Indonesia twenty-five years ago. Perhaps, there are even those among us who did experience it, but do not remember much of it. Moreover, most of us do not have the time it would take to compare Indonesia with other countries that have suffered all kinds of setbacks in their development.

The reality is that many developing countries are having setbacks and lots of failures. Their economies are deteriorating and the living standards of their people are declining. People in some countries have even suffered beyond the limits of humanity. And not a few developing nations have gone through recurring turmoil and rioting. Tribal conflicts have deteriorated into civil wars in some of them. In some, rebellions have broken out in regions where people feel they have been treated unjustly. Other nations have experienced frequent changes of governments. There are also wars between neighbouring countries.

There are several reasons for these tragic situations. One of them is the strong feeling of suspicion among tribes, followers of religions, and among newly independent neighbouring nations. Other reasons are the world's economic turbulence and the policies of industrial nations that are placing heavy burdens on developing ones. In addition, natural disasters, such as droughts and pest attacks, have delivered devastating blows to crops and on harvest plans, sending living standards plummeting.

Another crucial cause of the failure of development efforts in some of the developing nations is the failure of their leaders to address the huge challenges facing their countries. Some of these countries have not been capable of nurturing a sense of unity as a nation, or of enforcing the responsibilities of statesmanship, or of building a consensus on ways to run the country, or of nurturing tolerance toward neighbouring nations.

Against the backdrop of those countries, it is clear that Indonesia stands out with regard to what it has achieved under the leadership of President Soeharto. One thing that has won Pak Harto constant attention from the very beginning is his nurturing of our sense of unity as a nation. It stands to reason that Pak Harto, along with other Indonesian leaders, have always fostered the collective perspective and judgment of the people of Indonesia in dealing with problems facing the nation. Pak Harto has always relentlessly tried to unify the outlooks of the Indonesian people from all walks of life. With laudable patience, he has nurtured a consensus on how to run the country and has instilled a sense of civil responsibility. Similarly, he has nurtured the true meaning of a gradual, well-planned and sustainable national development carried out in the long run. Also, Pak Harto has always paid much attention to encouraging the followers of different religions to remain tolerant toward one another.

Pak Harto's emphasis on carrying out development in every region across the country reflects his persistence in nurturing and safeguarding the unity of the nation. Diverse developmental problems in the regions have never escaped his attention. Direct distribution of part of the development budget allocations to provinces, districts and villages under the Inpres programmes, which are constantly increasing in number, are measures consistently prioritized by Pak Harto to guarantee equity in the distribution of the benefits of the development process. Furthermore, as a way of improving the people's welfare, access to education and healthcare is now spreading out equally across the nation.

In reality, the failure of some developing nations to make a success of their development programmes may have something to do with the failure of their leaders to guarantee equity in their development processes; equity that reflects social justice; equity in job opportunities, equity in business opportunities, equity in justice, equity in sharing the burden of development, and equity in enjoying the benefits of development. Most people in those countries do not have a sense of ownership or involvement in the development activities, let alone have the opportunity to enjoy the benefits. Also, there is often no effective forum for the people to channel their complaints or suggestions, or opportunity for them to assume active roles in the development. Consequently, disappointment, unrest and social discord have escalated in many countries, often leading to turmoil.

The failure of leaders to set out consistent priorities as to what steps to take is another factor causing the inability to address economic challenges in some developing countries. Or their leaders simply fail to reach a compromise in setting out priorities. Even if they did reach an agreement, they would then fail to hold to the priorities and to execute them consistently. The result is that they have executed programmes that were not priorities and sacrificed the opportunity to carry out more effective programmes; clearly they were working without a clear scale of priorities. In some countries, the leaders want to develop and build everything all at once. Numerous large projects are being carried out at the same time, as if there is no limitation to funding or their capacity. In the end, many programmes are left unexecuted and projects abandoned amid an uncontrollable surge in inflation.

This all stands in sharp contrast to the circumstances in Indonesia that has since emerged from the economic devastation it faced twenty-five years ago. At that time, 1966, the legislators gathered for the General Assembly of the Provisional People's Consultative Assembly (MPRS) reached a consensus on what measures should be taken to tackle the country's economic woes. The agreement was stipulated in MPRS Decision No. XXIII on the Reform of the Foundation for Economic, Financial and Development Policies, dated 5 July 1966. This document makes a clear distinction between short-term programmes for stabilization and rehabilitation, and long-term programmes for development.

In executing the stabilization and rehabilitation programmes, the Ampera Cabinet spearheaded by Pak Harto as the Presidium Chairman held firmly to a simple yet realistic and effective scale of priorities:

(1) inflation control;
(2) sufficient supply of food;
(3) rehabilitation of economic facilities;
(4) improvement of export activities; and
(5) a sufficient supply of clothing.

In line with those priorities, Pak Harto emphasized inflation control by introducing extremely tough and painful measures. First, this was undertaken through controlling the main sources of inflation, namely the budget for state expenditure and banking loans. Discipline in state expenditure had reached its lowest level at that time. Not only had state expenditures far surpassed state revenue, creating a huge deficit; the resulting deficit had also become so big that it surpassed state revenue. In 1964, the state deficit equaled 150 per cent of state revenue; worsening to 174 per cent in 1965.

To uphold discipline on the expenditure side, so that expenditures would remain well within the limits of state revenue, Pak Harto made many tough and painful decisions. Among others: the sharp increase in the prices of fuel and other goods controlled by the state, in power tariffs, and in transportation fares, and so on. All the while, revenue was boosted through taxes, excise, import duties and so forth. Interest rates for bank lending were also significantly adjusted upward to more realistic levels. Those painful and tough measures managed to bring down inflation, from 650 per cent in 1966 to less than 10 per cent within three years.

Pak Harto also paid particular attention to food and clothing supplies by increasing domestic production and facilitating flows of imports. Next, a series of actions were taken to boost exports by setting the exchange rate of the Rupiah at a more realistic level, among other things. Meanwhile, no new projects were built. The entire budget for development was allocated to rehabilitating existing facilities and infra-structure. Not until three years later, after the stabilization programme had been running well for some time, did the development programme kick off. Pak Harto's strong commitment to the priority scale made it possible for the stabilization and rehabilitation programmes to be fully executed, which then facilitated the start of the development programme.

In reality, leaders in developing countries have to make plenty of difficult and painful decisions to deal with economic turbulence. But often they delay those decisions on the grounds they call "political reasons," an oft-repeated and over-used excuse. Things usually get a lot worse because of that. The longer the delay, the tougher it is to make the necessary decisions, and the more painful the impacts will be. When, eventually, those decisions have to be made, the public responds violently with rioting and turmoil.

As President of the Republic of Indonesia, Pak Harto has made so many hard and painful decisions in the field of economy. Some of those decisions have been aimed at strengthening Indonesia's economy to support efforts to improve the people's welfare. There have also been those made to steer Indonesia's economy clear of the grave impacts of the world's economic turbulence. Each of those tough and painful decisions made by Pak Harto has been based on a choice from among many alternatives. In this decision making process, each alternative is thoroughly analyzed, compared with others and the odds of achieving the desired objects meticulously calculated. The various impacts of those decisions, including their side effects, are always thoroughly calculated by Pak Harto. As well, Pak Harto also scrupulously analyzes the possible impacts if those decisions were not made, or if they were delayed, or not fully implemented.

To provide illustrations on how hard and painful the decisions Pak Harto has had to make in the field of economics, the following will describe two particularly difficult ones. The first decision was made in 1968, while the second was made in 1986.

Tough and Painful Measures in 1968

It was 24 April 1968. On Wednesday evening Pak Harto, for the first time since he had been elected by the MPRS to become the President of Republic of Indonesia in March 1968, spoke directly to the Indonesian people through radio and television broadcasts. The President began by thanking the people for giving him their trust. He later described how important it was to build unity in perspective and judgment in facing the big problems affecting the lives of the majority of the people.

He emphasized the need for an understanding among the people of why the government needed to take certain steps and what it was trying to accomplish. Then Pak Harto explained in detail the gravest problem facing the country at that time; the extraordinary rise in rice prices. This had been caused by insufficient domestic rice production, exacerbated by unfavourable weather conditions.

In order to overcome this problem, it would be necessary to secure rice stocks in a large amount under the direct control of the government. The stocks were needed to fulfill the allocations of rice for civil servants, regional government employees, and members of the Armed Forces (ABRI), as well as for sale to the people at large in the markets. It was expected that such actions could control and stabilize rice prices.

It was an enormous amount of rice. Part of it came from domestic purchases and the rest from imports. Because the rice prices were high, the amount of funds needed to make the purchases was huge. Fund for rice purchases has actually been allocated in the state budget, but the recent rice price hikes dwarfed the allocated amount. That was the challenge at that time.

Against that backdrop, Pak Harto put into plain words the three options that the government could take. The first option was that the government could print more banknotes so that it could finance the necessary rice purchases. This would clearly trigger another round of surging inflation at a time when inflation had gradually come under control. Printing new banknotes would only delay the danger; and it could even invite much bigger problems in the future.

The second option was that the government could limit the purchases of rice to equal funds allocated in the budget for that purpose. The volume of the rice bought would be much lower than what was actually needed. This would again result in the rise of rice prices, especially during the non-harvest seasons, which would eventually bring about more damaging impacts.

The third option was that the government would look for additional state income to enable it to make the rice purchases as needed. The sources of income that could still be optimized were corporate taxes, excise, import duties and export taxes. Still, these sources of income would not be adequate to buy that vast amount of rice. Another potential source of income was imposing levies on fossil fuel, or oil.

Pak Harto reasoned that the prices of processed oil, or oil fuels, could be raised because they were quite low, even lower than the prices for the basic staple goods that the people could still afford. Pak Harto pointed out, as an example, how at that time the price of one liter of gasoline was cheaper than that of a glass of tea with sugar. It was fully understood that the fuel price increase would lead to a rise in transportation tariffs and the prices of other goods. But, Pak Harto went on to say that if properly calculated, coupled with the absence of attempts to take advantage of the situation to reap huge profits, the gasoline price increase would have a relatively small impact on the prices of other goods.

Pak Harto said that it was not a matter of being "contented" or "not contented", nor "pleased" or "not pleased." The problem revolved around an obligation to choose one of two directions; to make a difficult and painful decision now for the sake of a healthier economy in a relatively short period of time, or to hold off on taking any action for fear of painful consequences, a decision that would eventually exacerbate the problems shaking the economy and be much harder to heal.

Of the two possible paths, Pak Harto was opting for the immediately painful one. The other option, added Pak Harto, especially if it was only a way of delaying the inevitable or was merely encouraged by the desire to be "popular", would drag the people down into deeper suffering; it was a decision that would, in fact, betray the people.

Furthermore, Pak Harto expressed his conviction that no matter how heavy the burden the country had to shoulder, if the people could be made to understand the difficult situation and the necessities faced, then the desired outcome would be accomplished and the burden alleviated. At least, at that time, we were all willing to suffer a bit more if it meant resolving our problems eventually. We had to understand that it would be impossible to carry out development otherwise. And, without development, it would be impossible to achieve collective prosperity. Therefore, Pak Harto expressed his hope that the decision would be well received by the people, as it was being for the sake of the people's interests in the first place.

That was the essence of Pak Harto's speech on Wednesday evening, 24 April 1968, that was broadcast directly to the people of Indonesia. On that evening, it was announced that the price of gasoline was being increased by four times, from Rp4 to Rp16 per liter. The price of kerosene was raised from Rp1.75 to Rp4 per liter, of diesel fuel from Rp3.50 to Rp12.50, of diesel oil from Rp1.25 to Rp6.50, of fuel oil from Rp1 to Rp5, of aviation gas (avigas) from Rp4 to Rp25 and of avtur fuel from Rp4 to Rp20.

Tough and Painful Measures in 1986

In the government's explanation on the 1986–87 Draft State Budget (RAPBN) on 7 January 1986, Pak Harto said that despite a decrease in foreign exchange income due to declining prices of oil and other exported goods, the government would not and would never devalue the rupiah. This statement had come in response to the development in the oil prices on international markets at that time.

From the early 1970s to 1981, fossil oil prices had sharply increased in the world's markets. The price of Indonesia's main oil product, Minas, rose from US$1.67 per barrel in January 1969 to US$13.90 in January 1979. It rose further to US$27.50 in January 1980 and peaked in January 1981 at US$35 per barrel. The price started to decline in the following years; in November 1982 to US$34.53, in February 1983 to US$29.53 and in February 1985 to US$28.53.

Foreign exchange incomes from oil and natural gas, which totaled US$18.8 billion, peaked in the fiscal year of 1981–82. Foreign exchange income from oil declined in the following years, with the oil price declining from US$28, to US$14.5 billion and US$14.0 billion in the fiscal years of 1982–83, 1983–84 and 1984–85. In 1985–86, incomes from oil and natural gas dropped further to US$12.4 billion.

By the end of 1985, both oil exporters and importers predicted a further decline in oil price from US$28 per barrel to US$25 in 1986. If the trend continued, according to the prediction, the price would hover at around US$20 per barrel. With these prices, Indonesia's income would certainly decrease. However, even with oil prices at US$25, or even as low as US$20 per barrel, Indonesia's economy would be resilient enough to face those challenges, so a rupiah devaluation would not be deemed necessary. That's why on 7 January 1986, Pak Harto stated in his speech that the government did not view a devaluation of the rupiah as necessary and had no intention of taking such an action.

During January 1986, the oil price moved downward, but was still above US$25 per barrel. In February, it continued to decline but remained above US$20 per barrel. However, in March 1986 oil prices started to drop quickly and deteriorated further and even faster in the following months. By July 1986, the price had gone down to US$10.25 per barrel and in August it hovered at levels below US$10. A decline of oil prices had been widely predicted, but a plunge at such a pace in that short a time was something beyond the forecasts set out by both the oil exporters and importers.

Faced with such a calamity, Pak Harto gave out clear signals to the people in his state address on 15 August 1986. Pak Harto reminded the public that oil price has been indeed predicted to decline, but what had happened in the past few months was not an ordinary decline, but a sharp plunge tinged with uncertainty. Pak Harto stressed: "To face reality in this adversely uncertain situation means, on one hand that we prepare ourselves for the worst; and on the other hand that we try our best to make the best of these unfortunate circumstances." That was the strong signal delivered by Pak Harto to the Indonesian people on how serious the situation was and the need to prepare for the worst.

About a month later, 12 September 1986, at 8 o'clock in the evening, the government announced a 45 per cent devaluation of the Rupiah from US$1 = Rp1,134 to US$1 = Rp1,644. Later, during the year-end address in 1986, Pak Harto explained that the sharp, quick decline in oil prices had severely eroded foreign exchange incomes, putting a heavy burden on Indonesia's balance of payments. That had led to the difficult decision to devalue the rupiah in September.

A more detailed explanation was delivered by Pak Harto when he presented the 1987–88 Draft State Budget (RAPBN) to the DPR (House of Representatives) on 6 January 1987. It had been stated a year previously that the government had seen no need for devaluation and had no intention of doing that, but, in reality, the government had eventually done so. Pak Harto said that the devaluation, which seemed to be inconsistent with the previous statements made, was done in an emergency situation that could not have been predicted beforehand. Pak Harto said:"I consider it more responsible and morally acceptable to say things as they stand to the people and consciously make a painful decision for the long-term interest of the development, than to not make such a decision merely because I do not want to retract my own words." Pak Harto stressed that a decline in oil prices had been foreseen beforehand, but the actual sudden, sharp drop was simply beyond any predictions. Nobody from any country anywhere in the world had managed to foresee such a drastic decrease in oil prices. This was the explanation given by Pak Harto.

In a more detailed explanation, Pak Harto spelled out the impacts of the oil price drop. Income from oil dropped by 47 per cent, or by almost half, from US$12.4 billion in 1985–86 to US$6.6 billion in 1986–87. Non-oil export income indeed increased, but not too significantly at that time. In total, income from oil and non-oil exports decreased by 30 per cent. Pak Harto said the 30 per cent drop in income in such a short time, without any sign of any improvement in sight, was an extraordinary circumstance with massive consequences.

The oil price plunge had to be dealt with through an equally extra-ordinary measure. That measure, Pak Harto explained further, was devaluation; a very difficult step that had negative effects, but was actually the best move possible to safeguard the sustainability of development. Pak Harto made it clear that the 30 per cent income decline in a short time without prospects of improvement in the near future could trigger an explosion in foreign exchange speculation, which would cause even more severe impacts. To prevent that from happening, the devaluation decision was made to prevent a situation that would be even more damaging and more difficult to handle.

Next, Pak Harto explained that the oil price debacle had been caused by the failure of producing nations to control themselves. Those who have big production capacity had increased their output sharply, flooding the market which eventually pushed the prices down. Pak Harto, therefore, conveyed a message to the leaders of oil producing nations that a reverse in price trends could only happen if each country could control its production and consistently implement the agreement on their respective maximum output limits.

Preparing For the Worst, Trying to Achieve the Best

The economic measures taken in 1968 and 1986, as described above, were only a few examples of the many difficult and painful economic decisions made by Pak Harto in leading the country. The decisions aimed to bolster the resilience of Indonesia's economy and to prevent or reduce the severe impacts of various incidences of economic turbulence. Pak Harto often stressed out that making and implementing the tough decisions was not a matter of being "contented" or "not contented", nor "pleased" or "displeased". The choice was between making painful and difficult moves to deal with the adverse economic situations laid bare in front of us, or not taking such actions for the sake of avoiding painful consequences at the expense of a worsening economy. It was also stressed that if the necessary measures were postponed — even though those measures eventually had to be taken — then when the time came, those measures would be even harder to carry out, and their consequences would be even more painful.

The option of making tough and painful decisions in the economic sector has never been fun, satisfying, pleasing, or popular. As Pak Harto has said: opting to delay to retain his popularity was in fact an action that would push the people further into misery. That's why in facing those alternatives, Pak Harto had chosen to tell things as they were to the people by describing the actual problems, and the available options, along with their consequences. Afterward, without delay, Pak Harto would make the necessary decision, albeit a very difficult and painful one.

In this context, Pak Harto always underlined the importance of the people having a proper understanding about the background of the measures taken by the government. He emphasized that if the people understand the circumstances and the need to take the measures, as well as the outcome to be accomplished, the burden would be lighter as willingness to collectively share that burden would emerge. This emphasis mirrored the ceaseless efforts on his part to foster a unity of perception and assessment among the people in responding to the grave challenges facing the nation.

Along the same line, Pak Harto has always provided early warning signals to the people prior to the announcement and implementation of difficult economic decisions. Such signals illustrated the challenges faced by Indonesia, their magnitude and the difficult situation the country was in. Those signals would invariably culminate in a message, which, in essence, would tell us to prepare for the worst, while at the same time trying to achieve the best possible situation under adversely unfavourable conditions. Those signals were given to prepare the people before the hard decisions were made, as well as to foster unity in perspective and judgment in dealing with the challenges, as well as adverse situations.

As mentioned in the beginning of this commentary, many developing nations suffered from failures in their development programmes. The comparison of what Indonesia and those countries have achieved clearly shows how important and vital the roles of leaders are. All developing nations experience various challenges and economic turmoil that drive their economies into dire and critical conditions. Those challenges can only be overcome when the leaders of the countries in question possess the ability, patience, courage, and wisdom to make difficult and painful decisions in the field of economy. Indonesia's experience in the past twenty-five years speaks by itself.

NOTE

[1] "Making Tough and Painful Decisions" is a foreword of the book "Among Friends. Pak Harto 70 Years". Publisher: PT Citra Lamtoro Gung Persada, 1991, pp. 620–33. This article is translated by Harry Bhaskara.

13

RESPONDING TO VARIOUS DEVELOPMENT PROPOSALS (1997)[1]

Introductory Note: *Studying the attitude and habits of Bapak Sudharmono, S.H. in handling the various matters he faced over the years would be a good idea for those who are in charge of approving, rejecting or improving various kinds of proposals to build development projects; or of purchasing goods and/or equipment; or of hiring contractors; or of providing certain goods or services, etc.*

The original heading of this article was "Is It Necessary?" a contribution in a book titled Impressions and Recollections from Friends — 70 Years H. Sudharmono S.H.

Bapak Sudharmono was the Vice President of the Republic of Indonesia for the period of 1987–93. He had formerly held the post of Minister/State Secretary for many years, and he had earlier served in the government in various capacities for a very long time. He began his close cooperation with the state economic team in 1966.

The way Bapak Sudharmono worked was fruitful and brought huge benefits for the nation and the country and could be a model not only for the Indonesian people but also for the peoples of other nations, who are trying to develop their countries.

"Is it necessary?" That was always the first question Bapak Sudharmono raised when someone was proposing a project or operation of a grand scale. The manner and the way in which he formulated this question might have varied from time to time, but the essence was always the same.

The question posed in an inquiring tone often made the applicant uncertain about whether the project was really necessary after all.

However, if the applicant could explain why the project was necessary, another question would be sure to follow: "Do you think the high-cost is justified? Can you make it smaller?"

If the applicant came up with an answer to that, Pak Dharmono would then ask: "Do you really need it now? Is it that urgent? Isn't there another thing that is more urgent?"

If there was an answer to these inquiries, still another question would follow: "Can't you make the cost lower? Have you made a real effort to save money?"

And if all of the questions were met with reasonable answers, Bapak Sudharmono would call for a feasibility study, adding that: "I will ask experts to review the feasibility study. I will let you know the results later."

Bapak Sudharmono never approved a proposal instantly. He explored every aspect of the proposal before asking experts to review it. And *Pak* Dharmono had many difficult questions for the experts. If some of them did not agree on a certain issue or if their reports were questionable, he would turn to more experienced experts.

He also always had a lot of suggestions related to the improvement, expansion or construction of infrastructure; or on the production of certain goods and services; or the purchase of goods; or the procurement of contractors' services, and so forth.

Because of his habit of making various suggestions, the experts who were asked to make the reviews were technical experts in respected areas like financial experts or accountants, etc.

As for proposals on procuring goods and services, Pak Dharmono often reminded applicants about the importance of marketing. "What is important is not only the fact that we can produce the goods or services we want, but whether we can sell them, whether there is a buyer, whether there is a market to absorb them, what about the competition within the market, what about the competitiveness of the goods and services that we produce?" he would always ask.

The experts would review each proposal intensively, yet it would almost always turn out that most of the proposals they had reviewed still needed revamping. Certainly, some would pass the scrutiny, but others would be considered as never having meeting the set requirements no matter how much revamping was done.

The above explanation briefly describes the exceptionally systematic way in which Bapak Sudharmono worked: every proposal or report was always critically reviewed and then checked again, and rechecked. In some cases the proposals might have important feature and an urgency that could have been used as a basis to approve them without such in-depth consideration. However, this would have meant that the principle of working with clear-cut priorities could be set aside just for prompt facilitation. If that were the case, the development programme would have the potential to tumble into chaos, followed by economic decline.

That is what happened in many developing countries, especially in Latin America. When the level of their economic development was still low and the capacity limited, each country was cautious and keenly adhering to their priority list in carrying out their development. As their economics grew, they became so overconfident that their alertness was eroded. Each sector tried to outdo the others in developing projects, and the government would finally dispose of their priority list to make things happen. In the end, the limits of their capability were surpassed and economic crisis set in with all of its consequences. This is what happened in Argentine, Brazil, Colombia, Venezuela, and in Mexico in particular.

Likewise, many private sector enterprises in those countries used foreign loans to finance their activities without official guarantees from the government. However, because the loans were spent to finance projects that had a great deal of interest to the government or big companies belonging to the government, a sort of indirect guarantee from the government would kick in. Then, when the foreign debt crisis set in, much of the burden of the private foreign debts — including the short-term ones — became the burden of the government. All of this was due to the loss of caution in the implementation of development programs.

Therefore it is really beneficial for us to study and to consider the way that Bapak Sudharmono, who served as State Secretary/Minister of the State Secretariat and was then appointed by the People's Consultative Assembly to the post of Vice President of the Republic of Indonesia in 1988, worked so responsibly and systematically. Not only for the sake of Indonesia, but also for the many other developing countries whose capacities have started to grow.

His handling of so many proposals was related to projects or activities in his capacity as Head of the Control Team for the Procurement of Goods and Services for the Government, which is widely known as the Team of Presidential Decree No. 10 (1980–88). The Control Team was initially established to make the best use of the additional budget and to facilitate what was called the "crash programme". Afterward, the team was tasked to control the procurement of goods and equipments needed by the government using the state budget and by state-own companies using their respective budgets.

Because there were more and more funds available in the state budget, the Coordinating Minister for Economics, Finance and Industry/Chairman of the National Development Planning Board (Bappenas) and the Minister of Finance proposed to the President that the additional funds be used to accelerate the implementation of the equitable distribution programme, particularly as related to equity in opportunity for education and health services, as well as electricity in villages, and other infrastructure in all regions. They also suggested the establishment of a team to manage the programs comprising members from various institutions, and chaired by the State Secretary.

Bapak Sudharmono immediately threw his full support behind the idea to spend the additional budgetary funds to accelerate the equitable distribution programme and the idea to establish the Control Team. But he said that he was very reluctant to become the chairman of the team. In front of the President, he said that it was beyond his duty as the State Secretary to do so, and suggested that the Coordinating Minister for Economics, Finance and Industry/Chairman of the National Development Planning Board head the team instead. However, the President made a very exact and wise decision stipulating the establishment of the Control Team and appointing the Minister/State Secretary as Head of the Team and the Minister/Deputy Chairman of the National Development Planning Board as the Deputy Head of the Team. Because this was a presidential decision, true to his character, Bapak Sudharmono carried out this duty with a full sense of responsibility.

As Head of the Control Team, Bapak Sudharmono regularly reported on developments in the implementation of the team's tasks and discussed matters regarding those tasks with the President. Therefore, if an applicant submitted a proposal coupled with the comment "The President has given his approval," Pak Dharmono would treat the proposal just like the others and not give it any special treatment. Why? Because in the end, he would report all proposals to the President.

One of the accomplishments of the Control Team led by Bapak Sudharmono was the growing inclination of government officials to use locally made equipment and goods and the opening of more opportunities to Indonesian contractors to work on government projects and state-owned company projects.

In this case, Bapak Dharmono's unforgettable questions were: "How big is the share of local products? Can't you increase that share? Have you tried in earnest? Is it true that the quality of local products does not meet the requirements? Is it true that the prices are higher? It is true that the delivery of the goods is not reliable?"

And, even more questions: "How many jobs will you give to Indonesian contractors? Have you tried your best? Is it true that the quality of work does not meet the requirements? Is it true that the cost is higher? Is it true that the work delivery schedule is not reliable?"

Those are some aspects of Bapak Sudharmono's implementation of his tasks as Head of the Control Team for the Procurement of Goods and Services for the Government for eight years.

From the time he was appointed as Secretary of the Ampera Cabinet Presidium in July 1966, Bapak Sudharmono was careful to familiarize himself with state economic issues and to stay abreast of all trends. To cope with the uncontrollable economic conditions of the time, it was necessary to take firm measures in the areas of finance, foreign trade, prices, interest rates, and so forth. Those pragmatic steps had to be formulated into regulations based on the existing laws. This is where Pak Dharmono's reputation and experience as a tough legal expert came crucially into play. One of his key contributions was his role in appropriately formulating — from the legal view — the first economic policy made by the New Order Government, namely the famous 3 October 1966, Economic Policy, which was then followed by a series of economic policies designed to uphold Indonesia's economic stability.

One example of Bapak Sudharmono's sharpness in reviewing economic issues is as follows. In the 1980s, the government planned to abolish the obligation of exporters to hand over the foreign exchange they generated from their exports to Bank Indonesia. In this way, the foreign exchange traffic would be freed up. Consultation about the issue with Pak Dharmono took place during an exchange of ideas and preparations toward formulating the necessary regulations. The first question raised by Pak Dharmono was about the impact of the abolishment upon Bank Indonesia's foreign exchange reserve. However, even before the answer was forthcoming, he came to the conclusion from the available figures that the impact to the foreign exchange reserve would not be significant. This was because of his accurate observation that the abolishment would only affect 30 per cent of all of the foreign exchange revenue from the exports. In those years, 70 per cent of the foreign exchange revenue from exports was from fossil oil and natural gas, which all together belonged to the government and was directly handed over to Bank Indonesia. Relieved that there would be no negative impact, Pak Dharmono prepared the necessary regulations.

These are just a few excerpts from the career of Bapak Sudharmono and the important role he played, which we can use in our efforts at upholding and boosting the acceleration of the Indonesian economy.

NOTE

[1]   "Responding to Various Development Proposals" was originally titled *"Is It Necessary?* in an article from the book *"Impressions and Recollections From Friends"*, 70 Years H. Sudharmono S.H. Publisher PT Gramedia Widiasarana Indonesia, Jakarta 1997, pp. 7–12. This article is translated by Harry Bhaskara.

PART **III**

FACING VARIOUS
ECONOMIC CRISES

14

THE INTERNATIONAL MONETARY CRISIS (1971)[1]

Introductory Note: *In 1971, an international monetary upheaval prevailed. This monetary fluctuation involved the currencies of a number of industrialized countries. Tensions peaked on 15 August 1971, when the United States declared that it was no longer committed to the 1944 agreement with other industrialized countries on the determination of currency exchange rates (Bretton Woods Agreement).*

Although this upheaval resulted most immediately in the fluctuation of the currency rates of industrialized countries, its impacts were also felt in developing countries. In the case of Indonesia, the changes in currency exchange rates between the U.S. and several European countries, as well as Japan, could be expected to bring a negative impact to Indonesian exports because those various countries were Indonesia's major export destinations. In order to be able to immediately take appropriate action, the government consistently monitored the latest developments in the world economy. Therefore, the government needed to take appropriate action immediately to prevent negative consequences. In matter of days, the government on 23 August 1971, announced that it would be taking several steps. In order to be able to take appropriate action, the government consistently monitored the latest developments in the world economy. In order to reduce confusion in media reporting and uncertainty in society, the government's timely announcement included an explanation that core economic elements (including the free flow of foreign exchange) remained unchanged.

Among the most vigilant in monitoring international monetary developments was Professor Dr Ali Wardhana, a Minister of Finance for fifteen years (1968–83) and Coordinating Minister for Economics, Finance and Industry for five years (1983–88). He was ever on the alert and always ready to take necessary action. At that time Indonesia was a member of Group 20, which gathered together ministers of finance for both industrial and developing countries. Professor Ali Wardhana was elected chairman of this group.

To deal with the impacts of international monetary volatility, the Government of Indonesia has taken a series of measures to safeguard Indonesia's export growth and simultaneously also safeguarding foreign exchange reserves for the financing of national development.

Since the international monetary crisis of May 1971, with the floating of the currency exchange rates of West Germany and the Netherlands, and the revaluation of some other European currencies, uncertainties have gripped the international monetary system, resulting in a decline in international trade.

The atmosphere of crisis was exacerbated by a series of measures introduced by the United States on 15 August 1971. The measures aimed at generating positive impacts on the economic growth of the United States, which in the long run would also boost the export performance of developing countries. Even though the import constraints imposed by the United States in the form of extra import duties were not applied to most of Indonesia's exports to that country, the action has led to a major change in the international economy, causing short-term problems that require immediate responses. In particular, the short-term problem at present is the volatility of the international monetary system that has led to a slowdown in economic activities in the countries to which Indonesia exports most of its products.

Countries are now taking steps to overcome those short-term problems, such as adjusting the exchange rates for their respective currencies. This process takes time and all the while strengthens that sense of uncertainty in the international monetary market. Therefore, even though an agreement could be reached between the United States and European countries, as well as Japan, on ways to adjust the various exchange rates, the uncertainty in international trade can be expected to continue for some time.

A similar impact could occur in the case of countries revaluing their currencies, which, in the short-term, would result in a decline in economic activities in the respective economies.

For Indonesia, the problem is that the countries that could revalue their currencies, or are taking steps in that direction, are its main export destinations.

It is now clear that the current international monetary crisis is bringing about unfortunate short-term consequences for Indonesia's exports.

Against this backdrop, it is of utmost importance for Indonesia to deal with this international monetary shift and to take steps to safeguard the sustainability of Indonesia's domestic economic development in general and its export growth in particular.

To boost Indonesia's competitiveness in the international market, the Government has put in place a series of measures, which have reduced obstacles to exports and increased export revenue. The reduction in export obstacles has taken the form of, among other things, the reduction or elimination of export duties, rehabilitation fees, and survey expenses, while the export revenue increase involves adjustment of the currency exchange rate.

In Jakarta's currency market spot on 23 August 1971, Bank Indonesia bought and sold foreign currencies on the pricing basis of:

(a) Buy M.T. Rp. 414 per US$1
(b) Buy T.T. Rp. 414.50 per US$1
(c) Sell M.T. Rp. 415.50 per US$1
(d) Sell T.T. Rp. 416 per US$1

So the median rate is Rp. 415 per US$1 (M.T. stands for mail transfer and T.T. telegraphic transfer)

The exchange rate adjustment and export obstacle reduction are expected to safeguard Indonesia's exports from the negative impacts of international monetary volatility amid weakening international trade.

Shielding Indonesia's exports against the international monetary crisis, and renewing discipline in domestic monetary policies has enabled the stability and maintenance of the new Rupiah exchange rate.

The exchange rate adjustment has not modified Indonesia's foreign exchange system at all.

The current foreign exchange regime will be retained so that the freedom to convert the Rupiah into foreign currencies, and vice versa, is preserved.

An adjustment has also been made to foreign exchange rates for credit, bringing them onto the same level with those of regular foreign exchange rates.

Meanwhile, in order to boost investment toward the expansion of job opportunities, a change has also been made in the calculation of investment credit repayment. The repayment for the principal of investment credit is no longer tied to foreign currency rates.

This greatly reduces the burden of repayment of investment credit and will eventually generate more robust economic development activities.

In the face of the international monetary crisis, the Government has also taken steps to safeguard the supply of the nine basic foodstuffs of high importance to the people. The current stock is quite adequate, significantly minimizing the risk of scarcity.

The amount of state revenue derived from the sales of imported goods, such as rice, grain, flour, cotton, woven thread and fertilizers, has not changed, so the calculation of prices for those commodities remains stable.

An import facility in the form of partial reimbursement of import activity expenses has been provided in order to increase the flows of the certain strategic imported goods. This is expected to boost the importation of the goods necessary for economic development.

The world's economy is currently experiencing a shock because of the volatility in the international monetary system. Indonesia's economy has the resilience necessary to handle that volatility, as long as steps are taken in the right way at the right time.

With the Government taking these measures, Indonesia's position in the world's market has been strengthening, thus safeguarding exports toward the sustainability of economic development.

NOTE

1   Deliberation as chairman of BAPPENAS on the government's moves to overcome the upheaval as a result of the international monetary crisis of mid 1971. This article is translated by Harry Bhaskara.

15

FOOD CRISIS (1972)[1]

Introductory Note: *A food crisis occurred in 1972. It was known as the "rice crisis" in Indonesia, a country where most of the population considers rice as the staple food. Rice prices jumped uncontrollably. Rice production had declined far below that of earlier years. It had been the policy of the government in previous years to handle price increases by selling its rice buffer stock to the public. At that time (1972), however, the rice stock was so limited that it could not cushion the impact of the soaring prices for rice in the markets. The problem was that there had been reports from senior agricultural and regional officials that the rice production was quite high; contrary to reports from the Central Statistics Agency, which said that the production was actually lower than in previous years. Because there were such great contrasts among the various reports, it was stressed, time and again, that the benchmark was to be the rice price level at any given harvest time. If the rice price at harvest time was higher than that of the year before, this would be considered an indication of lower production rates. So, what we used as a guideline was the rice price at harvest time and not the confusing paddy production forecast reports.*

However, apparently certain senior officials at the agriculture ministry and in regional administrations were reluctant to report that the rice production in their areas was lower than in the years before. There was also another problem that worsened the government's buffer situation. That was the requirement for farmers to sell the higher quality rice or unhusked rice to the government, so it could be preserved longer. This caused the government's rice and unhusked procurement from the farmers to drop. To deal with the declining production, the government took various actions, all of which required time to implement. The impact of this time gap was exacerbated by continued confusion in the production reports and the stringent requirement on rice quality. After undertaking some fruitful policies, including importing rice on a large scale, the government then decided to convey a comprehensive explanation of the problem to the House of Representatives and the public. Eventually, the prices could be brought under control. The government's explanation was conveyed by the National Planning Agency (Bappenas) on 14 December 1972.

The government's hearing on the problem of rice at the House of Representatives of the Republic of Indonesia, delivered by State Minister for National Development Planning/Chairman of Bappenas on 14 December 1972.

Rice is a national issue. Any failure to solve any problem related to rice will influence the course of our development. Rice is a very important factor in the Indonesian economy, precisely because rice is one of the foundation elements of our economic stability, a pre-requirement to our achievement of development.

In this connection, we need to thoroughly review our experiences in this sector, its ups and downs and its stability and dynamism, in order to give us an understanding to ensure our agricultural development in the future; at least to prevent recurrence in the coming years.

In line with this thinking and its goals, the government is grateful that an appropriate time has presented itself in which to explain the background of the rice crisis to the revered members of the House and the public. The government is now attempting to give a candid explanation; nothing but the reality.

Several key questions come to mind as we look back at the rice problem as it has unfolded over the last few months. The first one is: What were the reasons behind the recent price increases? Next: Hadn't those reasons been anticipated before hand and were they unavoidable?

Then, still another question arises: What measures were taken by the government to overcome this critical situation? Were those measures enough to answer the challenge? And lastly: What measures have been taken by the government to prevent the recurrence of this critical problem?

The government is aware that there is still a long list of questions that mirror the feelings and aspirations of the people in connection with the rice price increases.

With these questions in mind, the government will give an explanation to answer those key questions whose main purpose is to enable us all to comprehend the fundamentals of the problem we are facing and trying to overcome.

The price of rice is an important component in the daily living expenses of the people. Therefore, a fixed rice price is the key to economic stability. In this connection, it is very helpful to understand the nature of rice production. As we all know, rice production is seasonal and this explains the ups and downs of rice prices. In addition, there are elements of uncertainty in rice production because it is heavily dependent on climate, weather, rainfall, plant diseases, natural disasters, etc. Meanwhile, demand for rice increases all the time due to population growth, social and cultural development, and higher incomes for the people due to the advancement of development.

Based on these facts and considerations, the government has been determined from the outset to control rice prices in the market by creating a buffer stock, thus ensuring that an adequate volume of rice is available at all times. This means the government has never had any intention of letting the market decide the rice prices. On the contrary, the government has purposely influenced rice prices in the market based on the laws of economics.

The lowest and highest prices of rice stem from this policy. It aims to ensure an appropriate level of prices that, on the one hand, will boost production because of the benefit given to the farmers and, on the other hand, will ensure that prices remain within the purchasing power of the people. The government will promptly buy rice in the market when prices are approaching the lowest level and sell them to the market from its buffer stock when rice prices are approaching the highest level.

In addition, the government is also duty bound to ensure that rice is available in non-producing regions and those places that are less attractive to traders, as well as providing rice for civil servants and members of the military. The government is aware that such a policy costs a lot of money, both for stockpiling rice for the buffer stock and for selling this stock in the market. But the huge cost is rewarded by economic stability that is a pre-requisite for development. The efforts that must be made now and into the future are toward efficiency and effectiveness in the implementation of this policy.

We can conclude that the purpose of all the policies is to reach these basic goals:

(1) Keeping prices from falling below the lowest acceptable level in producing regions during harvest time.
(2) Keeping the price from exceeding the highest acceptable level during times of shortage in supply, and in regions that do not produce enough rice.
(3) Supporting and encouraging healthy rice trade.
(4) Guaranteeing the rice supply for civil servants, police and the armed forces.
(5) Guaranteeing the distribution of rice and other staple foods in disaster areas.

With the above description of the current situation, the main question asked by the people recently has been: What was the cause of the price increases?

The rice price increase of late was caused by the fact that the rice supply in the community could not match demand, while, in the past few months, the government had not been able to prevent price fluctuations due to the insufficient rice stock on hand.

As for the rice supply failing to meet the demand, this was because in 1972, for the first time since the implementation of the REPELITA Five-Year Development Plan, the production of rice was actually lower than estimated. During the first three year of REPELITA, the rice production kept on increasing sharply, so that each year it always managed to reach or even surpass the targets set. However, the rice production was clearly below expectation this year, caused firstly by a dry session that was not only severe but also prolong in various areas. That resulted in a big blow to paddy production, especially in the central part of Java, southern Sulawesi, southern Sumatra, and eastern Nusa Tenggara, as well as some other areas. The extraordinarily long and severe dry season, along with the floods that hit certain parts of the country at the start of the year, was responsible for the damage of 160,000 hectares of crops in Java from January to August 1972. These losses were twice as large as those occurring in the same period in 1971 or in 1970. Although the paddy production in Java this year is likely to be higher than in the same period in 1971, the production in the following months is expected to be affected severely by dry conditions. The government has received signals of this potential difficulty from regional reports and the trends in rice prices.

Apart from the impact of the long and severe dry season, the government also has pinpointed weaknesses in the application of the Mass Guidance and Mass Intensification for Self-Sufficiency in Food (Bimas and Inmas) programmes as the causes of the lack of success in the rice production this year. The government also acknowledges that coordination among agencies involved in the Bimas programme, both at the central and regional levels, requires a lot of improvement.

Despite this gloomy description, there is still some encouraging news. There remains the potential for adequate production and good harvests in Aceh, North Sumatra, West Sumatra, Bali and West Nusa Tenggara this year (1972). This positive trend can also be seen in the increased usage of high quality seeds, a higher crop yield per hectare in well-irrigated rice fields, and improvement in rice milling capacity.

It is clear that the long and severe dry season was the main cause of the decrease in rice production this year. In conjunction with that fact, the country's ability to forecast weather trends must be enhanced with a focus on the field of agriculture.

The long dry season in the middle of this year also affected the harvest of non-staple food crops, so their production this year will also not reach the targets. This means that the contribution of the non-staple foods to the food stock will be lower than usual.

Moreover, with rainfall not yet occurring by October and early November, the farmers have been forced to delay the planting of non-staple food crops. This will further hurt the food stock in the next January and February because the harvest of non-staple food crops, which usually falls in those months, will be delayed.

This means that we can predict food supply difficulties in the first months of 1973 before harvest time.

Because the food stocks, covering rice and non-staple foods, can meet neither demand nor expectations, the next question to answer is: Why did the government not have enough stock to prevent the rice price increase?

Although the government's rice stock in the early fiscal year of 1972–73 stood at 387,000 tons, which was actually enough for about three-months' needs, the stock volume declined in the following months because the government's procurement of domestic rice was smaller than earlier estimated. This had to do with changes in requirements and procedures for procurement.

Aiming to curtail storehouse losses due to damage by ensuring a higher quality of rice in stock, the government upgraded the quality of rice it would buy. Besides that, the government also set up different procedures in the procurement process to improve its rice trading capability. The new procedures and requirements took effect in April 1972. In May, June and July, domestic rice procurement was small in quantity.

What steps did the government take to cope with this situation?

In early August this year, the government restored the previous procedures and requirements as an effort to increase the level of domestic rice procurement. The effort failed to deliver the expected results. In addition, due to the late timing of the purchase, the government has had to acknowledge that weaknesses still occur in relation to the procurement of rice domestically.

Then, after learning that the prolonged dry season was continuing to put food stocks in jeopardy, the government immediately decided to import rice in addition to continuing its efforts to boost domestic rice procurement.

We first tried to import rice through food assistance programmes from various countries that supported Indonesia under the IGGI. Prioritizing food assistance programmes rather than immediately resorting to commercial imports is understandable because this conserves the country's foreign exchange reserves. However, upon considering that importing through food assistance programmes could take much more time, the government also tried to strengthen its supply of rice through commercial imports.

It is understood that during a meeting in the middle of December last year, a deal was reached among members of IGGI that Indonesia would get food assistance, which would be tied to the country's food production in 1972. In other words, the food assistance was to be flexible in amount, unlike assistance in the form of projects or credits. If the food production is successful, the government will not need to use the entire amount of pledged assistance. The segments of unused assistance can be used in the following year instead. This happened in the fiscal year 1971–72, where parts of the pledged assistance were used in the following year. On the contrary, if production does not reach the expected target, there is an opportunity for the country to get a bigger amount of food assistance. Such agreements are made based on alertness to every possible occurrence in the food production process, especially in the face of unpredictable season changes and disasters. The flexibility of this food assistance enables us to customize our food stock in line with actual demand.

The government and the members of IGGI had jointly set the amount of food assistance for the fiscal year of 1972–73 in the previous meeting by taking into account the rise in rice production during the first several years of the REPELITA Five-Year Plan. They also took into consideration the fact that the assistance remaining from the allocation for 1971–72, amounting to 169,500 tons of rice, was still available for 1972–73. With this year's food production less than encouraging, some members of IGGI, in line with the flexible characteristics of the agreement, have stated their willingness to increase food assistance for Indonesia.

The government of the United States said it is willing to add 50,000 tons of rice to the previously promised 100,000 tons. The American government actually wanted to give more, but that country has a limited stock, as they had also given out large amounts of rice to the Philippines and Bangladesh due to disasters and armed conflict. America also gave help to South Vietnam, the Khmer people, South Korea and many others. The American government then decided to provide another form of help to Indonesia. It agreed to assist Indonesia with supplies of cotton, so that it did not need to import cotton commercially and could use the saved funds to import rice.

The Japanese government has also expressed their willingness to raise its food assistance to Indonesia by 150,000 tons of rice, based on a long-term soft loan agreement. This volume would come on top of the 230,000 tons of rice agreed to previously. We will sign the additional assistance agreement in the next several days and it will be implemented starting in January next year. One of the difficulties the Japanese government has encountered in increasing the volume of its food assistance to Indonesia is the limitations faced by milling facilities in Japan. At present, besides being used to meet Japan's own domestic needs, the milling equipment is being used to process rice to be sent to the Philippines and Bangladesh because those countries are struggling to handle recent disasters. In order to save time, the additional assistance to be shipped to Indonesia was to be in the form of brown rice, or rice that had not been fully processed. This was agreed to after we tested a sample and ascertained that the rice could be cooked and eaten without any further processing. That is why, once the rice arrives in Indonesia, it will immediately be made available in the market.

The Dutch government has also provided additional assistance of 10,000 tons of rice. Holland does not produce rice, so they have bought it from Thailand.

The previous Australian government agreed to provide assistance of 4,900 tons of rice from that country's own production. Australia cannot give more extensive assistance because their rice production has also declined due to the long dry season.

The current Australian government has also stated their willingness to increase the level of rice assistance to Indonesia. Due to the county's limited production, they are providing foreign exchange reserves that can be used to procure around 20,000 tons of rice outside of Australia.

The French and Italian governments have agreed to increase their food assistance as well, by 4,000 tons and 6,000 tons of rice, respectively.

Please let us use this opportunity to thank all those countries once again. We feel that the added assistance reflects a good bond of friendship between Indonesia and those countries, and proof of their seriousness in helping to strengthen the economic stability and development of Indonesia.

Meanwhile, we have also received help in the form of a loan of 20,000 tons of rice from our neighbour, Malaysia, although that country is actually a rice importer. After our rice production recovers, we will immediately repay this rice debt to Malaysia. Malaysia's support shows the solidarity existing among members of the Association of Southeast Asian Nations (ASEAN).

So in total, foreign food assistance for the 1972–73 fiscal year reaches more than 750,000 tons of rice, apart from other forms of food assistance.

Because we are not able to satisfy the domestic demands as yet, the government has tried to find other alternatives apart from food assistance by importing rice commercially. It is this awareness of its duty to ensure rice availability that has pushed the government to import rice from wherever possible.

In the past several years, Indonesia's commercial rice imports have come from Thailand and Myanmar. That was why we first tried to import rice from those two countries. But their crops also have declined due to bad weather and they are limiting rice exports to prevent rice price increases there. Nevertheless, the two countries have tried to export some rice to Indonesia. In the first stage Thailand exported 126,000 tons of rice, while Myanmar sent 20,000 tons. On top of that, two days ago, a deal was signed on the purchase of an additional 250,000 tons of rice from Thailand, which will begin arriving in January. We deeply appreciate the attention of these two countries to our problem.

One of the other countries with the capability to export rice nowadays is Pakistan. From Pakistan, we imported 157,000 tons of rice. The Indonesian government also procured 115,000 tons of rice from China in Hong Kong and 20,000 tons of rice from Taiwan.

This procurement will add almost 1 million tons to the volume of rice imports for the fiscal year of 1972–73. About half of this imported rice comes from food assistance, while the rest comes from commercial imports. We are currently in talks with several countries on the possibility of importing more rice, which we can do when we need it.

It is clear that the effort to increase the level of rice import is not an easy task. Countries that are able to help turn out to have the responsibility to help other countries that were hit by disasters, like the Philippines and Bangladesh. Meanwhile, countries that usually export rice have to limit their exports because their productions are on a decline due to unfavorable weather. This shortage of food increases demand, which makes competition in the world's food markets even tougher.

The successful effort at providing an adequate stock of rice, whether from food assistance or commercial imports, does not mean that the rice shortage problem can be entirely resolved immediately. The transportation of this rice from the various countries to Indonesia has encountered a number of obstacles. Many of our ships used to transport rice from other countries are aging. The shipping sector in Indonesia is in need of rehabilitation. We have started to take some steps to resolve this matter, but we realize that the fleet upgrading process will take some time. That is why we also use ships from other countries to transport the rice here. However, this is not a simple matter either. At present, the global demand for ships to carry food is also rising. This is caused by the shortage of food suffered by many countries, and they too need ships to carry rice from other countries.

The shipment of rice from Pakistan hit still another snag in relation to disputes over labour issues in the country. This has resulted in very slow progress in shipments.

As the result of those transportation problems, rice imports for November were delayed. This is certain to influence rice distribution in the domestic market. However, recently we have begun to be able to overcome those transportation problems. Our efforts to find enough ships are beginning to bear fruit. The Pakistani government has also begun prioritizing our rice shipments for facilitated transportation service to Indonesia through Karachi harbour. Also in Indonesian ports, ships carrying rice get ultimate service, with the rice unloaded from the ships being moved directly to trucks and distributed to the designated locations. Nowadays, both sea and land transportation vehicles are focused on serving rice distribution.

The government tries to distribute the imported rice to regions that need it in a timely manner. In addition, we are also paying close attention to the food situation in regions with much lower income than others. For people in those areas, the availability of rice is not yet a complete solution as they have a limited purchasing power. That is why we also have to provide non-rice staple foods that they can still afford to buy in those areas. The government therefore welcomes America's assistance in the form of 560,000 tons of cracked wheat and corn that can be expanded up to 150,000 tons if necessary.

With the currently adequate level of rice imports, we have started distributing large amounts of rice to the markets since the first week of this month. For Jakarta, which often becomes the benchmark for rice prices for other regions, at least 1,500 tons of rice is being distributed in traditional markets every day. Meanwhile, at least 120,000 tons of rice is being distributed nationwide every month. The volumes are considered sufficient to push the rising rice prices downward. As a result, prices have started declining in Jakarta.

Unfortunately, the government has witnessed some irregularities in this process of decreasing the price of rice. For example, some traders and retailers have been charging more than the set retail prices for the imported rice being "dropped" into the market to keep prices down. It is obvious that some people are trying to benefit from the difficult situation. To deal with that, the government has taken the necessary measures, including preventive and repressive actions. We have increased the rice distribution flows and disciplined the dealers and retailers who have been violating the existing regulations

With a sufficient volume of rice being maintained by the government and the continued flows of rice to the market to meet demand, it is expected that the prices of rice will ease down consistently over time.

The above import figures show us the seriousness of the problem we are facing now. However, those figures also show how extensive the efforts have been to deal with the problem.

It is true that the amount of rice being imported paints an unpleasant picture of the economic situation in Indonesia. However, that does not mean that it will continue to be hot and dry forever. There are signs enough that Indonesia's economy is still moving forward. One of those signs is our ability to import rice in large amounts. Yet, it goes without saying that it would be better for us if we could do a better job in increasing the production and supply of foods this year, so that the foreign exchange we need to import rice could be used for development.

Even in this difficult time, we have higher foreign exchange reserves than initially projected, partly because of an adjustment we made in August last year in an effort to counter the impact of the international monetary crisis.

Now this brings us to question: What steps has the government taken to prevent a similar crisis from happening again in the future?

Based on the analysis of what caused the rice crisis, the government's steps focus on efforts to increase rice production and to better secure the rice stock held by the government.

The government has anticipated the need for better preparation for the planting season in the 1972–73 fiscal year. Learning lessons from the current difficulties, we have been paying more attention to improving coordination among the various stakeholders at the center and in the regions, as well as to ensuring proper supervision of technical operations.

We are especially focusing on making certain that the Bimas and Inmas programmes will be implemented in the regions that are adequately prepared for that, so that farmers can receive the necessary production facilities in the appropriate number and at the right level in a timely manner.

Apart from that, the government is trying to improve irrigation facilities, including through the repair of channels and many other actions. The financial assistance given to subdistricts and villages is being focused on irrigation.

The government is also preparing for the stockpiling of high quality seeds through facilitating the efforts of the farmers who produce seeds and by raising the level of production of seed agencies.

The demand for fertilizer for the 1972–73 planting season is estimated to reach 420,000 tons of urea and 116,000 tons of TSP. Up to now, most fertilizer has been distributed to subdistricts and will soon be distributed to villages. The government has also improved patterns and procedures for the distribution of the fertilizer so the farmers can receive adequate amounts of the right kind of fertilizer at the appropriate times. The fertilizer prices remain at the same level as in previous years. For areas outside Java, where extra transportation costs are incurred, the government is also providing a transportation subsidy. We also provide fertilizer for non-paddy plants to guarantee that the supply of fertilizer for rice intensification is sufficient.

Pesticides and preparations for the possibility of pest attacks have also been prepared; including light airplanes that are used to spread the pesticides in order to curtail outbreaks.

Efforts to improve access to credit for farmers have also been made. Credit is directly channeled to farmers by Bank Rakyat Indonesia (BRI) officers, meaning that the loans go directly to the individual farmers, who are responsible for repaying them directly to the bank without the intervention of any third parties.

The procedures for credit have also been simplified to cut short the processing time. The government has also decided that the farmers who do not own land are to be given an opportunity to enjoy credit and other production facilities. Although this programme remains selective, the loan requirements are not as stringent as in the past. It has been decided as well that the repayment of Bimas credits will be extended from one planting season to two. This means the farmers do not have to directly sell their crops at harvest time to pay back the debt. In addition, the amount of loans to cover the farmers' cost of living has been increased; and so have the credit levels for seed procurement. During the 1972–73 planting season, the number of BRI units in the villages has been increased to 1,300 units.

It is the intention of the government to develop the Village Cooperative Unit (BUUD) programme, which will mean that the people of each village will own and manage their own cooperative units. With this policy, the cooperative, which is a reflection of Indonesia's economic cooperation principle, can be expected to truly grow up from bottom all the way. The government realizes that the path toward that goal will take time to traverse, and that the return of public confidence in cooperatives will require well-trained and loyal cadres. That is why the government has started to encourage the cooperative movement by forming the BUUD. As farmers work together to take care of the production, milling, marketing, and other facilities by themselves, they will benefit more than ever before from their own efforts. Although the BUUD is currently directed at increasing rice production and improving the farmers' lives, in the future, after these cooperatives have become stronger, they will be upgraded into KUD (Village Cooperative Units) which will become the main forums for rural economic development.

With regard to the government's attempts to secure adequate food supplies, preparations have also been made for further purchases of rice from both domestic and overseas sources. The domestic procurement policy includes making sure that even the lowest price levels set are attractive enough to the farmers to encourage an increase in production that will enable the government to secure an adequate rice stock. To accomplish this, the government has returned to the employment of past procedures and requirements for domestic procurement. Apart from that, the BUUD will be used as one of the agencies for purchasing paddy. In that way, the floor prices for farmers can be better secured.

The preparations to import rice, both in the form of assistance and commercial procurement, are based in solid projections that rice production for next year will continue to be influenced by negative weather conditions, meaning that crop planting and harvest levels cannot be expected to improve.

The government itself considers the rice crisis as a sign for us to remain alert in the future. The implementation of government policies in the field will be better monitored and thoroughly evaluated. Therefore, the execution procedures and the activities of the implementing agencies at the central and regional levels must also be improved so that they work effectively and efficiently to deal with any problems relating to the production of rice.

The government is now consistently and continuously monitoring the people's feelings and thoughts out of a sense of responsibility and in response to the recent rice crisis. With the spirit of working together to find a way out of this problem, the government also wishes to express its appreciation to the respected members of the House of Representatives for their serious attention to the problem.

In this case, the government had been purposely waiting for the perfect time to "openly" convey the government's explanation to the House of Representatives (DPR) about the rice issue by stating the situation clearly "as it is", just as I am doing right now. There are several reasons for this:

First, the government needed to undertake intense analysis of the situation to determine the cause of the problem and the best solution. Without that analysis, the government would not be able to give a proper explanation, thus exacerbating the situation. And without a clear description of a solution, the people would only become more concerned and anxious.

Secondly, once we realized that the only immediate solution would be to import rice, the government considered it unnecessary to publicly announce that effort until there was certainty about the availability of adequate rice stores for import. Any mistimed announcement would only further raise rice prices — which were already on the rise — on foreign markets, while the prices of domestic rice would keep rising because of speculation and rice hoarding.

There has been no intention whatsoever on the part of the government to conceal the truth. The extremely careful steps on our part were because we truly realized that the rice problem is at the center of interest to most Indonesians, in particular those with low levels of income. The successful handling of the rice problem is a must for the sake of economic development, a task that the government has tried to carry out to the best of its ability.

The government is convinced that the respected members of the House will agree with us that the recent rice problem is a national misfortune. In handling this matter, the government expects the people at large, and businesspeople in particular, as well as all elements of the state apparatus, to respond to this situation with a sense of responsibility, service and the sharing of national development goals, by eschewing all temptations to benefit and gain personally from the difficult situation the people of Indonesia are facing in their daily lives.

With this explanation, the government is convinced that our collective sense of responsibility and cooperation will strengthen, especially among the executives of the nation, the legislators, and all members of the state apparatus, as well as between the government and the public. We hope that this solidified sense of cooperation and responsibility will further strengthen our joint efforts to overcome this rice crisis.

NOTE

[1]   The government's explanation of the rice shortage to the House of Representatives, Republic of Indonesia, delivered by Minister/Chairman of the National Development Planning Agency (BAPPENAS) on 14 December 1972. This article is translated by Harry Bhaskara.

16

PERTAMINA CRISIS (1975)[1]

Introductory Note: *On 25 June 1975, I presented the Government's Explanation on the Pertamina crisis to the members of Commissions I, VI, VII, along with the State Budget, in a joint session of the House of Representatives.*

The Pertamina crisis stems from measures taken by Pertamina that ran counter to the Law on Pertamina and other Government regulations; among these regulatory infringements were:

1. *Undertaking huge construction projects outside of the Company's scope of duty;*
2. *Financing those projects by short-term foreign loans which it failed to repay;*
3. *Failure to submit to the Government taxes paid by foreign oil companies in the form of fossil oil;*
4. *Failure to pay the Company's own corporate taxes.*

On top of the above infractions, there have been a number of other measures taken by Pertamina, whose purpose and motivation remain unclear, and which are currently under an in-depth and broad investigation at the time this explanation is being delivered to the Government; these include leasing and purchasing agreements for a great number of huge oil tankers.

The government has taken a great number of measures to resolve the Pertamina crisis. Among the lessons learned from this crisis are that state-owned companies should strictly abide by existing laws and regulations at all times, and that they have a duty to promptly submit comprehensive reports to the government.

To complement the account in Chapter 16 on the Government's Explanations on 25 June 1975, on the "Pertamina Issue", the following three attachments have been placed at the end of this chapter:

Attachment I: Excerpts from Government Deliberation on the 1976/1977 State Budget at the House of Representatives delivered by the President of the Republic Indonesia on 7 January 1976. (page 315)

Attachment II: Excerpts from State of the Nation Address by President of the Republic Indonesia Soeharto at the House of Representatives on 16 August 1977. (page 320)

Attachment III: Excerpts from Chapter 44 "Resolving Pertamina Crisis" from the book titled: Pikiran, Ucapan dan Tindakan Saya (My Thoughts, Words and Deeds), an autobiography by Soeharto as told to G. Dwipayana and Ramadhan K.H. (pages 304 to 306). Publisher P.T. Citra Lamtoro Gung Persada, Jakarta 1989. (page 322)

THE GOVERNMENT'S EXPLANATION ABOUT THE ISSUE OF PERTAMINA IN THE JOINT MEETING OF THE HOUSE OF REPRESENTATIVES' COMMISSIONS I, VI, VII, AND THE STATE BUDGET COMMISSION OF THE HOUSE OF THE REPUBLIC OF INDONESIA, DELIVERED BY COORDINATING MINISTER FOR ECONOMICS, FINANCE AND INDUSTRY/CHAIRMAN OF THE NATIONAL PLANNING DEVELOPMENT AGENCY, 25 JUNE 1975

First of all the Government wants to thank the House of Representatives for giving it the opportunity to fulfill the Legislature's request that it deliver an explanation about the current issue of the State Oil and Gas Company (Pertamina).

The Government thanks the House of Representatives for their request on the issue. The Government also thanks the public and the press for the various ideas and reviews that have been expressed regarding the issue.

In this case, the Government is of the opinion that the House and the public are fulfilling their sense of belonging and sense of responsibility for the safety and the survival of this important state company and for the sustainability of the ongoing national development. The Government also has the same goals and initiatives. Therefore the Government will deliver an explanation about the issue in the same spirit.

This explanation is expected to clarify this matter upon the appropriate basis so as to avoid any possible ambiguities and baseless assumptions regarding it.

The Government is aware that the House and the people are paying serious attention to this matter because of the importance of oil to state revenue and foreign exchange. What happens to our oil has much to do with the state economy and development activities in general. Therefore, soon after Pertamina began facing difficulties, the Government conducted a thorough investigation and took the necessary measures. Of course, the complete resolution of the matter will take time. Now, the Government deems that the time has come to make a clear explanation; only after its investigation has yielded sufficient results, and after the execution of the necessary actions has taken place.

A brief review of the development of this state owned company in the past few years shows that Pertamina has grown into a big company with a lot of activities and huge investment in a short time. Motivated by the intention to make the best of its capability in national development activities, the company has expanded its investments into various areas. Pertamina's rapid expansion was in tandem with the fast growth of the international money and capital markets. This expansion has resulted in the availability of adequate funds to finance various activities. Such a situation, along with the rapid growth of the Indonesian economy and Pertamina itself resulted in the willingness of international banks to provide more loans to our state company, especially because the Government itself had not borrowed any commercial loan from international banks. The abundance of funds available in the financial and capital markets worldwide also encouraged Pertamina to sign development contracts for massive projects, even though there was no guarantee that all of the necessary financing would be fulfilled.

In the meantime, the economic developments worldwide underwent change. The once-abundant money market and international capital has now shrunk and become limited. Long-term loans from the international banking world have been harder to get. In its efforts to find a solution,

Pertamina has obtained short-term loans, with a less-than-one-year return period, to finance its long-term investment projects in the hope that the short-term loans could always be extended. Meanwhile Pertamina needed more capital to complete its various and newly kicked-off projects. Unfortunately, the money market and the level of capital available internationally did not recover fast enough. The expected new long-term loans were never disbursed, while the company found it very difficult to extend its short-term loans. It then tried to meet the needs of its various projects by spending part of the state revenue from oil. However, the situation worsened even further when it had difficulties repaying its short-term loans.

Meanwhile, the company's poor administration exacerbated these difficulties. The company's administrative systems had failed to accommodate its rapid expansion and to cope with its widening range of activities.

In March 1975, the Government took a series of necessary measures to address the situation. This series of measures was implemented immediately and correctly considering the important role of oil for national development and the need to maintain the trust of the business community in the country and outside Indonesia. It is tremendously important to maintain trust in order to ensure that the years of effort spent on cultivating it will not have been wasted.

The measures taken by the Government cover three main areas:

(1) to resolve Pertamina's difficulties;
(2) to secure the state revenue, which means to secure development; and
(3) to secure the balance of payments of Indonesia.

The three measures were executed simultaneously and harmoniously because the development of the oil sector has direct impacts on state revenue and foreign exchange. By implementing the three measures swiftly and in tandem, it is expected that unexpected impacts will be mitigated in a short time.

The actions taken by the Government to cope with Pertamina's difficulties fall into three categories:

(1) to provide financial aid from the Government to Pertamina so that it can fulfill its obligations to pay back domestic and foreign debts;

(2) to make a thorough re-examination of Pertamina's investment programme for its projects in numerous sectors; and

(3) to make efforts to improve the administration and finances of the company in order to improve its administrative capacity. All of this is in accordance with the implementation of Law No. 8/1971 on State Oil and Gas Mining Companies.

The Government's financial aid is aimed at enabling Pertamina to pay back its domestic and foreign debts in due time. The aid was in the form of funds from Bank Indonesia. In this case, it is necessary to explain that the Government did not take over Pertamina's debt. What the Government did was help Pertamina by providing a huge amount of funds to pay back the debt. As for the domestic debt, special attention was given to the payment of contracts regarding service provision, including construction work. The reason for this prioritization was that construction work is labour intensive in nature, so that payment would ensure the provision of employment opportunities. The amount of the domestic debt related to the payment process was about Rp47 billion, while the short-term debts owed to foreign banks and companies was about US$1.5 billion, and the long-term debt was about US$0.8 billion. Based on development research data, the domestic and foreign debts are being paid back regularly.

In this case, it is necessary to make a more careful examination of every commercial debt, including the debt to companies and contractors from inside and outside the country. Presidential Decree No. 15/1975 assigned the Trade Minister, assisted by several officials, to make inventories, and to examine and evaluate all of Pertamina's commercial debts. This assignment was based on the need to get an overall picture of Pertamina's obligations, especially in the settlement of its commercial debts.

In addition, to ensure order and coordination, the Government has decided that Pertamina and other state-owned companies should not apply for foreign loan by themselves. All foreign loans for state-owned companies will now be decided solely by the Government. The only possible exception will be the financing of cost deficit in certain projects.

One of the recent problems has arisen from Pertamina's grandiose investment plans, both for ongoing work and for projects yet to be carried out. Therefore, the Government considers it important to reevaluate all of Pertamina's investment plans. A distinction is being made in the evaluation between the gas and oil projects on one hand and projects in other sectors on the other. In line with the provisions on business as stipulated in the law, projects for the exploration, exploitation, refining, processing, and transportation, as well as the sale of oil and gas should get first priority. Projects in other fields are to be re-evaluated based on the merits of each project, their linkages to the whole framework of development, and whether or not their level of financing would be burdensome.

This evaluation is currently being carried out. Basically, some projects will be continued, some others will be carried out on a more limited scale, while some will be postponed, and some others will be halted. A review is also being done to see if certain projects will be continued by Pertamina or taken over by other Government institutions. This is part of the implementation of Law No. 8/1971.

Another series of important actions is related to the efforts to put things in order in the areas of administration and finance to improve the company's administrative capacity. This includes the company's budget, control system, and others.

In connection with the Government's efforts to help cope with Pertamina's difficulties, based on Presidential Decree No. 11/1975, a technical team was established, comprising Lieutenant General A. Hasnan Habib, Major General Piet Haryono, and Brigadier Geneneral Ismail Saleh, who have been assigned to examine and evaluate Pertamina's 1975 budget plan; both for its routine budget and its budget for financing development projects. Besides this, the team is also assigned to examine and evaluate the development projects undertaken by Pertamina and its affiliated companies.

Based on Presidential Decree No. 13/1975, the Minister for Administrative Reforms, assisted by a number of officials, has been assigned to make a thorough review and evaluation of programmes and implementation of the project regarding the construction of a steel plant, PT Krakatau Steel, including related infrastructure projects in order to bring them into line with Government policies. The next assignment is to renegotiate with suppliers and contractors of PT Krakatau Steel in order to finish the project in accordance with the policies set out by the Government.

Several supervisory teams have also been set up based on Presidential Decree No. 14/1975: the Supervisory Team for Natural Gas Project in Aceh and East Kalimantan, the Supervisory Team for the Fertilizer Plant in East Kalimantan, and the Supervisory Team for the Oil Refinery

Project in Cilacap. The tasks of the supervisory teams include evaluating the projects' physical plans and financing plans, whether these are in accordance with the need and the available financial sources. The teams are also assigned to monitor the company's spending to determine whether it is in accordance with the set project plans.

As is the case with the previously mentioned teams, the supervisory teams are also accountable to the President.

Meanwhile, Presidential Decree No. 16/1975 stipulates that the Fertilizer Plant in Jatibarang (Cirebon) is a Government project under the auspices of the Ministry of Industry. The Minister of Industry has been appointed and assigned to continue the implementation of this development of the project in accordance with the physical plan and policies set by the Government. It has also been decided that the source of financing for the implementation of the project will be decided by the Government.

Besides this, Presidential Decree No. 17/1975 assigns the Minister of Industry to immediately take preparatory steps to implement the construction of Fertilizer Plant PUSRI-IV, in accordance with the physical plan and policies set out by the Government.

Based on Presidential Decree No.14/1975, a review has been made of several regulations on capital and the business model of the Petro Kimia corporation in Gresik.

In pursuance to the policies set out by the Government, Pertamina has undertaken various measures to improve its administrative and financial departments, as well as its operations and personnel departments, in order to achieve various targets, such as securing state revenue, prevention of the taking out of more loans, stricter control of operational cost spending, more intensive supervision of budget and work plan implementation, the prevention of waste, the improvement of job efficiency and productivity, and the limiting of business scopes to a minimum, as well as the halting of all kinds of spending that has nothing to do with minimum operational needs. To further straighten things up, a Budget Committee has been established to coordinate, examine and decide business priorities, to make plans and to monitor and control all of the spending of the company's funds. Another action is the establishment of an "internal audit" mechanism to check and examine the implementation of procedures, management policies, financials, and the treasury. Along with these efforts to improve the administrative and financial systems, upgrading is also being done in relation to organizational and personnel matters.

In order to accelerate the drafting of the company's balance of payments and profit and loss accounts, an accounting company has been assigned to help with the implementation of a financial management and supervisory system and to prepare for the execution of a thorough and complete audit.

Besides the actions taken by the Government to help cope with Pertamina's difficulties, the Government has also made efforts to secure state revenue in relation to the implementation of the State Budget, as well as securing the state's balance of payment, particularly foreign exchange revenue. These efforts are complementary to each other and will be elaborated upon at the same time.

As explained earlier, Pertamina did not hand over all its oil revenue to the Government last year. Therefore, the government received less revenue and foreign exchange than it should have. The shortage amounted to around US$850 million. In response to this situation, the Government has decided that such shortfalls in submission of funds must not recur in this year's budget, nor in the years to come. Therefore, various actions have been taken.

It is understood that in oil-related activities in Indonesia, we recognize working contracts, production sharing and the activities of Pertamina itself. State revenues from oil and taxes on the oil company have been set on the basis of certain formulations. In the case of a working contract, part of the payment is made directly by the related company to the Government. The rest is in the form of crude oil handed over to the Government through Pertamina. Revenue from the oil, including that from oil exports, is then handed over by Pertamina to the Government. It was this revenue that Pertamina failed to hand over in full to the Government last year.

In the case of production sharing, crude oil is set aside for the Government. Pertamina processes the crude oil on behalf of the government for domestic needs or for export. Last year, Pertamina also failed to deliver all of the revenue from this sector to the Government.

Like other companies, Pertamina has the obligation to pay taxes to the Government for its own oil-related activities.

To prevent further unexpected incidents and problems, the Government has taken several actions. All Letters of Credit for Pertamina's oils export must now be opened through Bank Indonesia. Thus, Bank Indonesia acts as a central institution to collect the oil export revenues of Pertamina. In the case of imports, the Letters of Credit are also opened through

Bank Indonesia. These measures are taken to allow Bank Indonesia to have a comprehensive picture about Pertamina's obligations and their payment.

In this connection, Presidential Instruction No. 12/1975 has stipulated procedures for the handing over of state revenues derived from the execution of working contracts and production sharing contracts, as well as the monitoring of all of Pertamina's overall activities. It has been decided, among other things, that all of the Government's revenue is to be recorded directly by Bank Indonesia and place in the Government's account at that bank.

This series of measures is expected to provide a higher level of certainty in securing foreign exchange and state revenue in order to facilitate the execution of the State Budget, so that the final outcome is more in line with expectations.

That is the explanation of the Government regarding the issue of Pertamina in response to the House of Representatives' request. The Government is convinced that the series of measures taken will contain the problems in the way we have all expected. Hopefully, the cooperation between the Government and the House of Representatives will become stronger in facing all difficulties and challenges in our development.

Attachment I:

Excerpts from Government Deliberation on the 1976–77 State Budget at the House of Representatives delivered by the President of the Republic Indonesia on 7 January 1976.

In the meantime the problem of Pertamina is partly related with that world economic upheaval. The intention of Pertamina to exploit its potentials for national development efforts has induced it to undertake big investments in different and vast activities. Those big investments were made with the expectation to obtain its financial sources from the international capital market, particularly with the availability of an enormous amount of petrodollars, which at that time indeed provided sufficient funds to finance various major undertakings. In such situation Pertamina concluded contracts for the construction of big projects, although the funds required had not been entirely secured.

Later as it turned out the world economy had undergone changes. The money and capital market became tight and limited. Pertamina sought a way-out by borrowing short-term loans in order to finance long-term projects. while the need for capital to complete the already started projects became greater, the international money and capital market has hardly improved. Moreover the long-term loans anticipated by Pertamina did not come forth. Difficulties in complying with the financial requirements of various projects were also attempted to be solved by utilizing part of the oil revenues which were initially intended as state earnings derived from contracts of work and production sharing.

Meanwhile the difficulties aggravated due to the company's administrative inadequacy, especially in managing such a fast growing enterprise with equally vast activities.

The difficulties suffered by Pertamina had wide repercussions, especially as they involved huge amounts of money. Besides affecting the company itself, they also created a series of serious consequences to the stepping up of national development activities in general. These consequences affect state revenues, foreign exchange reserves, foreign loans and domestic credits.

It is known that state revenues originating from the sector of crude oil is playing a very important role. These state revenues from crude oil are for the most part produced from contracts of work, another part from production sharing, while a minor portion from Pertamina's own production. Thus, the problems encountered by Pertamina would not have great repercussions on our state revenues, if only the transfer of state earnings from contracts of work and production sharing was not obstructed.

Because during 1974–75 and the beginning of 1975–76 foreign exchange originating from contracts of work and production sharing, which should have been delivered to the Government through Pertamina, were not entirely transferred and this had its impact on state revenues, thus reducing the ability to accelerate the pace of national development. Consequently the Government took a series of measures to prevent similar recurrences. These measures among others consisted of regulations on transfer procedure of state revenues from crude oil, namely that all state revenues from crude oil should be directly credited by Bank Indonesia on the Government's account to said Bank.

It was also stipulated that all exports and imports by Pertamina should be carried out by opening Letter of Credits (LC) through Bank

Indonesia. With this series of measures the Government is convinced that state revenues from crude oil will be better ensured, for the sake of accelerating development implementation.

The Pertamina problem also has its impact on our foreign exchange reserves. State revenues originating from crude oil are almost totally in the form of foreign exchange. Since state earnings from contracts of work and production sharings by Pertamina were not entirely submitted to the Government, the increase of our national foreign exchange reserves did not materialize accordingly. Besides, the Government had to assist Pertamina in overcoming its debts repayment by using the foreign exchange reserves accumulated over the past few years. Thus the national foreign exchange reserves which should have rapidly increased and could have been used in accelerating the realization of REPELITA, has suffered a setback. The Government, therefore, had to take a series of measures in order to replenish the national foreign exchange reserves. One of these important measures was securing loans from international capital markets.

These foreign loans, aimed at strengthening the foreign exchange reserves within the scope of tackling the Pertamina problem, amount to approximately US$1 billion and consist of loans on commercial terms. These are Government loans executed by Bank Indonesia. These huge amounts of commercial loans have greatly affected the efforts for stepping up development. We are aware that progress achieved in the realization of national development has increased the ability to accelerate the pace of REPELITA. In this respect, apart from soft-terms foreign loans, those based on less-concessional terms have also started to be used for various development projects in different sectors. In obtaining these less-concessional loans we must be very cautious that the repayment of these loans in the future would not go beyond our ability. Such cautiousness is furthermore required as huge amounts of foreign commercial loans are obtained in the efforts to solve the Pertamina problem. To prevent repayment of overall Government foreign loans from exceeding beyond our ability, the Government has stipulated a policy for limiting the number of foreign loans based on less concessional terms for development projects.

Meanwhile part of the domestic financial obligations of Pertamina at home is in the form of rupiah. To assist Pertamina in meeting this obligation, the Government has provided rupiah funds through Bank Indonesia. The amount needed is enormous. On the other hand the increase of overall bank credits needs to be carried out within the normal limits, so as not to jeopardize the economic stability greatly required for the smooth realization of development. In this connection the provision of credits for other sectors are controlled more tightly while still taking into account development priority. Hopefully the financial assistance to Pertamina in rupiahs on the one hand can be carried out, while on the other hand the increase of bank credit in its totality can still be executed within proper limits.

Due to these rather far-reaching consequences, measures already taken by the Government were not merely aimed at the solution of Pertamina problem, but also at limiting the detrimental effects that disrupt the stepping up of development; and simultaneously to prevent similar recurrences. The Government strongly believes that with all these measures which have been carried out convincingly, God willing, the Pertamina problem can be solved and the acceleration of development during 1976–77 and onward will proceed as expected.

Attachment II:

Excerpts from State of the Nation Address by President of the Republic Indonesia Soeharto at the House of Representatives on 16 August 1977.

By adhering to the same basic principles we are also trying to find a solution for the debts incurred by Pertamina. Part of the loans secured by Pertamina have indeed been used for productive projects like the Liquefied Natural Gas (LNG) plant, oil refineries, oil exploration and exploitation, distribution infrastructures and so on. But some of these loans have been utilized not in compliance with the policies adopted by the Government and some were even beyond the knowledge of the Government, while the terms or loan agreements which have become a burden were for the most part extremely unfavourable for Pertamina, terms which seemingly would not appear in ordinary agreements. These heavy loans/debts run into billions of dollars.

Therefore, as soon as the Government found out about the difficulties Pertamina was in, it took the necessary measures to save the state finances, to rescue Pertamina from bankruptcy and to reform the **entire** management and administration of Pertamina. These efforts have so far produced satisfactory results. Pertamina's debts — their reimbursement is assisted by the Government — have been reduced to a minimum, so that Pertamina can continue its function properly.

Similarly the hire-purchase contracts of ocean-going tankers which we regarded as not only being inconsistent with the Government's policy, but they were even very harmful to Pertamina, apparently were not based on terms which are customary in sound agreements. If we continue to deal under these contracts, they would cause heavier burden on Pertamina. Therefore — in view of safeguarding the state's and Pertamina's finances and of exercising an overall control — there was only one alternative that the Government had to take, namely to find a way to cancel these contracts, either through negotiations with the parties concerned, or, if deemed necessary, through court proceedings.

Thanks be to God, we have succeeded in most of our efforts. So far, as a result of the measures taken by the Government, the debts incurred by Pertamina as a consequence of the hire-purchase contracts of tankers, which originally would have reached to around US$3.3 billion, have been reduced to a minimum. A settlement has been reached with regard to 27 tankers at an original hire-purchase value of US$2.8 billion. After the cancellation of these contracts, Pertamina's obligations amounted to US$255 million. For the remaining hire-purchase contract of 9 tankers at a value of about US$470 million similar efforts for a solution are now being pursued, which, hopefully, would be successful in the near future, thus reducing Pertamina's debts even more. Meanwhile, steps to put Pertamina's internal organisation in order are still being continued, including legal actions againts those who are found guilty in connection with the Pertamina crisis.

Attachment III:

Excerpts from Chapter 44 "Resolving Pertamina Crisis" from the book titled: *Pikiran, Ucapan dan Tindakan Saya* (My Thoughts, Words and Deeds), an autobiography by Soeharto as told to G. Dwipayana and Ramadhan K.H. (pages 304 to 306). Publisher P.T. Citra Lamtoro Gung Persada, Jakarta 1989.

"Difficulties arose when I found in 1975 that Pertamina had borrowed money to finance its projects. The revelation of the state oil company's debts, which were linked to local and overseas contracts amounting to US$10.5 billion, had resulted in an uproar. Meanwhile, newspapers were attacking the policy of the top leader of Pertamina. I had to dig deeper into the problem. I knew I had to be impartial, while at the same time I was fully aware about the nature of fraud in big businesses, such as those in the oil sector. Pertamina had many enemies overseas who were envious of it.

I did not cover up the serious problems stemming from the Pertamina crisis.

I was coaxed to do something. But I know for sure when it is the right time to take action, or to not do something, or merely to admonish someone.

It was true that we had an acute problem at that time, but it was not unsolvable. We found a way out and we followed that path with utmost care. Pertamina was in a serious crisis mainly because it was trapped by its obligation to pay back its debts, which was beyond its capacity at the time. The massive amount of its obligation stemmed from the activities it had extended beyond its core oil business.

It is true that the government was aware and had even approved a number of Pertamina's activities outside its oil business. However, this knowledge and approval was given on the understanding that the activities would expedite its core tasks, and with the condition that any expenses should not burden the company, let alone the government.

All of a sudden and without government knowledge, Pertamina, perhaps out of its desire to finish its projects, had become haunted by huge financial obligations beyond its means. These included short term obligations, as well as those needed to finance its grandiose business activities. And this had become extremely burdensome; for example, the lease-purchase scheme for ocean tankers and the construction of other projects that had incurred huge business debts.

Had the government not taken prompt action to salvage Pertamina, it would have faced bankruptcy because it was impossible for Pertamina, considering the weight and gravity of its financial situation, to resolve its own problems. In turn, this would certainly have led to serious damage to our economy and state financial conditions.

The measures taken by the government at that time were internal disciplinary action at Pertamina, on one hand, and assisting it in resolving and reducing its burden in an optimal way on the other hand.

Apart from that, the government had also decided that Pertamina must sell part of its excessively large amount of assets to both the government and the private sector.

Therefore, the view or concern pervasive among the people that the government had been forced to devalue the rupiah because of Pertamina's enormous debt is not true, and is, in fact, baseless. We would not have and had never seen the need to devalue the rupiah at that time.

In sum total, this episode constituted more than a financial hurdle. The Pertamina crisis was a bitter experience and had to become a lesson for all of us; the government apparatus, as well as the state-owned companies. Even if we had wanted to speed up development, in the absence of prudent execution, such an action would end up in trouble or even in failure.

Some time later, I put forward my standpoint when I presented the 1976–77 State Budget. The government was confident about all the measures it had taken; the Pertamina crisis had been resolved and development during the year 1976–77 and beyond could move forward as planned. We had found the way out then and the Pertamina problem was handled appropriately.

I resisted the strong public pressure for me to do something immediately. I let the boiled water cool down first before I would be able to drink it. As soon as public attention shifted to another issue, a leadership change in Pertamina took place.

I decided to keep almost all members of the board in place to ensure constancy and to facilitate the company's operations. Meanwhile, Ibnu Sutowo was replaced by Piet Haryono.

I detest unnecessary disturbances, which could be dangerous and devastating. But, of course, I would also constantly assess capability and loyalty in the execution of tasks to ensure that Pertamina achieved its goals.

NOTE

[1] The Government's explanation about the Issue of Pertamina to the House of Representatives, Republic of Indonesia, delivered by Coordinating Minister for Economics, Finance and Industry/Chairman of the National Development Planning Agency on 25 June 1975. This article is translated by Harry Bhaskara.

17

DEVALUATION OF THE RUPIAH (1978)[1]

Introductory Note: *Devaluation is the official decreasing by the government of the value of a given country's currency against a foreign currency. If a currency's value decreases solely due to market forces and entirely without government intervention, the decline in a currency's value is called depreciation not devaluation. On 15 November 1978, the Government of Indonesia officially announced the devaluation of the Rupiah against the U.S. dollar from Rp415 per US$ to Rp625 per US$. The Rp415 rate had been in effect since 1971. Various explanations were given to the public about the policy. One way of conveying these explanations was through a television interview that took place on 22 November 1978. The interviewer was Drs. Sumadi, M.EC., a graduate in economics at an Australian university, who would later become the Director General for Radio, Television and Film, and then go on to serve as Indonesian Ambassador to Mexico, a post which also covered Cuba and Panama. The government prepared several anticipatory moves before making the decision. Two of the most important things involved were the sufficient stockpiling of foreign exchange reserves and food supply (rice) all across the country. Therefore after the devaluation announcement took place, every request for foreign exchange and/or food could immediately be fulfilled.*

Sumadi: Good evening to you all. As we are all aware, on 15 November 1978, the government introduced a new policy in the economic and monetary fields, and since then there have been a multitude of reactions from the public. Therefore, I now invite you to observe a question and answer session with the Coordinating Minister for Economy, Finance and Industry, and Chairman of BAPPENAS, Bapak Prof. Dr Widjojo Nitisastro.

Pak Widjojo, even though the government has explained the policy that was announced on 15 November 1978, many parties in our society do not yet fully understand it or the reasons behind it. It's therefore timely for Pak Widjojo to re-emphasize the essence of the policies that were stipulated on 15 November.

Answer: Thank you, Pak Sumadi. On 15 November, the government put in place a new policy, which relates to foreign exchange. As we all understand, when we trade with another country, our currency, the rupiah must be converted into a foreign currency. That's why there is something called the exchange rate. For instance, previously one U.S. dollar equaled Rp415. Then on 15 November we made a revision, so that one U.S. dollar is now equivalent with Rp625. This revision also occurs in relation to the currency of other countries, such as the Singaporean dollar, the yen of Japan, the mark of Germany, and so on.

Apart from the foreign exchange rate revision, a change was also made in the exchange rate system. This can be explained as follows: Since 1971, the exchange rate of the rupiah against the U.S. dollar had been fixed at Rp415 per one dollar. This had been going on until the 15 November, 1978. From that point on, the rate has no longer been fixed; now it can fluctuate instead. However, the government will try to see to it that any fluctuations are not significant. So, the rupiah will not be fixed at Rp625 per dollar and will be allowed to fluctuate, albeit in minor ranges.

This is what is called a managed floating exchange rate. This means the rate is not persistently constant and that it floats within a managed range. It is not be let loose to go up freely or down arbitrarily, but is managed. That was the second point.

The third is the emphasis that the foreign exchange regime in Indonesia remains fully free. That means that the public can draw on an unlimited amount of foreign exchange abroad and vice versa. In other words, if any of us needs foreign currency, such as the yen or any other currency, they can purchase it from the banks. And those banks can buy those currencies, in any amount, from Bank Indonesia. No matter how much it is, it can be bought and if you want to take the currency outside the country, there will be no problems. This is also the case if you want to sell foreign currencies to Bank Indonesia; you will be served.

As for the fourth point; it relates to raw material imports used for domestic production. The import duties for those raw materials were cut by 50 per cent. The taxes on import sales were also cut. The raw materials covered are used to produce goods for domestic needs or exports. Whenever the produced goods are sold overseas, or exported, then those raw materials will be exempted from import duties and import sales taxes. That is basically the essence of this policy.

Sumadi: This policy was met with strong public response after it was launched on 15 November. In the current situation, in particular by the people at large, questions are being asked concerning the government's aim in introducing this policy. In other words, what is the government is trying to accomplish with this action?

Answer: Every policy has its objectives of course. What the government is doing in the context of our task framework is carrying out national development. It is understood, that our national development has two objectives, first, to improve the welfare of the people, and second, to lay a sound foundation for further stages of development.

One of elements of the people's welfare is the level of income. We want to increase their income and create more equal distribution of income. Income is closely related to job opportunities. Someone can only secure income if she or he works; no work no income. So it is our duty to create as many job opportunities as possible. Obviously job opportunities do not present themselves on their own. We have to create them.

How? When there are vigorous economic activities, when investments are made, when factories are built, when the agricultural sector yields more produce, and transportation activities come to life; then, and only then, are jobs created.

Now, what will drive factories to be built; the agricultural sector to increase production, and the other activities necessary to growing the economy and providing the need jobs? A market for the various industrial and agriculture products being produced is imperative. If you produce goods but cannot find a market for them, you will sell nothing. Then the factories will have to shut down, and no matter how bountiful the harvest in the agricultural sector, the farmers will suffer losses instead of prospering. In the past, farmers often cultivated cassava and produced dried cassava (*gaplek*), but the price of *gaplek* declined. Production then dwindled.

We have often heard that the goods produced domestically are struggling to compete with the imported ones. So we have to create a market for our own goods; it is imperative that we create a viable domestic market.

We import so many goods because we need to because we have not yet managed to produce what we need on our own. But there are also goods being imported into Indonesia, which we could actually produce and sell at competitive prices. Unfortunately, there is a tendency in society to regard imported goods as of higher quality than the locally produced ones. In fact, many of our goods are on par in quality with imported products, and the prices for both are competitive. This requires protection of our domestically produced goods. How? By slapping on high import duties, up to 100 per cent or even higher or imposing import bans. But what has happened? The goods keep coming in despite the bans. And, the high import duties have no impact because many items are being smuggled in. Banning only seems to induce people to resort to smuggling.

There are similar issues with our export goods, whether that would be natural rubber, tea or the other commodities that we sell abroad. Our goods have to be able to compete with other goods produced by other countries on the international market. In reality, what our exporters — and also our farmers who are the producers of those export goods — get in rupiah is undervalued. This is because they export the goods in foreign currencies (the yen, dollar, gulden, and so on) while the value of those currencies in rupiah is too low. The results of our exports are then below expectation.

Moreover, we need to remind ourselves that out exports are divided into two categories: oil, including liquefied natural gas and non-petroleum goods. During the past Repelita II (National Five-Year Development Plan II), our revenue from oil increased sharply, as oil prices soared. At first, the oil price was US$3 per barrel, then climbed to $6, $8, $10, $12, and is now at $13.3. So during the Repelita II period, oil prices increased more than four times. For the upcoming Repelita III years, we do not expect the oil price to jump as it did during Repelita II.

Yet the oil exports are not enough, we need to boost our non-oil exports in a variety of sectors because we need foreign exchange to import industrial equipment, and machinery for the mining, transportation and other industries as well.

We need to create job opportunities. This can only be done if there are economic activities. The economic activities will be there if markets are available. Such markets will exist if our goods on our domestic market can compete with imported ones, while our exports on the international market can compete with similar products from other countries.

With improved exports, our income from foreign exchange will increase. And when our goods can compete favourably with imported goods, a reduction in the importation of such goods will occur. That will help us save our foreign exchange. This is very important as we need plenty of foreign exchange to import the necessary equipment and machinery.

Now, why can't our products compete well in the domestic market? Why is it that our export products cannot compete effectively with similar products in international market? Why? This needs a thorough analysis.

Of course there are plenty of reasons; we could make a long list. One of the most important reasons is the comparison in value between the rupiah and foreign currencies. Because the U.S. dollar is the currency most commonly used, the exchange rate of the rupiah against the U.S. dollar, which was Rp415 to one dollar, required reviewing.

The upward revision of one dollar being valued at Rp625 creates far better opportunities for our products. Why? First of all, if one dollar becomes Rp625, then imported goods become more expensive.

For instance, there are people among us who like to purchase foreign made goods, in particular those with French names on them. Our products have to compete with such goods. If the imported products become more expensive, ours will surely be more accepted in the domestic market. If our products sell better, production will increase, economic activities will accelerate and employment opportunities will soar.

Our exporters and farmers who produce rubber and other export products will get more rupiah. If exports used to yield Rp415 per dollar, now they get Rp625. Therefore, they will be encouraged to boost production and exports. If that is the case, employment prospects in Indonesia will be brighter. As mentioned earlier, improvement of the people's welfare has much to do with the expansion of employment opportunities.

Sumadi: The rupiah is no longer tied with the U.S. dollar, so it floats against foreign currencies, including the dollar. Please explain, what will happen to the rupiah if the value of the dollar declines or, conversely, increases. This needs an explanation since people are asking how long the new exchange rate of Rp625 per dollar can prevail.

Answer: That is a logical and understandable question, as this phenomenon seems to be a new one for the public. In fact, it is not very new at all, because, before 15 November, the only currency that did not float against the rupiah was the U.S. dollar. The Singaporean dollar, the Hong Kong dollar, the Japanese yen, the Australian dollar, the West German mark, and all the others have long floated against the rupiah. So the only flatly fixed exchange rate was that of the U.S. dollar. Now the rupiah is not only tied with the U.S. dollar, but also with a basket of currencies of significance to Indonesia's international economic relations.

That group of currencies fluctuates, with the exchange rates of certain currencies rising and those of others declining. Sometimes the pull to go up is stronger and another time the pull to go down is stronger. That's why that even though the whole group of currencies fluctuates, these overall fluctuations are never as severe as for any of the given individual currencies on their own. Because the rupiah is tied with that whole group of currencies, then it will fluctuate in line with their collective movements, but not with steep volatility. Therefore, being tied to a whole basket of currencies will make the rupiah more stable.

In addition, the exchange rate of the rupiah is also monitored and controlled by the government. If the overall value of the basket of currencies jumps, while the government thinks it is best for the rupiah to not fluctuate sharply, then the government will step in to manage and control the exchange rate of the rupiah. However, should a fundamental or structural change occur in the world's economy, a change in the exchange rate would perhaps be in order. What is certain is that the government will not allow the rupiah to fluctuate wildly.

So if the question is how long the Rp625 rate per dollar will last, then the best answer is to let us just see in reality, whether or not the volatility can be controlled. If we tell the people that we have nothing to worry about, they will say that we are only saying what they want to hear. Therefore, let us look straight on at the reality. What is clear is that no matter how much foreign currency people want to buy, Bank Indonesia will be at their service. So there should no longer be any worries about the possibility of foreign exchanges shortages, or that foreign exchange will become too expensive, or that their rates will rise again.

Sumadi: In short, to provide certainty for businesspeople, the government will control the fluctuation of the rupiah against other currencies. Now, how does the government do that? Pak Widjojo, you always say that it is a controlled floating rate. How do you do that Pak?

Answer: The rupiah is tied to a basket of currencies. Each individual currency relates to one another. Each currency has a different role in our economic relations.

Any change in the rates among those foreign currencies, will certainly have an impact on us. However, the changes in the rates occurring among those currencies differ from one another in that as one rate increases another declines. Such changes, therefore, will have a relatively small impact on the rate of the rupiah. Even so, when the rupiah does fluctuate, the fluctuation must be kept within certain limits. So we will not let it fluctuate starkly.

A controlled exchange rate is not a simple matter and indeed it is not easy for the general public to understand, but that's basically the principle of the concept.

If we look at how this has been progressing since 15 November — if we read the newspapers and make comparisons — there have been some changes. However, those changes have not involved the U.S. dollar, but rather it has been the Japanese yen that has fluctuated against the rupiah.

Sumadi: It has been explained that with this new policy, namely the rate change of the rupiah to the dollar, imported goods will eventually become more expensive. But in reality, we are witnessing that the new policy has pushed up the prices of goods for domestically made products. How can we prevent the prices of these domestic products from rising too much?

Answer: As it is with everything else, when something that has stayed the same for a long time, suddenly changes, a sense of a shock emerges. This is understandable, as a new system has been introduced. In the first few days we did, indeed, see the prices of various domestic products soar. People purchased goods, while those in possession of the goods tried not to sell. This is the result of a reaction to the transformation from one situation to another.

Hence, concerns could, indeed, emerge during a time of adjustment, but over time they will eventually ease. If we compare the situation today with that of a week ago, we will see that such worries have diminished; we are all calmer now than we were a few days ago. If the prices go up, we will inform each other, but if the prices go down we think it's normal. A price going down is not news; if it is going up then that is news.

It is, therefore important, for us to stay calm and rethink the situation before yielding to the feelings of surprise, shock, or panic. Take our rice supply as an example. The rice reserves are sufficient and the price of rice has returned to its previous level.

We need not worry because our rice stock is plentiful. In this case we just need to calm down and avoid unnecessary actions. For instance, buying rice in large amounts and stockpiling it at home. What for? If it is held for too long the rice will spoil. So will any other goods we try to hoard.

Those of us in our business circles who have become accustomed to having a fixed rate for the U.S. dollar may well have some worries. Besides that, there have also been people who have tried to take advantage of the change. It is very common in every economy that some people will always attempt to reap benefits out of any situation if they can. So it has been rumored that our domestically made products will be affected in this or that way, with the result that prices for local goods have been pushed upwards.

It is, of course, not always easy to push the prices of goods up, because, basically, this depends, at core, on the balance between supply and demand. Even if prices can be nudged up, there is no way that they can be maintained at the higher levels because the demand is bound to remain stable, and, as long as supplies are also steady, the prices will adjust back to where they should be. As we have certainly seen in the past few days, the prices have, indeed, started to ease down.

Sumadi: I also have questions that represent the interests of civil servants, members of the Army and, most predominantly, pensioners. How can they cope with the rising prices?

Answer: Try it this way; let me ask you a question. For instance, the government announces today: the salary of civil servants will be raised by a certain percentage. What will likely happen?

Sumadi: I think there is a big possibility the prices will go further up.

Answer: That's it, exactly! We have consistently witnessed this over the past years. Every time we have even considered announcing a salary increase, prices have begun rising immediately. This is because people owning goods have held them back or hoarded them, waiting for the actual increase to take place. So such an announcement is not really sensible. Of course, we are always looking for ways to improve the salary levels of our civil servants. However, this can only be done within the limits of our expenditure budget. There are just so many other expenses apart from civil servants' salaries that we have to cover, including building schools and hospitals, as well as repairing roads and water pipes. We have to consider these expenses carefully in order to effectively prioritize toward moving development forward. However, if we try really hard, we are certain that our economy will strengthen, and so will our incomes. This, of course, increases the possibility of a salary increase for civil servants as well. We must see such an increase as a result of our joint effort to improve economic activities overall. So, for now, there has been and will be no announcement from the government with regard to any salary hike. So our business community should not try exploit the current situation or to speculate any further.

Sumadi: Can I say then that the salary hike will be done secretly?

Answer: That would be difficult to do, because the state budget (APBN) has to be discussed and jointly decided with our people's representatives at the DPR. So it has to be included in the state budget draft (RAPBN) which will be submitted to the House of Representatives (DPR) next January. All will be decided there, at that time.

Sumadi: Now with regard to development. What will happen to the development projects, both from the government and the private sector, in particular projects that use plenty of imported materials such as equipment and machinery? Will they be reviewed?

Answer: Every activity has its priorities; there are projects of high priority that must go ahead despite the need of imported goods. There are also activities that do not use imported goods, but are not too urgent; so they can be delayed, or their completion dates put off. We need to look at one project at a time, case per case. They cannot be generalized.

Sumadi: So if it's not a priority, meaning not too important, and the available funds will not be enough to carry out or complete the project, that particular project will be put on hold: is that it?

Answer: Yes, if it's not that urgent. But if it is very important, of high priority, we will try to continue. The same policy applies in relation to imported goods; not all are urgent, but some indeed are. So we have to calculate and be selective about prioritizing imports.

Sumadi: If you don't mind, I would like to discuss the current public opinion that although the government announced the new policy on 15 November, it is not yet ready to deal with all the consequences. What do you think?

Answer: As I explained before, the monetary matters and the foreign exchange rate and all the other financial issues are very important for every economy. Whenever there is a change, it has to be done carefully and with the best preparation. However, we all must keep in mind that it is impossible for a government — any government — to announce a timeline, say a week, for any revision of the exchange rate. That is simply impossible. So there is no other alternative but to announce such changes when they are ready for implementation, although it may seem sudden. Indeed, the announcement and the actual implementation are done suddenly. Any early announcement of such a move must be avoided.

So, what preparations had to be made for this? First, the objectives had to be clear. On top of that, there were also side effects, for instance the possibility of concerns and anxieties, which could push the prices up and so on. Therefore we had to make sure that the supply of basic foods; in particular rice, the main staple food in Indonesia, was adequate. Therefore, we have stockpiled large amounts of rice.

We have now 1.6 million tons of rice stocks across Indonesia and they are now starting to hit the market. So, even though the prices of rice jumped in the first few days after the announcement, we can see now that they are going down. Of course, the rice being made available is not the deluxe varieties, such as Cianjur rice, or Cianjur Kepala or Rojolele, but, rather, good, medium quality rice, which can be purchased at reasonable prices.

In the past few days in Jakarta, 6,000 tons of rice has been made available. This amount can be increased to 10,000 tons or more, if necessary. So if the public wishes to buy rice, it is available. That's called preparation, which took time to do, but it needed no publication.

Other preparations were related to the possibility of people rushing to buy the U.S. dollar for fear its rate might go up again. The government had to be ready with large foreign exchange reserves. At present the government has a foreign exchange reserve of US$2.5 billion. Anyone wishing to purchase dollars please do so, and in any amount.

Those were the most important preparations: Do not let fear over the availability of rice grasp society; do not let apprehension over our foreign exchange reserves haunt the business community. Those are the two main things of the utmost concern. In addition to that, there were other preparations, such as the reduction in duties for imported raw materials.

Sumadi: I would like to speak with you about this more extensively, but time is against us. Maybe other opportunities will arise for us to get a further explanation from Pak Widjojo, or some other senior officials. For now, let me express my gratitude for the explanations made. Well viewers, for tonight we're done listening to government's explanation; in this case from the Coordinating for Economics, Finance and Industry; Chairman of BAPPENAS, Bapak Widjojo Nitisastro. Good night, till we meet again.

NOTE

[1] Recording of the interview made by Coordinating Minister for Economics, Finance and Industry/Chairman of BAPPENAS with TVRI on 22 November 1978, with Drs. Sumadi M. Ec. acting as interviewer. The later subsequently became Director General of Radio, Television and Film and Indonesian Ambassador to Mexico, which includes coverage of Cuba and Panama. This article is translated by Harry Bhaskara.

18

FUEL PRICE INCREASE (1982)[1]

Introductory Note: *BBM is the local term for oil based fuel, while APBN stands for the State Budget of Income and Expenditure. Over the years the BBM and APBN were topical subjects, often causing a great deal of tension in society. The problem was the government plan to increase oil prices, which constituted an extra burden for consumers.*

Every year a new state budget was announced by the government, one of the elements receiving public attention would always be the oil fuel subsidies. Therefore, it was very important for the public to obtain the most comprehensive explanation about those two matters and their relationship to one another. In this context, I tried to provide as complete as possible a description of the current situation and the thinking and actions concerning the budget and the subsidies, through, among other channels, television interviews. The interviewer for the programme featured below was Drs. Sumadi, who finished his study of economics in Australia and then became Director General of TVRI and later represented the country as Ambassador to Mexico, concurrently Cuba and Panama.

One very important thing for the people to realize was the benefit to be gained through the reduction of oil fuel subsidies. So I made it clear that the decrease in fuel subsidies in 1982–83 enabled the construction of 22,600 new primary schools (compared with 15,000 in the previous year), 35,000 new classrooms (compared with 25,000 in the previous year), 20,000 houses for school principals and teachers (compared with 9,500 in the previous year), and the publication of 30 million reading books (compared with 15 million in the previous year).

Sumadi: Good evening viewers. I wish you a Happy New Year. May the new year of 1982 bring success, health and happiness to us all. At present the increase in the prices of oil based fuels or petroleum fuels is a topical issue in society, as is the Draft State Budget of Income and Expenditure, or RAPBN for 1982–83, which was delivered by the President to the House of Representatives yesterday, 5 January 1982. In this context, various questions and responses have arisen from the public. Therefore, this evening, I would like to invite you to observe a question and answer session with the Coordinating Minister for Economic, Financial and Industrial Affairs (EKUIN) concurrently Chairman of the National Development Planning Agency (BAPPENAS), Professor Widjojo Nitisastro.

Pak Widjojo, the two issues, which constitute the **problem of new fuel prices within the framework of the Draft State Budget for 1982–83**, appear to be very important. In order to provide viewers with a clear view, I would like to request your explanation about **the broad framework of the 1982–83 Draft State Budget** to start this programme. Please take your time.

Answer: Thank you, Pak Sumadi. As we are aware the Draft State Budget is compiled annually and later ratified as the State Budget of Income and Expenditure (APBN). As every family certainly has a budget and every company has a corporate budget, a state also has a budget called the State Budget of Income and Expenditure (APBN). As is the case with the household budget, the APBN is also composed of two parts: the part of income (or revenue) and the part of expenditure. The same is true of a company. There is corporate income and corporate expenditure.

Because the expenditure of any given household is adjusted to income, the principle of State Budget management is also that of expenditure adjusted to income. This is the principle of any balanced budget.

Let us examine several tables that we can use to better understand the essence of the State Budget. We will start with **Table 1: State Budget of Income and Expenditure (APBN)**.

TABLE 1
State Budget of Income and Expenditure (APBN)

State Income:	State Expenditure:
1. Domestic Revenue	1. Routine Expenditure
2. Foreign Revenue	2. Development Expenditure

The APBN consists of two parts: State Income and State Expenditure. State Income is composed of Domestic Revenue and Foreign Revenue. State Expenditure is also composed of two parts: Routine Expenditure and Development Expenditure.

State Income comprises Domestic Revenue and Foreign Revenue. Domestic Revenue is divided into two parts: oil receipts and other receipts that come from taxes, import duty, excise and so forth. Receipts from oil constitute the largest revenue source. If we produce and sell crude oil, we earn income for the State Budget. Foreign Revenue comes from external loans, provided on the basis of soft terms, which are totally utilized for Development Expenditure.

State Expenditure is made up of Routine Expenditure and Development Expenditure. Routine Expenditure is broken down into Personnel Expenses, Logistics Expenses, Regional Subsidies, Oil Based Fuel Subsidies and so forth. Personnel expenses are expenditures for salaries and food supplies for civil servants. Logistics expenses are expenditures for office equipment purchases and so forth. Regional subsidies are subsidies or aid provided for regions, because regional revenue is not very large. Such regional subsidies are meant to assist in the disbursement of salaries to regional civil servants, most of whom are teachers. Then there are the fuel subsidies that are currently a topic of great interest. Other expenses are food subsidies, foreign loan repayments and other costs. Development Expenditure covers expenses for building bridges, ports, schools, hospitals and so forth.

Now let us take a look at State Income, comprising Domestic Revenue and Foreign Revenue. Domestic Revenue consists of oil receipts and other receipts, which are derived from taxes, import duty, excise and so forth. See **Table 2: State Income, 1979–80 and 1982–83.**

TABLE 2
STATE INCOME, 1979–80 and 1982–83
(Rupiah trillion)

	APBN 1979–80	APBN 1980–81	APBN 1981–82	RAPBN 1982–83
A. Domestic Revenue				
1. Oil Receipts	3.3	6.4 (+94%)	8.6 (+34%)	9.1 (+6%)
2. Other Receipts (Taxes, import duty, excise, etc.)	2.1	2.6	3.7	4.7
3. Total Domestic Revenue	5.4	9.0	12.3	13.8
B. Foreign Revenue	1.5	1.5	1.6	1.8
C. Total State Income	6.9	10.5 (+52%)	13.9 (+32%)	15.6 (+12%)

In discussing the State Budget (APBN) we are usually discussing figures in the trillions of rupiah. As we are aware, a trillion equals a thousand billion. A billion equals a thousand million. And a million equals a thousand thousand. *So if we have a thousand rupiah multiplied by a thousand it becomes a million, multiplied by another thousand it becomes a billion, multiplied by still another thousand it equals a trillion.*

In the period of 1979–80, oil receipts reached Rp3.3 billion. In the period of 1980–81 the receipts increased to Rp6.4 billion, or by 94 per cent. In 1981–82 the receipts rose to Rp8.6 billion, or by 34 per cent. Next year the receipts are expected to increase by 6 per cent, because the price for our crude oil for export is predicted to remain unchanged in 1982. Other receipts have also registered increases from year to year.

State Income, as a whole in the period of 1979–80, totaled Rp6.9 billion, which rose to Rp10.5 billion, or 52 per cent, in 1980/81; to Rp13.9 billion, or 32 per cent, in the following period, and will increase to Rp15.6 billion, or by 12 per cent, in 1982–83. So it is apparent here that in 1982–83 our income can be expected to grow by only 12 per cent, whereas in 1981–82 it went up by 32 per cent, and in the previous period by 52 per cent. Why? This is because the receipts from oil for 1982/83 are projected to experience growth of just 6 per cent, against 34 per cent in the previous year and 94 per cent in the year before that. So our income in the coming fiscal year will not register a big increase. This is a challenge to us all.

Now let us check State Expenditure, which is also in the trillions of rupiah. See **Table 3: State Expenditure, 1981–82 and 1982–83**. We are comparing the 1981–82 State Budget with the 1982/83 Draft State Budget. Routine Expenditure comprises Personnel Expenses, which are projected to rise from Rp2.4 trillion to Rp2.5 trillion, Goods/Logistics Expenses from Rp1 trillion to Rp1.1 trillion, Regional Subsidies from Rp1.2 trillion to Rp1.3 trillion; Oil Fuel Subsidies, which are to decline from Rp1.5 trillion to Rp900 billion, and other expenses that will decrease from Rp1.4 trillion to Rp1.2 trillion. Routine Expenditure, therefore, is expected to decrease by 7 per cent from Rp7.5 trillion to Rp7 trillion. On the other hand, Development Expenditure is to be increased by 34 per cent from Rp6.4 trillion to Rp8.6 trillion. State Expenditure is set to be equal to State Income, growing from Rp13.9 trillion to Rp15.6 trillion, or by 12 per cent.

TABLE 3
STATE EXPENDITURE, 1981–82 and 1982–83
(Rupiah trillion)

	APBN 1981–82	RAPBN 1982–83
A. Routine Expenditure		
1. Personnel Expenses	2.4	2.5
2. Goods/Logistics Expenses	1.0	1.1
3. Regional Subsidies	1.2	1.3
4. BBM Subsidies	1.5	0.9
5. Others	1.4	1.2
6. Total Routine Expenditure	7.5	7.0 (−7%)
B. Development Expenditure	6.4	8.6 (+34%)
C. Total State Expenditure	13.9	15.6 (+12%)

We can see that the entire State Income rises by 12 per cent. So State Expenditure also increases by 12 per cent. But Development Expenditure grows by 34 per cent, while Routine Expenditure declines by 7 per cent. This is what we strive to achieve for the fiscal year of 1982–83. Why? This is because we deem it very important for development to proceed rapidly. Development efforts should not be slackening off.

What should be done in order to jack up Development Expenditure? For this purpose Routine Expenditure needs to be reduced. What parts of it have to be lowered? Naturally they are not personnel expenses, Goods/Logistics Expenses and Regional Subsidies. What can be reduced are the Oil Fuel Subsidies. The Oil Fuel Subsidies are being lowered from Rp1.5 trillion (or Rp1,500 billion) to Rp0.9 trillion (or Rp900 billion). Without reducing the Oil Fuel Subsidies — in other words, without increasing oil fuel prices — the amount of Fuel Subsidies would certainly be far greater. A far bigger total of Fuel Subsidies would mean an even more massive increase in Routine Expenditure. As we are supposed to maintain a balanced budget, the Development Expenditure would have to be considerably reduced. Consequently, we would have to curtail development activities. So, this is the broad framework of the 1982–83 State Budget.

Sumadi: Thank you Pak Widjojo. It has been made clear that the subsidies for BBM in 1981–82 reached Rp1.5 trillion. In 1982–83 they will be reduced to Rp0.9 trillion. What has actually prompted the government to reduce oil fuel subsidies by raising fuel prices?

Answer: With the fuel price increase, subsidies can be reduced and the difference, which is the total of the reduction, can be shifted to Development Expenditure. Let us scrutinize the consumption of oil fuels in our country, examining **Table 4: Consumption of Oil Fuels, 1972–73, 1977–78 and 1982–83**.

There are various kinds of petroleum or oil-based fuels and they can be grouped into eight types. First, Avgas, or Avigas, is the fuel for aircraft with propellers. Second, Avtur is the fuel for jet aircraft. Third, Super 98 is super gasoline. Fourth, Premium is premium gasoline. Fifth: kerosene. Sixth: automotive diesel fuel, which is now widely used for trucks, buses and so forth. Seventh: industrial diesel fuel, and eighth: fuel oil. So there are eight types of petroleum-based/oil fuels.

TABLE 4
Consumption of Oil Fuels (BBM), 1972–73, 1977–78 and 1982–83

Types of OIL FUELS (BBM)	Volume (millions of litres)			
	Increase			
	1972–73	1977–78	1982–83	
Average	1972–73 and 1982–83			per annum
1. Avgas	15	20	20	3%
2. Avtur	137	371	641	17%
3. Super 98	36	113	67	6%
4. Premium	1,772	2,816	4,448	10%
5. Kerosene	3,363	5,944	9,413	11%
6. Automotive diesel fuel	1,538	4,482	8,330	18%
7. Industrial diesel fuel	445	973	1,617	14%
8. Fuel oil	897	1,281	3,632	15%
Total	8,153	16,000	28,168	13%

Now let us look at the consumption of oil fuels. Ten years ago, in 1972–73, the country consumed 15 million litres of Avgas, 137 million litres of Avtur, 36 million litres of Super, 1,722 million litres of Premium, 3,363 million litres of kerosene, 1,538 million litres of automotive diesel fuel, 445 million litres of industrial diesel fuel and 897 million litres of fuel oil, so that the total reached 8,153 million litres. This was in the period of 1972–73.

What was the situation in 1977–78, five years later? Avgas consumption increased from 15 million to 20 million litres, Avtur from 137 million to 371 million litres, which was a sharp rise in five years. The utilization of Super also went up, and so did that of Premium. The use of kerosene rose from 3,363 million litres to 5,944 million litres; automotive diesel fuel also registered a big increase, so did industrial diesel fuel and fuel oil. In 1977–78 the total consumed was 16,000 million litres.

Next year (1982–83) Avgas consumption is estimated to remain unchanged at 20 million litres. The use of Avtur is predicted to soar. Whereas five years ago it reached 371 million litres, for next year it is projected at 641 million litres. Super is just expected to list a lower rate than five years ago. But Premium consumption will rise from 2.8 billion litres to 4.4 billion litres. Kerosene will record a level of 9.4 billion litres next year against 5.9 billion litres five years back. Automotive diesel fuel will also see increase consumption from 4.4 billion litres five years ago to 8.3 billion litres next year. This is also the case with industrial diesel fuel and fuel oil, making the estimate for fuel consumption next year (fiscal-1982–83) 28,168 million litres.

Therefore, ten years ago oil fuel consumption totaled 8 billion litres, five years ago 16 billion litres and next year it will be 28 billion litres. The annual percentages of average increases over the last ten years have been as follows: Avgas 3 per cent, Avtur 17 per cent, Super 6 per cent, Premium 10 per cent, kerosene 11 per cent, automotive diesel fuel 18 per cent, industrial diesel fuel 18 per cent, and fuel oil 15 per cent, with the average for all oil fuel consumption standing at 13 per cent a year.

The average increase of 13 per cent a year indicates that there has indeed been a considerable rise in oil fuel consumption. This can be understood because, as a nation engaged in development, we need automotive diesel fuel, fuel oil and industrial diesel fuel in large quantities, while our people, with their increasing incomes, are also consuming a lot more kerosene. The rise in BBM consumption is thus proper. But we need to take care that the use of BBM will not be excessive, in the sense of wasting the fuel, because it has to do with the problem of BBM subsidies.

It is worthwhile for us to take a look at the costs of Oil Fuel subsidies from year to year. See **Table 5: Costs of BBM Subsidies, 1972–73 and 1981–82**. Ten years ago, in 1972–73, no subsidies were provided, so that a surplus, totaling Rp31 billion, was recorded. At the time, the government sold Oil Fuels without providing subsidies. The government's income increased by Rp31 billion. In 1973–74 there was also an income surplus of Rp34.2 billion. In 1974–75 subsidies were first provided at Rp16 billion. In 1975–76 the subsidies dropped to Rp1.3 billion, in 1976–77 they rose to Rp10.4 billion, followed by a rise to Rp62.2 billion in 1977–78, to Rp197 billion in 1978–79, and to Rp535 billion in 1979/80, Rp1,005 billion in 1980–81, and to Rp1,511 billion, or Rp1.5 trillion, in 1981–82. These were the annual costs of oil fuel subsidies.

TABLE 5
Costs of Oil Fuel Subsidies, 1972–73 and 1981–82

Year	Costs of Subsidies[1] (Rupiah billion)
1972–73	(31.0)
1973–74	(34.2)
1974–75	16.6
1975–76	1.3
1976–77	10.4
1977–78	62.2
1978–79	197.0
1979–80	535.0
1980–81	1,005.4
1981–82	1,511.0

[1] Figures in brackets mean surpluses.

Now a question certainly arises: If the oil fuel prices for next year, the fiscal year of 1982–83, **are not raised, how big will the oil fuel subsidies be?**

The answer is contained in **Table 6: Costs of Oil Fuel Subsidies for 1982–83 Under Unchanged Prices for Oil Fuels**. We have listed the selling prices of the relevant types of fuel before the oil fuel price increase: Avgas is Rp150 per litre. So is Avtur. Super sells at Rp220 per litre and Premium Rp150 per litre. Kerosene costs Rp37.50 per litre, automotive diesel fuel Rp52.50 per litre, industrial diesel fuel Rp45 per litre and fuel oil Rp45 per litre. Thus are their selling prices.

What, then, is the actual production cost of fuel? The average cost is Rp132.69 per litre. So in order to produce BBM, we have to spend Rp132.69 per litre.

Now let us compare the relevant selling prices with this production cost. It turns out that we have been selling Avgas, Avtur, Super and Premium (before the price change) at more than cost. The cost is Rp132, while the selling prices are respectively Rp150, Rp150, Rp220 and Rp150. But kerosene, automotive diesel fuel, industrial diesel fuel, and fuel oil are respectively sold at prices far below the production cost. The cost is Rp132, while kerosene is sold at Rp37.50 and automotive diesel fuel at Rp52.50, while industrial diesel fuel and fuel

TABLE 6
Costs of Oil Fuel Subsidies for 1982–83
Under Unchanged Prices of Oil Fuels

OIL FUELS	Selling Price (Rp/liter)	Quantity (millions of litres)	Costs of Subsidies[1-2] (Rupiah billion)
1. Avgas	150	20	(0.3)
2. Avtur	150	641	(8.5)
3. Super 98	220	67	(4.7)
4. Premium	150	4,448	(30.1)
		5,176 (18%)	(43.6)
5. Kerosene	37.50	9,413	899.3
6. Automotive diesel fuel	52.50	8,330	691.6
7. Industrial diesel fuel	45	1,617	141.8
8. Fuel oil	45	3,632	318.5
		22,992 (82%)	2,051.1
Total		28,168 (100%)	2,007.5
Average Cost Price	132.69		

[1] Figures in brackets mean surpluses
[2] Other costs have been calculated, namely pump holder margins, land transport and regional contributions.

oil are sold at Rp45 respectively. So four types of oil fuels are sold at prices above the production cost, while the other four are sold below cost level.

Let us now look at the quantities of fuel to be sold next year. The total of Avgas, Avtur, Super and Premium to be sold is 5,176 million or 5.2 billion litres. The amount of kerosene, automotive diesel fuel, industrial diesel fuel and fuel oil will reach 22,992 million litres or almost 23 billion litres for sale next year. The total amount of oil fuels to be sold next year will come to 28.2 billion litres. The 5.2 billion litres constitute only 18 per cent of the total of 28.2 billion litres, while the 23 billion litres cover 82 per cent of the total oil fuel to be sold.

So what is noticeable? We sell Avgas, Avtur, Super and Premium at prices above production cost, yet they account for only 18 per cent of the entire sales. Conversely, we sell kerosene, automotive diesel fuel, industrial diesel fuel and fuel oil at below cost, while the quantity sold is 82 per cent of the entire amount of oil fuels sold. So the types sold at prices above production cost involve a small quantity of the total, while those sold below the production cost involve a very large quantity. The situation, therefore, has resulted in the problem of subsidies.

We sell Avgas at Rp150, while the cost is Rp132, which will produce a surplus of Rp300 million. In the absence of oil fuel price changes next year, the sale of Avgas would bring in a Rp300 million surplus, of Avtur Rp8.5 billion, of Super Rp4.7 billion and of Premium Rp30.1 billion. So a surplus would accrue from selling these products at prices higher than the production cost. The surplus would then total Rp43.6 billion.

On the other hand, kerosene is sold at Rp37.50 while the cost price is Rp132.69. There is thus a shortage. And this shortage has to be subsidized by the government. How big are fuel subsidies? Since a large quantity of kerosene is sold, reaching 9,413 million liters, the subsidy is also large at Rp899 billion. The other subsidies are: automotive diesel fuel Rp691 billion, industrial diesel fuel Rp141 billion, and fuel oil Rp318 billion. The total subsidies for kerosene, automotive diesel fuel, industrial diesel fuel and fuel oil reaches Rp2,051 billion.

So, on the one hand subsidies worth Rp2,051 billion are needed, while on the other hand, there is a surplus of Rp43.6 billion. In this way the subsidies total Rp2,007 billion. In the case of no change in the prices of oil fuels next year, the subsidies required will reach Rp2,007 billion or Rp2 trillion. Thus the question of the total amount of subsidies needed without changing oil fuel prices is answered.

Sumadi: Now there is of course a question from our society: **Can't the cost price of Rp132 be pressed down or reduced?** If we can lower the cost, there would not be much of a gap between it and the selling prices, so the subsidies would not be that big either.

Answer: The question from the public is appropriate, and it was the question I asked for the first time myself. Let us examine **Table 7: Calculation of Average Cost Price of BBM, 1981–82 and 1982–83**.

What are the costs to produce oil fuels? The first is the cost to obtain crude oil at home, which is our own crude, and the cost to procure crude oil from imports. I will explain why we import crude oil even though we have our own crude, and even export crude. Then there is the fact that we also import oil fuels. This could raise the question why we still have to import oil fuels. The second is the cost to process crude oil into oil fuels, the costs of distribution, sea transport, depreciation and so forth. If the two groups of costs are added up, we obtain the average cost of production. Or production cost.

TABLE 7
Average Cost Price of BBM, 1981–82 and 1982–83

Costs	1981–82 (Rp/litre)	1982–83 (Rp/litre)
Costs of Domestic Crude Oil, Imported Crude Oil and Imported BBM[1]	Rp95.16	Rp103.83 (+9.1%)
Costs of Processing, Distribution, Sea Transport, Depreciation, etc.	Rp30.58	Rp28.86 (–7.6%}
Average Cost	Rp125.74	Rp132.69 (+5.5%)

[1] Reduced by exporting of Residue

Let us check the costs in the fiscal year of 1981–82: What was the average production cost of oil fuels per litre? The total cost of domestic crude oil, imported crude oil, and imported oil fuels is Rp95.16 per litre, while the total cost of processing, distribution, sea transport, depreciation and so forth is Rp30.58, so that the average production cost for 1981–82 is Rp125.74, which was the cost for the period of 1981–82.

What is the situation in 1982–83? The total cost of domestic crude oil, imported crude oil and imported BBM next year can be expected to increase from Rp95.16 per litre to Rp103.83, or by 9.1 per cent. So the increase is 9.1 per cent rather than above ten per cent. The total cost of processing, distribution, sea transport, depreciation and so forth this year has been Rp30.50 and next year this will become Rp28.86; for a decline of 7.6 per cent instead of going up. The cost for next year is thus Rp132.69. Compared with the previous year, the increase is 5.5 per cent. It is obviously not so big. So the attempt to lower the cost, which will decrease by a total of 7.6 per cent, has been made particularly in relation to processing, distribution and so forth.

Naturally, the next question would be: **Why do we still have to import crude oil, when we have our own crude and export it?** The answer is: crude oil has different properties. Not all crude is the same. Some crude or fossil oil produces a lot of kerosene, automotive diesel fuel and so forth; other types of crude produce less kerosene and automotive diesel fuel. Indonesian crude produces a lot of what is called residue. Residue comes from refining, which is for the greater part exported rather than locally utilized. On the other hand, there is crude oil produced by other countries, especially Saudi Arabia, which contains a great deal of kerosene and automotive diesel fuel. Therefore, we import crude from Saudi Arabia, which is refined here and turns out considerable quantities of kerosene and automotive diesel fuel. As we are aware, the price of Saudi Arabian crude has risen from $32 to $34 per barrel.

The next question is: **Why do we still have to import oil fuels?** The reason is none other than the limited capacity of our oil refineries, while the demand in Indonesia keeps increasing at the rate of 13 per cent annually. Consequently, we have to import oil fuels. That is why we need to import crude oil and also oil fuels. It is also for this reason that we are now engaged in the construction of new oil refineries in Balikpapan, Dumai and also Cilacap.

Sumadi: One of the other questions the public may ask is: **If we raise oil fuel prices, to what extent can we save on or reduce subsidies?** So, if for instance, we increase the price of premium gasoline by Rp1, to what extent can subsidies be saved on or reduced?

Answer: To answer this, let us see **Table 8: Effect of Prices of Oil Fuels on Oil Fuel Subsidies, 1982–83**. This table shows the effect of oil fuel prices on oil fuel subsidies. So it shows: if the price of Avgas rises by Rp1 per litre, the oil fuel subsidies are reduced by Rp20 million. Any increase in the Avgas price by Rp1 thus enables us to save Rp20 million. If the price of Avtur for jetliners increases by Rp1 per litre, we save Rp64 million. If the price of Premium gasoline is raised by Rp1, we save Rp4,226 million or Rp4.2 billion. If the price of kerosene goes up by Rp1, Rp9.4 billion is saved because the volume of kerosene consumption in Indonesia is indeed huge. If the price of automotive diesel fuel rises by Rp1, Rp8.2 billion is saved. If the price of industrial diesel fuel grows by Rp1, we save Rp3.6 billion.

TABLE 8
Effect of Prices of Oil Fuel on Oil Fuel Subsidies, 1982–83

Price Increases by Rp1 per litre	Oil Fuel Subsidies Decreases by (Rupiah million)
1. Avgas	20
2. Avtur	640
3. Super 98	64
4. Premium	4,226
5. Kerosene	9,413
6. Automotive diesel fuel	8,205
7. Industrial diesel fuel	1,618
8. Fuel oil	3,632

Thus is the clarification. This is just to set forth the idea that by raising oil fuel prices by Rp1 we can save a lot of funds. But oil fuel subsidies are in fact very big. It is therefore necessary to adequately increase oil fuel prices if we wish to reduce oil fuel subsidies and shift them to the development budget.

That is all about oil fuel, Pak Sumadi.

Sumadi: So the problem of oil fuel in fact is not simple, Pak Widjojo. All right. In this context, the President in introducing the Financial Notes and 1982–83 Draft Budget to the House of Representatives yesterday **appealed that the public should be willing and prepared to bear the burden of development. In this case the burden is the increase in prices of oil fuel and possibly also prices of other goods and services.** So the question emerging in society is: If that is the case, **what development projects will be implemented, which will directly benefit the public sharing the burden of development,** in 1982–83. What do you think, Pak Widjojo?

Answer: The situation is like this: We raise oil fuel prices and in this way we can save on expenditure that would otherwise go to oil fuel subsidies. The expenditure saved on is fully shifted to the Development Budget. As we have seen, oil fuel subsidies will total Rp2 trillion unless oil fuel prices are increased. Now oil fuel subsidies remain at Rp924 billion. So the amount saved is over Rp1 trillion. This fund is totally shifted to the Development Budget. Let us now see **Table 9:**

Development Budget, 1981–82 and 1982–83, which describes the use of development funds.

TABLE 9
Development Budget, 1981–82 and 1982–83
(Rupiah billion)

Sectors	BUDGET 1981–82	DRAFT BUDGET 1982–83
1. Agriculture	941.9	1,252.5
2. Industry	330.4	366.1
3. Mining and Energy	683.6	938.2
4. Communications	1,098.4	810.3
5. Trade and Cooperatives	64.3	106.4
6. Manpower and Transmigration	435.9	605.9
7. Regional Development	612.5	740.6
8. Religious Affairs	46.5	60.3
9. Education	786.7	1,301.7
10. Health and Social Welfare	258.5	322.1
11. People's Housing	156.0	281.3
12. Legal Affairs	66.6	79.3
13. Defense and Security	481.2	568.7
14. Information	45.6	54.5
15. Science and Technology	100.2	121.9
16. Government Apparatus	190.2	223.0
17. Business Development	200.5	264.8
18. Natural Resources and Environment	188.2	220.1
Total	6,399.2	8,605.8

The Development Budget is divided into 18 sectors: Agriculture, Industry, Mining and Energy, Communications, Trade and Cooperatives, Manpower and Transmigration, Regional Development, Religious Affairs, Education, Health, People's Housing, Legal Affairs, Defense and Security, Information, Science and Technology, Government Apparatus, Business Development, Natural Resources and Environment.

Let us see the Development Budget for 1981–82. For 1981–82 the development budget for Agriculture is listed at Rp941.9 billion, Industry Rp330 billion, Mining and Energy Rp683 billion, Communications

Rp810 billion, Trade and Cooperatives Rp64.3 billion, and so forth. The figures involve tens or hundreds of billions of rupiah. The entire total is Rp6,399.2 billion or Rp6.4 trillion. If we try to find the largest of the figures, it is Rp941.9 billion for Agriculture. The second largest is Rp810.3 billion for Communications. The third is Rp786.7 billion for Education. So in 1981–82 the Development Budget for Education ranked third among the 18 development sectors.

Now let us have a look at the situation in 1982–83 as indicated in 1982–83 Draft Budget. Here are some figures: Agriculture Rp1,252.5 billion, Industry Rp366 billion, Mining and Energy Rp938.2 billion, Communications Rp1,098.4 billion, and so forth. So the figures involve tens of billions, hundreds of billions, and also trillions of rupiah. Three sectors register over Rp1 trillion, which are Agriculture Rp1.2 trillion, Communications almost Rp1.1 trillion and Education Rp1.3 trillion. So the draft Development Budget for 1982–83 totals Rp8,605.8 billion or Rp8.6 trillion. The increase is 34 per cent.

Among the eighteen development sectors, Education turns out to be the sector that will receive the largest Development Budget, worth Rp1.3 trillion. The second is Agriculture and the third Communications. The Development Budget for Education will rise from Rp786 billion to Rp1.3 trillion, an increase of nearly 66 per cent. So for next year the Development Budget as a whole grows by 36 per cent, while the Development Budget for Education expands by approximately 66 per cent.

Sumadi: All right Pak Widjojo, so the problems of education, agriculture and communications will receive priority respectively with the largest development budget allocations. Then we also must remember that the **majority of Indonesian people live in the regions, particularly in rural areas**. Therefore, I would like to request that Pak Widjojo explain **what Presidential Instruction (Inpres) based programmes are spread and applied over the various regions** to especially serve regional communities for the period of 1982–83.

Answer: Very well, Pak Sumadi. There are indeed Presidential Instruction, or Inpres, programmes, which are aid programmes for rural communities channelled through regional administrations. There are different Inpres programmes such as the Rural Programme, Regency Programme, First-Level Region Programme and so forth.

Let us now check the Rural Programme first. See **Table 10: Rural Programme, 1982–83**. Indonesia has a total of 65,127 villages. Each of them will receive Rp1,250,000 in aid. In 1981–82 the aid received was Rp1 million each. So the amount is raised from Rp1 million to Rp1.25 million. Of this sum, Rp250,000 is meant for Family Welfare Programmes (PKK), which are developed and carried out by housewives/women. For this purpose each village receives Rp250,000.

TABLE 10
Rural Programme, 1982–83[1]

Total of villages	65,127
Aid per village	Rp1.25 million [Rp1.0 million]
Total	Rp88.4 billion

[1] Figures in brackets are for 1981–82.

Then there is the Regency Programme. See **Table 11: Regency Programme, 1982–83**. Indonesia has a population of 150.9 million today, no longer 147 million. That figure came from the census of 1980. Now it has reached 150.9 million. The aid is provided per capita: this year it is Rp1,000 per capita, next year Rp1,150 per capita, increasing by 15 per cent. Some Second-Level Regions — regencies or municipalities — have small populations. The regencies and municipalities with small populations receive a minimum amount each; which was Rp160 million. This year the minimum sum is Rp150 million. That is all about the Regency Programme.

TABLE 11
Regency Programme, 1982–83[1]

Total Population	150.9 million
Aid per capita	Rp1,150 [Rp1,000]
Minimum Aid per Second-Level Region	Rp160 million [Rp150 million]
Total	Rp193.9 billion

[1] Figures in brackets are for 1981–82.

Now we go to **Table 12: First-Level Region Programme, 1982–83** and **Table 13: Road Infrastructure Programme 1982–83**. The First-Level Region

Programme for 1981–82 determines that each province received at least Rp7.5 billion, while next year the aid totals Rp9 billion. It is thus not a small increase. There is also the Road Infrastructure Programme for regency road repair. This year 6,000 km have been repaired and next year 8,000 km. Bridges are also covered: this year the total length of bridges repaired was 10,500 m and next year over 14,000 m.

TABLE 12
First-Level Region Programme, 1982–83[1]

Minimum Aid per First-Level Region	Rp9.0 billion [Rp7.5 billion]
Total	Rp253.0 billion

[1] Figures in brackets are for 1981–82.

TABLE 13
Road Infrastructure Programme, 1982–83[1]
(Regency Roads)

1.	Roads	8,485 km [6,285 km]
2.	Bridges	14,175 m [10,500 m]
3.	Total	Rp80.1 billion

[1] Figures in brackets are for 1981/82.

There is a very important Presidential Instruction (Inpres) Programme, which is the Primary School Presidential Instruction (Inpres) Programme. See **Table 14: Primary School Presidential Instruction (Inpres) Programme, 1982–83.**

TABLE 14
Primary School Presidential Instruction (Inpres) Programme, 1982–83[1]

1.	Primary School Construction	22,600 [15,000]
2.	Classroom Addition	35,000 [25,000]
3.	Primary School Building Rehabilitation	25,000 [25,000]
4.	Houses for Principals and Teachers	20,000 [9,500]
5.	Reading Books	30 million [15 million]
6.	Sports Equipment	50,000 packages
7.	Total	Rp589.2 billion

[1] Figures in brackets are for 1981–82.

The Primary School Programme is composed of various things, such as primary school (SD) building construction: this year 15,000 elementary school buildings have been put up, next year 22,600 buildings will be constructed. Then, classrooms in existing schools are added: this year 25,000 additional classrooms have been built, next year there will be 35,000 constructed. There is also the rehabilitation or repair of the existing elementary school buildings, totaling 25,000. Houses for principals and teachers in remote regions are also built, involving 20,000 next year and 9,500 this year. Reading books for elementary school students reached 15 million volumes for libraries this year, and will double next year to become 30 million. For the first time, primary school sports equipment will be provided, covering 50,000 elementary school units. The number is about a third of the total of these schools.

The question may be raised as to what the Primary School Programme is supposed to achieve. Once the Primary School Programme is implemented, it is expected that by the 1983–84 school year there will be additional classrooms for over 3.9 million children, so that in that year study rooms will be available to all Indonesian students aged 7–12. So we hope that parents and communities in regions will really benefit from the extra classrooms.

Apart from that, in secondary education, the number of schools will also be increased. Among other things, 1,000 junior high or middle school (SMP) buildings will be put up and 5,000 additional classrooms will be constructed. Once this is realized, in the school year of 1983/84, there will be over 400,000 extra classrooms.

With these measures we hope that all students aged 7–12 will be accommodated in primary schools, and we are also preparing to increase the capacity for junior high schools to receive grade school graduates, so that, in phases, all children wishing to go on to secondary schools in the years ahead and in the period of the Fourth Five-Year Development Plan (Repelita IV) will be accommodated in junior high schools and other secondary-level schools.

There is also the Health Programme for the development of public health clinics and so forth. We are also fostering the facilities. The priority is the supply of a lot more medicines in regions. This has become our main concern in this sector. Thus is the description of the Presidential Instruction programmes, Pak Sumadi.

Sumadi: Yes Pak Widjojo. So it is all about oil fuel subsidies and the total we can save from the reduction of oil fuel subsidies; with the funds from that being shifted to the development budget and various projects financed through the cutback. In that case, could you give a brief illustration of the **comparison between the oil fuel subsidies and the development budgets for several sectors?**

Answer: Sure Pak Sumadi. As we know, for the period of 1981–82, oil fuel subsidies reach Rp1.5 trillion. It is worthwhile to now look at **Table 15: Comparison between Oil Fuel Subsidies and Development Budgets for Several Sectors, 1981–82 and 1982–83.**

TABLE 15

Comparison between Oil Fuel Subsidies and Development Budgets for Several Sectors, 1981–82 and 1982–83

	APBN-1981–82		RAPBN-1982–83	
	Totals (Rupiah in billions)	Comparison with Oil Fuel Subsidies	Totals (Rupiah in billions)	Comparison with Oil Fuel Subsidies
A. BBM Subsidies	1,511.1	100%	924.0	100%
B. Development Budgets for				
1. Education	786.7	52%	1,301.7	141%
2. Agriculture	941.9	62%	1,252.5	136%
3. Communications	810.3	54%	1,098.4	119%
4. Mining and Energy	683.5	45%	938.2	102%
5. Regional Development	612.5	41%	740.6	80%

We can see that in the 1981–82 State Budget, the oil fuel subsidies total Rp1,511 billion. Now let us take a look at the Development Budget for Education in the period of 1981–82, which is Rp786.7 billion. Let us compare: if the figures for oil fuel subsidies are taken as 100 per cent, the Education budget figures constitute 52 per cent. So the Development Budget for Education in 1981–82 amounts to 52 per cent of the oil fuel subsidies. That is thus around half of the subsidies. Or the oil fuel subsidies can be said to be double the Development Budget for Education this year. The rate of Agriculture is 62 per cent. It is thus far lower than the oil fuel subsidies. The rate for Communications is also lower, so is Mining, and Regional Development, only account for 41 per cent of the oil fuel subsidies. The subsidies are two and a half times as big as the Development Budget for the Regions.

What about the situation in 1982–83? It is apparent here that the oil fuel subsidies register Rp924 billion, while the Education allocation is Rp1,301.7 billion. So if both amounts are compared and we cite 100 per cent as representing the oil fuel subsidies, the fund for Education equals 141 per cent. The Development Budget for Education is thus almost one and a half times as big as the amount for oil fuel subsidies. Likewise, the fund for Agriculture exceeds the amount of subsidies. So does the Mining budget. Such is the comparison between the oil fuel subsidies and the Development Budgets for several sectors.

Now we are reversing the situation: the Development Budget for Education had earlier reached about half of the oil fuel subsidies; now we are reducing oil fuel subsidies and the total saved from the oil fuel subsidies is shifted to the Development Budgets for Education, Agriculture, Communications, Mining, Regional Development and so forth. Thus is the essence of what we are striving for today.

Sumadi: Thank you Pak Widjojo. Now before winding up our talk tonight, I would like to ask another question being set forth by the public, which is about the building of oil refineries. As you have explained, some of the oil fuels we consume at home are still imported and this certainly depends on overseas price developments. Therefore, the question is **how the construction of oil refineries is to be undertaken so that in due course we will be able to reduce or discontinue oil fuel imports from abroad, and in this way we perhaps also further reduce oil fuel subsidies and price increases in the future.**

Answer: At present we are building oil refineries. We have some oil refineries but most — not all — of them are fairly old. So we are constructing three oil refineries: one in Balikpapan with a capacity of 200,000 barrels of oil daily, another in Dumai with a capacity of 85,000 barrels daily, and the third in Cilacap with a capacity of 85,000 barrels daily. These are large quantities; totaling 485,000 barrels daily.

The capacity of our existing oil refineries currently stands at 470,000 barrels daily, but not all of the refineries can be fully utilized owing to their age. So the capacity will be doubled. Then the refineries will make full use of Indonesian crude oil. Thus, the oil refined will not be imported crude oil from Saudi Arabia or other countries. In this manner, any problem that may arise in the Middle East will pose no difficulty to us because we will use Indonesian crude.

Especially in Dumai and Balikpapan, the refinery projects constructed will include what are called hydrocrackers. With hydrocrackers we can process residue, which is amply produced by Indonesian crude, and, as I have described, is now exported. The residue can be processed and then turned into kerosene and automotive diesel fuel. In fact, we are now still importing large quantities of kerosene and automotive diesel fuel. So we hope that later we will no longer need to import kerosene and automotive diesel fuel.

But this naturally will considerably depend on our fuel saving efforts. **So we need to cut down on fuel consumption. If anything is too cheap, we tend to be less prudent**. Now oil fuel prices are rising and we certainly need to save a lot more. We should use less premium gasoline, super gasoline and so forth, as well as less kerosene, automotive diesel fuel and other fuels. Although automotive diesel fuel is far cheaper than premium, those who own cars operated by automotive diesel fuel — like trucks, buses, jeeps and so forth — should also save fuel. It is very important for us to save fuel. If we do, the expenditure for oil fuel subsidies will also be further reduced to a lower level. And the difference can be transferred to the Development Budget in order to intensify our development. So that is all, Pak Sumadi.

Sumadi: All right Pak Widjojo. So we can conclude that on the one hand we are striving to increase the capacity of our crude oil processing into fuel for our domestic consumption, but on the other hand the public should remember that fuel consumption is growing from year to year, so that it is necessary to save fuel. If both efforts later converge, we will hopefully be able to manage our oil affairs better than we do today.

Well, thank you Pak Widjojo for all of the explanations. I hope that with this description and clarification of the various aspects of current budgetary issues and the future national development process the public has obtained additional information, which may have been needed by them to interpret and understand the measures adopted by the government to reduce oil fuel subsidies by raising oil fuel prices.

Widjojo Nitisastro, Bapak, Coordinating Minister for EKUIN/Chairman of BAPPENAS.

NOTE

[1] Television interview on the increase of fuel price and its linkage to the State Budget of Income and Expenditure in January 1982. This article is translated by Harry Bhaskara.

19

WORLD'S OIL-BASED FUEL PRICES DIVED (1986)[1]

Introductory Note: *Throughout the 1970s, oil prices went up sharply, particularly in the period of 1973–74 and in 1979. In 1982 the prices began to decline and in 1985 the market for crude oil began to weaken. In 1986 global oil production began to soar resulting in rapid decline of oil prices. The following description is meant as a warning to the public to always be on the alert about falls in oil prices on the international market and the disastrous impact of this on foreign exchange income as well as state income.*

The Indonesian economy is facing a tough challenge nowadays. The source of this challenge is the sharp decline in oil prices occurring within an abbreviated period of time.

During a span of six months in 1986, oil prices have dropped by more than 50 per cent, from US$25 per barrel in January to less than US$10 in July. Meanwhile, two third of Indonesia's export revenue comes from oil (including natural gas). It also makes up 60 per cent of domestic income in the state budget.

Although there has been a tendency for oil prices to decline in the last few years, a very sharp drop in a very short time, as is occurring now, has never happened before.

In the 1970s, oil prices shot up twice (1973–74 and 1979). These oil price increases caused two significant developments:

(a) the gradual decline in demand as a result of the successful efforts of consuming countries to convert to other sources of energy (coal and nuclear and hydro resources, etc).

(b) the increasing supply of oil from the countries that had managed to increase their production (including England whose production rose from 250,000 barrels per day in 1976 to 2.1 million barrels in 1982; Mexico from 800,000 barrels to 2.7 million barrels; Norway from 280,000 to 500,000 barrels; and the People's Republic of China from 1.6 million to 2.0 million barrels).

Between 1976 and 1982, world oil production dropped from 57 million barrels per day to 54 million. Of the total, the production of non-OPEC members rose from 26 million barrels to 35 million barrels, while the production of OPEC members dropped from 31 million barrels to 19 million barrels per day.

As long as the prices were increasing or still high, a decline in production would not cause a problem for OPEC members, as the income would remain high. And the fossil oil or petroleum reserves not yet extracted remained a precious stock for the future. But when the prices started to go down, as was the case in 1982, this posed problem for OPEC, and it was forced to determine an oil production quota for each of its members.

Before determining the quota for each member country, the total production of all OPEC members was established on the basis of global oil market conditions, with the goal of achieving and/or maintaining a certain range of prices. Afterwards, the total production was divided according to the number of members and a quota set for each member. Among the OPEC members, there was an agreement that Saudi Arabia, as the largest oil producer, would act as a "swing producer." That means that if the market allows for OPEC to raise its production, Saudi Arabia will increase its production, or vice versa. This allows other OPEC members to produce oil in accordance with their respective quotas. In March 1983, a deal was reached that the production level would be

17.5 million barrels per day, while in October 1984, the production was set at 16 million barrels per day.

In general, global oil prices have been on the decline since 1982, although there have been seasonal fluctuations affected by stronger demand ahead of winter in the northern part of the world. Two signals have emerged in the wake of the weakening oil prices:

(a) OPEC members have begun to feel it unfair that they must shoulder the burden of maintaining global oil prices, while non-OPEC members could better enjoy the high prices and continue to raise production levels;

(b) OPEC members have become suspicious with regard to violation of production quotas and price level requirements.

The market remained weak throughout 1985. OPEC's production averaged 15.8 million barrels per day. In August, demand was approximately 14.5 million barrel per day. In that month, Saudi Arabia, as the "swing producer," produced only 2.3 million barrels, although its quota was 4.3 million barrels.

The next development resulted in great turbulence in the global oil market. Several producing countries sharply increased their production. This forced Saudi Arabia to take the following steps:

(a) stating that it would no longer be willing to act as a "swing producer";

(b) stating that it would raise production in line with its quota;

(c) abandoning the agreed to pricing and targeting mechanism and replacing it with the "netback pricing" scheme.

Saudi Arabia's production, which in the middle of 1985 was 2.3 million barrels, rose to 4.3 million barrels in early 1986 and reached 5.5 to 6 million barrels per day in August 1986. OPEC's total production in the first quarter of 1986, which was 17 million barrels per day, jumped to 20.3 million barrels per day in August 1986.

The abundant supply of oil, which was sold with the "netback pricing" system, eventually resulted in a sudden and sharp decline in oil prices.

It's a relief now that we have reached an agreement among the OPEC members to cap production again and adopt a production quota for each member (with an exception of Iraq) for the upcoming period of September and October. However, the market which has been disturbed by the flood of cheap oil, is curious to observe:

(a)   the actual implementation of the agreement;
(b)   whether an agreement can be achieved for November and the months ahead of winter season, or whether the individual members will raise as they did last winter; and
(c)   whether the countries with massive production capabilities will raise their production again in the future irrespective of the agreement.

The oil price situation of 1986 has shown how major changes can occur in the oil market, and how fragile it actually is. For that reason, it is appropriate for Indonesia, in addition to always trying its utmost to keep oil prices at stable and decent levels together with other producing countries, to prioritize efforts to boost its foreign exchange revenue from non-oil and gas exports.

NOTE

[1]   A description meant as a warning to the public to always be vigilant about the impact of a sudden drop of oil prices (1986). This article is translated by Harry Bhaskara.

PART IV

SETTLEMENT OF FOREIGN DEBT

20

OLD AND NEW DEBTS (1969)[1]

Introductory Note: *When any change of administration occurs in a country, like that in our country in mid 1966, there will be a tendency to accrue new debts on top of old ones. The old debts are those incurred by the old administration whose repayment has yet to be fully settled. The settlement of these old debts is the responsibility of the new administration. If the new administration is in no position to assume this responsibility and does not consider the debts as its responsibility, the governments of other countries will be in no position to extend fresh loans to the new administration and will even sue it in their domestic courts or international courts of law. They can even seize the property of the new administration, such as aircraft and vessels that happen to be in other countries. Therefore, there is no alternative for the new administration but to acknowledge the debts of the old administration as theirs and try to find the best solution possible. It is the obligation of the new administration to find a way to solve the problems of old debts in the best possible manner, while avoiding the accrual of further debts burdens.*

There are a number of questions about offshore loans. On this occasion, I find it in place to dwell on this problem.

In fact, our loans come in two types; past loans (those of the past administration) and the loans of the present administration. There is a line of demarcation here; that being 30 June 1966.

All loans, or all debts, incurred prior to 30 June 1966 are old debts and those incurred on 30 June 1966, or afterwards, are new debts or loans. Old debts, incurred prior to 30 June 1966, come in several types. Among them are the debts categorized as "debts incurred as compensation for nationalization"; these were incurred mostly in relation with the Dutch. In 1966, an agreement was reached with the Dutch government that the compensation for nationalization would be paid off within forty years.

Then there are other debts amounting to about $2.1 billion. Of this $2.1 billion, around $1.7 billion is the principal and $0.4 billion, the interest. This is just an approximation. The $2.1 billion in debts come from about thirty different countries, some small and some large. The major creditor countries are the Soviet Union, Japan, Britain and the small creditor countries are, for example, Tanzania and Hong Kong.

In 1966, in the case of debts, Indonesia actually was in arrears. In 1965 and 1966, Indonesia failed to pay back its debts. In 1966, a decision was made that if we were going to be unable to pay back our debts, we should at least be polite about it and talk the matter over with our creditors. So that year, negotiations began to postpone the payment of our debts, so that if we were not yet in a position to pay back our debts, we would simply say so and ask for postponement. So, we were now open about the problem and no longer refused to pay in secret.

These negotiations can be divided into two categories: negotiations with East European countries and those with West European countries, America and Japan. Negotiations were conducted individually with each of the East European countries: Czechoslovakia, Hungary, Poland, Soviet Union and so forth. In 1966, an agreement was reached with the Soviet Union that the repayment of our debts to that country would be postponed, and would recommence in 1969. So, repayment would be made in 1969, 1970, 1971, 1972 and so forth. So, the debts have not been waived, but their repayment has been postponed. Then we have also reached an agreement with some other East European countries (Czechoslovakia, Hungary, Romania) to the effect that the repayment of our debts has also been postponed and that repayment would start again in 1969.

The Western countries and Indonesia got together in Tokyo in September 1966 for negotiations on the postponement of Indonesia's debts. The Indonesian side stated that it would not be possible for it to repay the debts. No agreement was reached in this round of negotiations, and talks would be continued in Paris in December of 1966.

In the Paris meeting with the Western group, an agreement was reached as follows: the repayment of debts to each country that fell due in 1967 or before 1967, namely the debts in arrears in 1965, 1966 and so forth, would be postponed and repayment would be made between 1971 and 1978. In the first year, 5 per cent of the debts will be repaid, in the second year, 10 per cent, in the third, 10 per cent, in the fourth, 10 per cent, in the fifth, 15 per cent, in the sixth, 15 per cent, in the seventh, 15 per cent and in the eighth year, 20 per cent. So, 100 per cent of the debts would be paid in eight years after a grace period of three years. That was the agreement reached then. A moratorium on the interest rates, pushing them to as low point as possible at between 3 and 3.5 per cent, was also agreed.

Regarding the debts, there are several kinds. The first kind is the debts to foreign governments. For example, Indonesia has borrowed from the Japanese, the Dutch, and the German governments. There are also debts to foreign private circles. These debts fall into two categories: those guaranteed by governments and those not guaranteed by governments. The postponement that the governments referred to above have agreed covers only the debts that Indonesia has incurred with each of these governments and Indonesia's debts to private circles that are covered by government guarantees. These foreign governments refuse to be responsible for any of the debts owed to private parties that are not guarantee by their governments.

In this case, the Indonesian government held negotiations individually with the private parties who had come here to claim repayment of their debts. We told them we were not yet able to repay our debts and offered to repay them in rupiah, with the understanding that the funds must be used for investment in Indonesia. The reason given was that when they invested, they would need rupiah, not just foreign exchange. So the Debt Investment Conversion Scheme (DICS) has come into being. So, they are repaid in rupiah, but this rupiah must be used for investment, not for other purposes. Therefore, gradually, a solution has been found for some of our debts to private circles that are not guaranteed by their governments.

In addition, of course there are several countries, PRC for example, with which we have never held any negotiations. We have never met, so the problem has never been discussed until now. That's the situation as it is.

After the Paris Meeting, there was an agreement to hold bilateral negotiations as well because we had not incurred debts with a group of countries, but also with some individual countries. To this end, it is necessary to hold bilateral negotiations with each country until there is an agreement signed with each of them. This takes a lot of time, ideas, energy and so forth, but we can implement the negotiations with a single pattern of discussion.

For the countries concerned, this debt postponement is important, as otherwise they will have to take action. In the international finance world, if you have a debt and then fail to repay your debt and there is no agreement with your creditor, the creditor will reserve the right to take action. One of the actions would be to confiscate the exports of the country skipping payments. Another way would be to file a lawsuit in the International Court of Justice. If this were to be the case, we would have even more difficulties.

That's why the first step that we took was to negotiate this matter, both with the East European countries and with Western countries, so that there will be the impression that Indonesia really wants to abandon the old, irresponsible methods and would like to begin to act responsibly as a member of the world community. This was the idea behind the negotiations referred to above.

Then in 1967, debt negotiations were held once again, this time for the debts that fell due in 1968, so that their repayment could be postponed. It was agreed that the repayment of the debts that fell due in 1968 would be postponed to between 1971 and 1979. Then in 1968, there were negotiations about the debts that fell due in 1968 and the repayment of these debts will be postponed to between 1972 and 1980. The grace period is three years and repayment will be made in eight years.

This postponement allows something like a breathing space; the amount that we have to pay back is huge. The debts have fallen due and must be repaid; some are years in arrears. For example, in the first Paris Agreement, the debts that had fallen due in 1967 (these were debts incurred only to Western countries, not to say to Russia and other Eastern European nations), and the debts in arrears from the previous years, amounted to some 300 million dollars. We can imagine what would have happened if at that time we had to pay some 300 million dollars, while our exports, as we all understand, were limited, and could be expected to remain so in the following years. Therefore, there are only two alternatives in postponing the debts, namely failing to pay unilaterally with all the consequences, or to pay, which means that we cannot import as practically all proceeds from exports must be spent on repaying the debts. That was the condition at that time and today. So the alternative — in fact there is no other alternative but to negotiate and try to get the best results possible.

In the negotiations in 1966, 1967, 1968 we always said to our creditor countries that we were negotiating to postpone the debts. In the opinion of the Indonesian government the short-term postponements of 1968, 1970, and 1971, would not allow enough time for Indonesia to get to a place where it could repay its debts. For the time being this solution could be accepted; but it was a temporary solution, not a final one. This is what we always put forward to the creditor countries, be they the Soviet Union, Hungary, Czechoslovakia or Britain, France, Holland, Germany, the United States, Japan and so forth. Every year the same thing was said.

In October 1968, during the Paris negotiations, the Indonesian side stated again that postponement of repayment to 1971, 1972 and 1973 was actually still unrealistic, because Indonesia was yet to be able to make repayment. And, if we look at the current projections for our exports in the coming years and the projection of debt repayment every year, repayment looks even more unrealistic, because, in this world, if, to repay its debts, a country has to spend 20 per cent or more of its export proceeds, this country is already in a very difficult situation, and cannot undertake development.

The projection already made shows that in the coming years Indonesia, to repay its debts, must spend over 20 per cent of its export value. This is obviously unrealistic. Therefore, we have asked our creditor countries to resort to an ostrich-like solution, but a serious one.

Of course, there is like and dislike of this alternative. However, at the end of the day there has come an agreement from the Western creditor countries to ask an independent expert to conduct research on Indonesia's debts. So, this expert will not just listen to Indonesia's opinion, but will conduct research. We have agreed. At first the creditor countries asked a famous Dutch expert, Dr Holtrop, who used to be the Governor of Dutch Central Bank, to do this, but he had other things to do so they asked Dr Hermann Abs of Germany, who is famous in the international finance area. Dr Abs has conducted his research and examination. In his research, Dr Abs obtained technical assistance from two international agencies, namely the International Monetary Fund and the World Bank, but it was Dr Abs who was accountable for the research.

Dr Abs has completed his work. The result of this work, called the Abs Report, has been put forward in the negotiations in Paris and submitted to the creditor countries and also to Indonesia. The problem that Abs has to solve refers to the debts that Indonesia incurred prior to 30 June 1966.

The Abs Report is a confidential report. Why it is confidential to the creditor countries is easy to understand: the loans extended to Indonesia, either the old loans or the new ones, mostly come from their state budgets. Whereas we would call these funds "the people's money", they call such funds their "taxpayers' money". They call it the taxpayers' money because their entire state budgets come from taxpayers. So, if their governments lend it to another government, the lending government is obligated to ensure its repayment, and should not just agree to postponement. As this is the taxpayers' money, it has to be repaid. So they are highly dependent on the provisions of the law there and cannot just agree to allow postponement as they must account for this to their own parliaments.

Second, some of them have been facing financial difficulties themselves. Take Britain and France. Their financial condition is very difficult. This has made it difficult for them to agree to our request for a postponement of repayment. Some others face balance of payment difficulties. So there are two types of financial difficulties: budget difficulties and balance of payment difficulties. Budget difficulties are related with the state budget, balance of payment difficulties are connected with foreign exchange conditions. The United States, for example, has its balance of payment problem, Japan has no balance of payment problem, but it has a state budget problem. Britain faces difficulty with both its balance of payments and the state budget. France particularly has a problem with balance of payments. Germany has no problem with its balance of payments, but it has a problem with its state budget. So, every country has its own financial difficulties. There are also legal difficulties, as well as financial difficulties.

Third, are the difficulties that they are having with other countries that have also taken loans from them. Ghana and others have also taken loans; not just Indonesia. Ghana used to borrow from here and there and make unproductive things. So, it was not much different from us then. There are also a number of Latin American countries (Colombia, Peru and so forth) which have piles of debts. There are also some Asian countries: India and Pakistan, whose debts are very huge, and the longer the debts are sustained, the bigger they become. Then, there is also Turkey, which has incurred large debts. These are some that are quite prominent; there are many others.

All these debtor countries are paying serious attention to see what Indonesia can get in relation to the postponement of its debt repayment. Because the moment Indonesia gets some leniency, they will immediately raise their hands. Around the time of Indonesia's negotiations in Paris in 1966, 1967, Ghana was undertaking negotiations in London. The chairman in London was Britain, in Paris the chairman was France. Ghana saw what happened with Indonesia, and of course Indonesia also saw what happened with Ghana. That was logically understandable. However, we always said our condition was worse than Ghana's. This is the problem of precedent and it is what the creditor countries are worried about.

This is one example: an agreement has been reached with Indonesia that the repayment of all Indonesia's debts to governments and its debts to private circles guaranteed by their governments will be 100 per cent postponed. The agreement reached with Ghana was not 100 per cent, but 80 per cent. Ghana protested: Why should Indonesia get 100 per cent and Ghana only 80 per cent? Then India, Pakistan, Turkey, Colombia and the others also protested. In our view, it is all right for them to make their protests as long as we get what we want. We do not have any objection to other countries also receiving the same term as ours, but we must get ours.

A similar thing was true of the Abs Report. One of the biggest difficulties for the creditor countries is the problem of precedent. They say, if we agree to Abs' proposals, the next day other countries will try to open our doors. So what must we do? We say Indonesia cannot be considered the same as other countries. What has made it different? We say: First, our debts, the debts which are an old legacy; debts that were not productive, spent either for military interests or economic interests. The debts said to have been spent on economic interests, however, were only so in name, as the majority of them were not productive. In addition, Indonesia has shown in the past few years that it can control inflation, and has now begun with real development. So, Indonesia's seriousness has been visible and proven. So, it is not just what we are potentially capable of doing, but what we have already done. To control inflation, extraordinary sacrifices have been needed and we have all felt these sacrifices in the past few years. This is evidence that the sacrifices are there and not just an empty talk. So, we are in a situation in which we should not be considered the same as other countries.

Then they have another reason. We have the problem of the law, this law, that law and so forth. It is not possible not to impose interest; there is no debt without interest. There is what is called the cost of money and this is the interest. Why should there be no interest? So, there are quite a lot of problems related with the law. When there is a problem related with the law, we say: if the government concerned is really convinced that Indonesia must have a chance in this respect, talk it over with the parliament concerned. We cannot talk with their parliament, but they have the obligation to do so.

Then there have also been other problems; extraordinarily difficult administrative problems. These have been great handicaps.

However, an agreement was reached in the Paris Meeting that each party would make a report to their respective governments and then get together again this coming December for further discussion. Of course, this is not something that can just lead to an agreement. It is not possible for us to get together again and simply expect that all will give their agreement. I don't think this will happen. What is important is that we take them step by step toward the conviction that this agreement is really necessary, as otherwise, well, Indonesia cannot repay its debts. If Indonesia repays its debts, its development will be disrupted. So, it is, indeed, necessary to have a process in which to explain the reason to them patiently. I think this process will take some time, perhaps we will still have to negotiate things for the entire next year (1970).

Then these nations will again try to convince their respective governments and their respective parliaments so that there will be an agreement. Of course, some are more progressive, while others are less so. Some can see difficulties, while others do not see any. Some see possibilities and so forth. All of this is a process that we must perseveringly and seriously respond to, and this requires time.

So much about the old debts; now it is time to discuss the new debts, or loans, or the new offshore aid. Part of this new offshore aid is, indeed, in the form of a loan, while the other part is in the form of a grant and need not be repaid. With Australia, for example, Indonesia has not sustained any debt, because Australia does not provide loans, but rather only grants.

Regarding the need for new loans, of course we will examine this; we will consider the projections that we make in our annual planning. The problem is as follows: offshore loans are closely linked with two things: First, they are closely linked with our export proceeds and our import needs. How big are our export proceeds and how big are our import needs? The second, they are related with our State Budget of Revenues and Expenditures. How much are our domestic revenues and how much are our expenditures for routine and development purposes? If we study these two things, the Balance of Payment and the State budget of Revenues and Expenditures, there seems to be a gap. The gap is a deficit because our exports are indeed low. As a comparison: our exports, excluding crude oil, in 1951, the year they were at their highest, were valued at over 900 million dollars, close to 1 billion dollars. Our exports in 1966, excluding crude oil, stood at some 400 million dollars. We can make this comparison. The size of the population has gotten bigger, our needs have increased, but our exports have dropped by half in these last fifteen years. So, we need foreign exchange, and in light of this, inflation is something logical; we simply do not have enough to afford imports. If we realistically view our import needs for example for purposes of rehabilitation and food (we have yet to be able to fulfill our need for food by ourselves), we can see quite a big gap. So, viewed from this aspect, there is indeed a need for loans, without reducing our activities toward boosting exports.

The problem is that there are no miracles in this world. We cannot just say a magic word and then boost our exports. We can only do this step by step. Therefore, our export target (beyond crude oil) stands at some 800 million dollars for 1972–73 in the five-year development plan. This amount, beyond the exports of crude oil, must be achieved in 1972–73. This is a target that is neither too high nor too low, but if we wish to develop the country, it is useless to set too low a target. We must set quite a high target so efforts will be more seriously made. This is just for 1972–73. We have yet to get to that, so our foreign exchange is indeed still insufficient and we need to increase it.

Although we must be austere about imports our import level is set at a certain level with our representatives overseas. If it is reduced further, the efforts toward our nation's rehabilitation will suffer difficulties. If we reduce the imports of cement, for example, the price of cement will soar, so that our efforts at rehabilitation will fall into confusion; likewise with fertilizer and other important goods and commodities.

In the area of state budget, we can see that revenues remained low in 1966 as had been the case for years. So, it is understandable that the Provisional People's Consultative Assembly (MPRS) in Stipulation No. XXIII prioritizes efforts to increase revenues. However, this targeted increase in revenues cannot be accomplished with the wave of a hand; it must be achieved step by step. In connection with this, we can see some progress in Law on State budget ratified by the DPR-GR.

In 1967, the state budget was balanced. In 1968, it was not only balanced overall, but the routine budget was fully covered by domestic revenues so that none of the offshore counter value would be required for routine purposes. In 1967 some had still been used for routine purposes; but that was not the case in 1968, nor has it been throughout 1969.

This means that all the counter value of foreign aid is now being used for the development budget. This is a step forward. Also in 1969, it has been planned that domestic revenues should exceed routine spending. This is a further step forward. Hopefully, in 1970, the surplus, which we call public savings, will be much bigger. And so on. This, certainly, will be satisfying to us because development will then be financed more by domestic revenues. To this end, efforts must be made to increase the state revenues. There is a dilemma here: the state revenues must go up, but we must also stimulate domestic investment. How can both be achieved?

So, our efforts are to ensure that the state revenues are increased, but investment and re-investment are also encouraged. This is not something easy to do but we have to do it. Seeing all of this, if we wish to be realistic, viewed either from the aspect of the Balance of Payment or the aspect of the State budget, and do not want to be like an ostrich, it is obvious that we need both offshore loans and aid.

Of course, there are problems. Wouldn't it just be possible to print more banknotes in place of taking out offshore loans? We could print the banknotes and use them for our budget. However, there are two things that we must contemplate upon very carefully: First, the problem is not just printing banknotes; aside from the quantity, how to distribute the money would also be an issue. At present, if we consider the amount of the money in circulation today — about 160 billion rupiah — we can see quite a large increase compared with one, two or three years ago. It is difficult to find for comparison in any other country that has so quickly increased the amount of money in circulation.

The core of the problem is where the money is channelled. This is what matters. In Indonesia, the money is channelled through the banks in particular. All revenues and state budget mean spending the money that the state has received. So, the state has revenues and these revenues are spent, so there is a balance. From the banks, the money is channeled out for short-term or mid-term loans. As this year we see the possibility of increasing the amount of the money in circulation, we have introduced an investment loan programme. So, banknotes are printed, but the money will be channelled through loans. These loans will be repaid a year, two years or three years later, and then it can be used again, so there is a quick revolving fund. In the case of state spending, the money need not be repaid. If the public works department builds or repairs a road, it need not repay the money. However, once the roads are in good condition, trade will be good and tax revenue will increase; both meaning income for the government. This is the first point.

The second point is that we need more than just rupiah; we also require foreign exchange. Foreign exchange cannot be printed, but must be obtained through exports. So printing banknotes is not an alternative to a loan. The appropriate alternative is to both increase state revenues and to boost exports. We must do this. However, this will take longer than just one, two, or three years.

Therefore, at present, loans are still needed. Of course, we will apply the lessons we have learned from the past, so that we will not repeat our past mistakes. What were the past mistakes in the case of loans? The first related to the terms and conditions of the loans. There are three kinds of terms and conditions: (1) interest (2) the timeframe within which the loan must be repaid and (3) a grace period.

Regarding the interest, in the past there were often loans with high interest rates of 8 or 9 or 10 per cent. Then there was the problem of time. Mostly the timeframes for repayment were short or medium term. Some loans were given for two–three years, some others for only 1 year, but there were also some loans given for six months or less. Others were given for four or five or six or ten years, often without a grace period. So the pattern is like this: we take a loan now and next year we start to repay it in installments. The mistakes we had made about terms and conditions.

Then, the use of the loans entailed quite a lot of problems. Take, for example, what would happen if we took out a loan for a project for which the equipment was unreasonably expensive? Such loans exist among the old loans that we now have to repay. The problem is not just about the prices, but also about project preparation. We must be careful about this, as there were many mistakes in this category in the past.

We still remember the Makariki project in Seram. This was a sugar mill project. If the project had been successful, the production costs at the resulting sugar mill would have been seven times higher than at existing sugar mills in Java. This is the calculation made by experts. That failed project has now become a debt.

Then there is the factory in Martapura. The construction of this factory has been completed, but there are difficulties with its location. Similar issues exist in the Pematang Siantar paper mill, which is too small and, therefore, not efficient enough.

Therefore, in taking out loans today, we are applying the lessons learned from the past. Regarding the conditions, we have carefully set a number of conditions for ourselves:

Interest rates must be no more than 3 per cent and the period of repayment must be twenty-five years, including a grace period of seven years. Well, what if a creditor offers a loan for ten years? We will say thank-you, but we won't take the loan. To this end, it is necessary to have self discipline so that we won't take a loan simply for the sake of taking a loan. In this case, we must be cautious, as there are many financiers and brokers out there ready to offer loans.

What matters is that once we lay down a provision, we must cling to it. Unless the rate is 3 per cent, or, perhaps, only slightly above 3 per cent, we won't take the loan. Unless the period is twenty-five years or slightly less, we won't take the loan. And the grace period must be seven years. These are the provisions that we must cling to.

Why are we imposing these provisions? Because, in our calculations, the period of time we are stipulating will not be too burdensome for Indonesia's economy. The interest is also something important. Take, for example, what would happen if we borrowed 500 million dollars at a rate of interest of 9 per cent per annum instead of 3 per cent? The amounts owed would be decidedly different. If the interest rate were 3 per cent, every year we would have to pay 15 million dollars for the interest alone, while if the interest rate were 9 per cent, we would be forced to pay 45 million dollars in interest per year. A difference of 30 million dollars a year is quite extravagant. We could use that 30 million dollars to build a cement factory larger than the one in Gresik.

At present, the conditions for our loans from various countries is 3 per cent, tweny-five years, including a grace period of seven years. In the case of loans from Holland, for example, two thirds are grants and one third are loans for twenty-five years, a grace period of seven years and an interest rate of 3 per cent. In the case of loans from West Germany, in the past we always got loans for twenty-five years, with a grace period of seven years and an interest rate of 3 per cent, but this year we get a loan for thirty years, including a 10 year grace period, while the interest rate is 2.5 per cent. In the case of loans from the United States, the loans are given for forty years, including a grace period of ten years, while the rate of interest is 2.5 per cent. In the case of loans from a subsidiary of the World Bank, the International Development Association (IDA), the period is fifty years, including a grace period of 10 years, and the loans are interest-free. In the case of loans from Japan, the period is not 25 years, but twenty years, with a grace period of seven years and an interest rate of 3 per cent for imports or 3.5 per cent for projects. These are the softest loans possible pursuant to the Japanese laws. Only two other countries, South Korea and Taiwan have enjoyed these credit terms and conditions besides Indonesia. As for Australia, as I have said earlier, they provide grants, not loans. Canada has also given us a grant. As for Britain, the loans are interest-free and given for twenty-five years, with a grace period of seven years. These are, then, the various kinds of debts or loans or aid that we have obtained.

The following covers the use of the foreign funds. There are three kinds of uses: for the importation of goods on the import list, for food, and for projects. As is understood, our import list contains two categories of items: Category A and Category B that cover essential imports, while Category C, is for non-essential items. We can use offshore loans known as BE loans for A and B category imports. In the case of aid, the country concerned provides the money, then we use the money for imports as long as they are for items on the list (categories A and B). The use is determined by the state of Indonesia's economy. So, if Indonesia's economic activities require spare-parts for jeeps, the BE loan will be used for the import of spare-parts. If Indonesia's economy needs electrical equipment or parts, we will use the loan for the importation of electrical equipment. If Indonesia's economy needs fertilizer, we use the credit to import fertilizer. This is a form of loan opposed by some circles in creditor countries. They do not like this kind of loan because they cannot determine what kind of goods must be purchased. In the relationship between developing countries and industrial states, we have forged new directions that other developing countries will follow.

If there is an opportunity, there is now a document available that would be very good to study; a report by Mr Pearson (former Canadian prime minister) along with four other people. They have studied the problems of aid and say that programme aid is good because its use is determined solely on the economy of the country concerned, not on the government, but on its economy. For example in Japan there are certain parties who want Indonesia to use the credit extended for the import of Toyota spare-parts, while what we need are Nissan spare-parts. It is not the Indonesian government, but, rather, the economy, that is dictating that the spare-parts must be Nissan. If Toyota spare-parts are needed, Toyota spare-parts will be purchased, but if Nissan parts are needed, Nissan parts will be bought. It all depends on our economy. This is also a shift in the system of offshore aid that has been opposed by some circles in the industrialized countries.

In some circles, both overseas and in Indonesia, there is sometimes a question as to whether it is true that when Indonesia take a BE loan that the funds will simply "disappear". Projects, after all, are visible. Jatiluhur, for example, or Cilegon, although that project has yet to be completed. In this context, BE assisted processes are not considered "visible". This is a mistaken idea. One of the uses of BE aid or credit is that foreign exchange is sold and turned into rupiah, which will later be used for purchases made through the state budget. Of course, it is still fresh in our minds that we need Rp123 billion for our budget this year. Of this 123 billion, Rp36 billion is the counter value of project aid, Rp87 billion is in the form of rupiah and of this amount about Rp22 billion comes from public savings; namely from the surplus of domestic revenues over routine expenditures, while Rp65 billion is the counter value of BE loans. So the value of BE loans is that they do not just bring in goods, but also produce rupiah for development.

Then there is the food aid. There is rice from several countries and there is flour from the United States. If there were no food aid, then the alternative would be that we would have to import food with our own foreign exchange and this would reduce our foreign exchange reserves. Importing food with our own foreign exchange would reduce our imports for other purposes. As we are yet to be able to meet our need for food, we must import food either through using our own money or by using BE funds. If we use BE assistance, the food provided can be sold so that the Government will have revenue that can be used for the budget. So, regarding food, the first policy is to import food, the second policy is to create projects aided by the proceeds from the sales of food. This is indeed a relatively new mechanism, not only in Indonesia but also in the world. Therefore, the understanding of this is sometimes still insufficient, not only in Indonesia but also in the creditor countries, and explanation will be needed, even though it is obvious that all this conforms to our needs.

Then, there is the matter of development projects. We must be prudent so as not to make the mistakes of the past. We must determine the projects ourselves. We do not want the loan or aid providers to determine the projects. We examine the potential projects that we deem necessary. We study these projects to see whether it would be best to get aid from this or that country for the selected projects. Then we negotiate with the country we have chosen. Then we make a feasibility study about this project. We also carry out price checks and so forth, with everything being done as carefully as possible because all of the funds or other assistance will have to be repaid in the future. So, we must be prudent.

In this context, the contracts for the projects that were kicked off in the past and are continuing now must be reviewed. Take, for example, the microwave project from Bandung to Semarang. This is an old contract. When we reviewed the contract, we also took into consideration current technological developments that would enable us, for the same cost, to expand the project to Surabaya. So we can benefit further from this project than originally expected with the network extending not only from Bandung to Semarang, but also on Bandung-Surabaya. We must be prudent in studying these projects. Likewise, with all the expansion projects, such as PUSRI, Semen Gresik, Karang Kates, and Riam Kanan, among others.

Take, for example, the road project that is now being funded with aid from the World Bank. Only the routes that will have guaranteed good economic impacts will be chosen for this project. We haven't started building new roads; instead, we have opted to concentrate on repairing and upgrading old roads that have been proven to have beneficial economic impact. To this end, we must reform our working system. The agencies involved in this project are not allowed to find their own loans. This is not allowed. Otherwise, this would create difficulties later. We will return to the habits of the old era. In 1966, it was very difficult to administrate our debts because they were scattered everywhere.

So, we must be prudent, and will not be allowed to find our own loans. Everything must be coordinated. Neither can we start developing a project the moment an idea strikes us. It just can't be that way. This was one of our weaknesses in the past. We are strong at coming up with ideas, but usually find it difficult to translate these ideas into projects that can be accounted for. So, also in the case of project aid, we now require that each government agency and institution prepare a well-examined feasibility study. The location must be appropriate; the size must be suitable; we must compare the various technologies being developed in many countries around the world. We should not just set up a factory and, then, run the risk of learning upon its completion that technology has changed and we have been left behind again, still unable to compete with imports. We must do all of this seriously and as carefully as possible.

If we look into the problem of project aid, we will see that, today, project preparations are being carried out as carefully as possible. What matters is not that the project must come into being, but that the project will be really useful and will not be too expensive. To this end, it is true that sometimes the implementation of project aid does not seem rapid enough, but wouldn't it really be better for us to move carefully, step-by-step, rather than to rush forward carelessly in too big a hurry. Slow but sure rather than in a hurry with the consequence that the project will fail to materialize while the debts pile up.

In 1970–71, much of the project aid we prepared in 1968–69 will be realized. In 1970–71 many project aid goods will come in. Now, in 1969, the quantity is still small. In 1970–71 the quantity will be big. We must be prepared and prevent the recurrence of past practices, namely that the goods arriving at the port are left to rust without ever being collected for use. This is a real problem. To this end, it is important to have the rupiah funds to enable the implementation of project aid. So the ministry obtaining project aid should get rupiah that can be used to collect the goods from the port. This is a local cost approach.

We should also prevent the following: lack of preparation for the implementation and/or utilization of materials or equipment or instruments that have arrived. For example: equipment — the value of which reaches108 million dollars — is being sent for road repair workshops. Prior to the arrival of these instruments, the workshops should be constructed and made ready to house the equipment. We should not wait to build the workshops until after the arrival of the instruments. So the rupiah spending for these workshops must be prepared ahead of time so that when the equipment arrives, it can be put to use immediately in the workshops. It is in this context that efforts are being made to use a network planning system. Hopefully, in the future, such networks will be more widely used so that all the above shortcomings can be overcome gradually.

NOTE

[1] Description given in capacity as Chairman of the National Development Planning Board (BAPPENAS) to the DPR-GR (Gotong-Royong House of Representatives), 15 November 1969. This article is translated by Harry Bhaskara.

21

A ONCE-AND-FOR-ALL SETTLEMENT OF INDONESIA'S FOREIGN DEBT (1970)[1]

Introductory Note: *When Indonesia was elected as Chairman of the Non-Alligned Movement of the Developing Countries in 1992, President Suharto gave special attention to the serious problems faced by the highly indebted developing countries and took a number of effective steps. First, he established the Non-Alligned Movement Ad Hoc Advisory Group of Experts on Debt chaired by Dr Gamani Corea (former Secretary General of the UNCTAD) and which later on published its Report. In 1993 President Suharto brought to the attention of the leaders of the seven industrial countries through a meeting with the Chairman of the G-7, the Prime Minister of Japan Mr Kiichi Miyazawa. In 1994 President Suharto convened in Jakarta from 13–15 August 1994 a Ministerial Meeting of Non-Alligned Countries on Debt and Development: Sharing of Experiences. The meeting was attended by ministers from 25 debt-distressed least developed countries (Benin, Bhutan, Cambodia, Cape Verde, Comoros, Djibouti, Ethiopia, Guinea, Guinea Bissau, Lesotho. Liberia, Mali, Mauritania, Mozambique, Myanmar, Niger, Sao Tome and*

Principe, Sierra Leone, Sudan, Tanzania, Togo, Uganda, Zaire, Zambia). The NAM Advisory Group of Experts on Debt was represented by Dr Gamani Corea and Dr Henock Kifle. The Indonesian delegation consisted of Coordinating Minister for Economic Affairs Dr Saleh Afijf, Ambassador Nana Sutresna, who was Executive Assistant to the Chairman of the Non-Alligned Movement, and the members of the Economic Advisory Team on Debt and Development Issues: Professors Moh. Sadli, Ali Wardhana, Radius Prawiro, Emil Salim, Suhadi Mangkusuwondo, Widjojo Nitisastro. In the meeting I delivered a presentation on Indonesia's experience: "A Once-and-for-all Settlement of Indonesia's Foreign Debt".

On the final settlement of Indonesia's foreign debt a crucial role was played by Dr Hermann J. Abs from the Deutsche Bank and on the Indonesian side by Mr Rachmat Saleh who was at that time Senior Deputy Governor of Bank Indonesia, later on Governor of Bank Indonesia and then Minister of Trade.

A once-and-for-all settlement of Indonesia's foreign debt was achieved in April 1970, while the above description was delivered in August 1994 at the Non-aligned Ministerial Level Conference whose very poor member countries were heavily indebted.

I am delighted to participate in discussions on the enormous external debt burden of the developing countries with a view to formulating common approaches. I doubt, however, whether I can contribute anything meaningful to the deliberations on the important topics of debt rescheduling, debt restructuring, debt refinancing and debt reduction. My familiarity with the settlement of foreign debts is limited to Indonesia's experience. Moreover, the last rescheduling of Indonesia's public debts took place one quarter of a century ago, from 1966 to 1970. Today, Indonesia is certainly one of the highly indebted developing countries in the world but fortunately Indonesia has been successful in preventing any foreign debt crisis during the past twenty-four years.

For whatever it is worth, let me try to describe the rescheduling of Indonesia's debts in the years 1966–70. In 1966 Indonesia was confronted with a severe foreign debt crisis. Debt payments due, including arrears, far exceeded total exports earnings. The payment obligations were due to twenty-two countries, including the Paris Club countries, the USSR and countries of Eastern Europe, and a number of other countries.

Political changes in 1966 enabled the country to adopt appropriate economic policies and to approach creditor countries to arrive at a rearrangement of debt service payments. The first meeting between Indonesia and the Paris club countries took place in September 1966 in Tokyo, followed by another meeting in Paris in December 1966, during which a settlement was agreed on.

The settlement provided for 100 per cent relief from payments of principal and interest due in 1967, including arrears, related to government and government-guaranteed credits. The amounts were to be repaid over eight years following a three-year grace period. An interest of 3 to 4 per cent was charged on the rescheduled amounts. The terms of this settlement were later on applied to maturities due in 1968 and 1969.

To accomodate private creditors whose loans had not been guaranteed by an official government agency in their countries, the Government of Indonesia introduced the Debt Investment Conversion Scheme (DICS) which permitted conversion of matured claims into local currency deposits which could be used for approved foreign investment projects in Indonesia.

The debt rescheduling agreement with the Paris Club countries made possible the convening of an aid group meeting called the IGGI (Inter-Governmental Group on Indonesia) in the Netherlands in February 1967.

Since the agreement of 1966 covered only the payments due in 1967, another meeting was held in 1967 for the rescheduling of payments due in 1968. Similarly, in 1968 another meeting was held for the rescheduling of payments due in the following year. Thus, it was necessary to have negotiations every year on the rescheduling of debt payments falling due in the following year.

Furthermore, every year after an agreement was reached at the Paris Club, further bilateral negotiations had to be conducted with individual creditors based on the agreement with the Paris Club. There were at that time 22 creditor countries, of which seven were participants of the Paris Club while the remaining were not. The latter had to be persuaded one-by-one to agree on the rescheduling of Indonesia's debt based on the terms of agreement with the Paris Club.

While the year after year rearrangement of debt provided some degree of relief, it was obvious that it could not become the basis of a viable long-term settlement of Indonesia's debt crisis. Not only were the grace period and the repayment period too short, but the amount rescheduled was limited to payments due in the following year only. Such an arrangement implied that rescheduling agreements had to be negotiated every year and that, soon, the rescheduled amounts would have to be rescheduled again. The continuing debt negotiations, year after year, created a never-ending climate of uncertainty, both for the government in working out its annual budget and its monetary policy as well as for the private sector which as a consequence kept postponing its investment decisions.

Not less serious was the fact that such an arrangement also had an impact of a different nature. At the time, during the late 1960s, Indonesia had a very limited number of people who had the capability to work out programs for economic recovery and growth. But they were totally preoccupied with the never-ending process of debt negotiation as a result of the year after year rearrangement of the country's debts.

It was fortunate for Indonesia that its Paris Club creditors also realized the serious shortcomings of such an arrangement. It was recognized that the 1966–68 year after year reschedulings were of an interim nature and could not become the basis for a viable longterm settlement of Indonesia's debt crisis. Without further postponement of rescheduled maturities, the payments burden of new loans extended to Indonesia would create another payments crisis in the early 1970s.

If another debt crisis was to be prevented, a more durable settlement had to be negotiated and agreed on. Such a durable settlement would enable Indonesia to have access to the necessary financial resources and to embark on a process of sustained growth. For that purpose there was a need for an assessment of Indonesia's debt problem, to be followed by proposals for a final settlement. It was strongly felt by the Paris Club creditors as well as Indonesia that such an assessment and proposals for settlement should not be requested from a creditor nor from the debtor, since both were parties to the debt problem. Instead it should be requested from a third party.

The Paris Club and Indonesia decided then to invite a third party to make an assessment of Indonesia's debt problem and to come up with proposals for a final settlement of Indonesia's foreign debts. The third party invited was Dr Herman J. Abs, the highly respected banker and authority on finance of the Deutsche Bank from Germany.

In preparing his assessment and in working out his proposals Dr Abs was assisted by a joint working group of staff members of the

World Bank and the IMF. The joint working group provided assistance in working out short range and longer-range balance of payments projections and in calculating the prospective effects of alternative debt rescheduling formulae on Indonesia's balance of payments and prospects for economic growth. A simulation model was prepared with alternative assumptions regarding aid levels and terms, debt rescheduling formulae and export growth rates. An assessment was made on the implications of the alternative assumptions on the balance of payments, including the capacity to service new external debt, and on the domestic economy including the prospective rate of economic growth.

Dr Abs submitted his assessment of Indonesia's debt problem and proposals for a final settlement based on the following considerations:

(1) There should be a "once-and-for-all" long-term debt settlement, not subject to periodic re-negotiations.
(2) The debt settlement should ensure the restoration of the creditworthiness of Indonesia.
(3) The debt settlement should be based on a strict application of the principle of non-discrimination.

As to the specific proposals. Dr Abs suggested the following:

(1) The principal sums owed by Indonesia were to be repaid in full over a period of 30 years in equal installments and with no grace period.
(2) Interest on old debts together with interest agreed upon in earlier rescheduling negotiations was to be cancelled.
(3) The new loan would be free of interest.
(4) No distinction was to be made between the different types of creditors as well as between the different purposes for which the loans had been extended: Paris Club and non-Paris Club countries; guaranteed and non-guaranteed debts; military and non-military uses.

A number of creditor countries had serious problems with some aspects of the Abs proposal. After further deliberations a number of amendments were introduced. The final settlement agreed upon in April 1970 between Indonesia and the Paris Club countries were as follows:

(1) Repayment of principal in equal installments in thirty years beginning in 1970 to 1999.

(2) Repayment of contractual interest in fifteen years beginning in 1985 to 1999.
(3) No further interest would be charged on the amounts deferred.
(4) Indonesia had the option to defer part of the payments of principal due during the first eight years to the last eight years, which was the period 1992–99, with payments of an interest of 4 per cent annually.

In August 1970 an agreement was reached with the USSR, and later on also with the other non-Paris Club countries, in accordance with the settlement agreed upon by the Paris Club countries.

Since 1970 no other rescheduling of Indonesia's foreign debts was necessary. Through careful debt management and timely implementation of economic reforms and structural adjustments Indonesia had been able to prevent another foreign debt crisis throughout the twenty-four years period.

The final settlement of Indonesia's debts twenty-four years ago could only be achieved because both sides, the creditors and the debtor, were determined to arrive at a once-and-for-all settlement by both sides doing their utmost. Thus, the debtor put its own house in order by carrying out effectively a comprehensive program of economic stabilization. On the other hand, the creditors made an all-out effort to explore and to work out a debt settlement which was truly a final settlement.

The following may illustrate the determination of the creditors. The final settlement of Indonesia's debt crisis as worked out in the Paris Club did initially not received the support of the Government of Japan since it was contrary to provisions in the existing laws of Japan. Had the Government of Japan at that time continuously opposed such a settlement in the Paris Club, no agreement could have been reached and the objective of finding a final settlement would not have been achieved. Instead, the Government of Japan made a determined effort to overcome such legal impediment by successfully introducing an amendment to the existing law. In today's language of development cooperation, it was an act reflecting a true spirit of cooperation between partners in development.

The rescheduling of Indonesia's debt in 1970 was a case of a fundamental settlement of a country's heavy debt burden which enabled the country to have access to financial resources and to move forward to a process of sustained growth.

Unfortunately, the Paris Club countries continuously stressed their strongly-held view that the settlement of Indonesia's foreign debts was a unique case and that it should not become a precedent for the settlement of the foreign debts of other developing countries. It is indeed hard to comprehend why it could not become a precedent for the settlement of the debt burden of other developing countries facing similar problems and carrying out development policies as effectively.

Of course, each country has its own specific features, but there are also many common features among developing countries, particularly with respect to their enormous debt burden. There are certainly unique features with respect to each country's foreign debt: the absolute size of each country's stock of debt is different; the ratio of debt to GNP, the ratio of debts to exports, the ratio of debt service to exports, and the ratio of interest payments to exports are all different; the composition of the outstanding debt is also different, in terms of public or private debts, short term or longer term debts, and guaranteed or non-guaranteed debts; the composition in terms of its sources of debts is also different: official creditors or private creditors, bilateral or multilateral creditors, concessional or non-concessional sources of credit; and in the case of private creditors: whether loans from banks or from other financial institutions, whether bonds publicly issued or privately placed, whether credits from exporters or from manufacturers.

Such differences has led the lending countries to give a disproportionate emphasis on the case-by-case approach, stressing the uniqueness of each case and oposing the use of a case as a precedent for similar cases.

An overemphasis on the uniqueness of each case results in ignoring the common features inherent in the challenge faced by all developing countries with a heavy debt burden. Actually, developing countries with a heavy debt burden are all facing the same challenge: how to arrive at a fundamental settlement of their heavy burden of debt which will enable them to have access to the necessary financial resources and to embark upon a process of sustained growth.

A country's fundamental settlement of its foreign debt problem may be achieved by a type of rescheduling with a very long maturity as was the case with Indonesia.

But probably for most developing countries with a heavy debt burden today only a substantial reduction of both the stock of debt and the debt service would stop the net transfer of resources from these countries and revive the development process.

Repeated reschedulings of foreign debts as is presently the case for many countries create uncertainties about future economic policies and performance, in particular since the debt overhang discourages effective reform efforts.

Perhaps today, twenty-four years after the final settlement of Indonesia's debt problem and in view of the still large number of developing countries with heavy debt burden, the Paris Club creditor countries and the international financial institutions may agree to apply the main features of Indonesia's debt settlement to relevant cases. The main difference is probably the fact that for most developing countries with a heavy debt burden today the rescheduling of debt is far from sufficient. A substantial reduction of both the stock of debt and debt service is a necessary condition for reviving the development process.

Repeated reduction of debt service payments or the provision of new loans instead of debt reduction create uncertainties which may become counterproductive for the investment climate. What is required for most severely indebted developing countries at present is a substantial debt and debt service reduction of the bilateral and multilateral debts in a single operation, instead of in stages, in order to arrive at a final settlement of their foreign debt problem. Moreover, in order to achieve a reasonable rate of economic growth, the final debt settlement and new flows of financial resources are to be worked out as integral components of a comprehensive external financing package.

In view of the urgency of the problem for the developing world it is of utmost importance that the developing countries continue to urge the lending countries and the multilateral financial institutions to arrive at fundamental settlements of the debt problem of the developing countries in order to enable these countries to embark on their sustained development process.

NOTE

[1] A presentation of "A Once-and-for-all Settlement of Indonesia's Foreign Debt" at the Ministerial Meeting of Non-Alligned Countries on Debt and Development: Sharing of Experiences, Jakarta 13–15 August 1994.

PART V

EQUITABLE DEVELOPMENT

22

EQUITABLE DISTRIBUTION PROGRAMME (1979)[1]

Introductory Note: *Equitable distribution of wealth is such an important element of development that it is often said it is one of the goals of development. However, if this equity should not materialize, and become just a mere slogan, this would ruin our development efforts. Therefore, equity and all facets of equal justice on all levels for all people should become an inherent element or an inalienable factor in development. In other words, equity must be transformed into a programme or programmes inseparable from development. Failing this, equity will become a mere catchword and our development efforts will not succeed.*

National development efforts put a great deal of emphasis on equity. This reflects the people's aspirations to uphold social justice.

The elements of equity in the Trilogy of Development are translated into eight programmes, known as the Eight Tracks to Equity, which comprise:

- equity in fulfilling basic needs. Because human needs are manifold, great emphasis is placed on three basic needs: food, clothing and housing.

- equity in opportunity to get education and health services. Hence, equity is not just a matter of the physical; it also covers the right to education and health.
- equity in income. Not in the sense of an equal amount of income, but of equity in income distribution.
- equity in employment opportunity. Employment is one of the fundamental issues in our national development.
- equity in business opportunity.
- equity in opportunities to participate in development, particularly for the younger generation and women.
- equity in the distribution of the development process throughout the country. Ours is a vast country. Equity in development is a must.
- equality before the law. This is a very important matter and should be transformed into a programme.

I repeat, the first equity programme is for the provision of basic needs, particularly food, clothing and housing; the second one is for education and health services; the third is for income distribution; the fourth is for employment opportunities, the fifth is for business opportunities, the sixth is for the opportunity to take part in development, particularly for the younger generation and women; the seventh is for development distribution throughout the country, the eighth is equity before the law. These, then, are the eight tracks to equity.

Let me now elaborate on these eight tracks to equity. In relation to basic needs, food comes first, not just polished rice, shelled rice, or unshelled rice, but foodstuffs of all kinds. Food has been purposely singled out because Indonesians are currently consuming more foodstuffs of a wider variety than previously. Our target is not limited only to boosting rice production, but to providing other kinds of food as well. This is closely related to nutrient enrichment.

In connection with this, one specific problem has emerged from among the others. Today, Indonesians not only consume the traditional basic foods, but also a rich diversity of foodstuffs. Corn is an easy example of this. Our corn production is on the rise. The corn harvest will be here soon. However, corn consumption has soared significantly. Not only is it consumed by people, but also by cattle and fowls. When we eat an egg, it comes from hens, who also consume corn. In this case, we are indirect consumers of the same corn. Not surprisingly, the demand for corn has been increasing remarkably. At this time there is also an attractive opportunity to export corn. This requires production and marketing skills. Other food items with good prospects are soybeans, nuts and sweet potatoes. Export prospects for sweet potatoes are good, but there are marketing problems in some regions.

The marketing of a product should also be based on the equal distribution principle to give producers a chance to get their fair share. For example, should there be a rise in our export of rubber; we want our rubber farmers to also gain from it, not only the exporters. In so doing, we are implementing the equity principle.

As far as clothing goes, we are experiencing what is called a "boom" in demand. We are hard put to meet this rising demand, particularly from overseas. It goes without saying that this demand also boosts domestic prices for garments and fabric, and we must not let a wide gap occur between overseas and domestic prices. We can overcome this problem by increasing our garment and fabric production. However, there is a disadvantage here; we depend almost entirely on imports of our raw materials for garment making. This is true for both cotton and synthetic materials.

Therefore, if there is one thing we need to seriously work on, it is our capacity to provide raw materials, both cotton and chemical-based synthetics, for our garment industry. The Aromatic Centre project in Plaju is now being revamped, and so is the olefin project in Aceh. The Aromatic Centre, in particular , is very important in the procurement of raw material for our textile industry.

We also want to fulfill another basic need, which is housing. We now have the Perumnas housing project. However, this does not mean that we will build houses for everyone using the state budget. There is not enough money; that would be completely impossible. We need to lay out a proper foundation and create an appropriate business climate so that our housing development will succeed.

Housing construction should use local materials to the fullest extent that this is possible, and should adhere to the principles of healthy housing construction. There is another important element in housing development, which is community development. The way we build houses, arrange the settlements, and so on, will determine the type of community we wish to create.

This is an important element indeed. Housing development is linked to the betterment of our people's living environments, both in urban and rural areas; especially in urban kampongs and rural villages whose residents are from the low-income bracket. Housing projects require a massive amount of energy, effort and activity; we can only hope that our production capacity for cement, bricks and other construction materials will be adequate to meet the demand for housing construction.

Then there is equity in opportunity to get an education. What is our target? Our target for the third Five-Year Development Plan has much to do with our achievement in the second Five-Year Development Plan. At the end of the first Five-Year Development Plan, about 57 per cent of children between seven and twelve years old went to school. At the end of the second Five-Year Development Plan, the percentage climbed from 57 per cent to 85 per cent. The question remains, however: 57 per cent out of how many and 85 per cent out of how many? There is a constant shift in the total number of children aged between seven and twelve. In the first instance the figure was 57 per cent out of 20 million, meaning 11.4 million, and in the second instance it was 85 per cent of 24 million, which is almost 20 million. In other words, during the second Five-Year Development Plan, we were able to provide access to education to only about eight million children.

Our target in the third Five-Year Development Plan is to provide primary school education to all children aged between seven and twelve. We have started from the elementary school level. No matter where these children are; whether they are on the tiniest islets or on top of a mountain, we should be able to provide them with educational opportunities. Then, even though they may have access to education, that does not necessarily mean that they will, in actual fact, study. This is because some of their parents want their children to help them in their work.

It is, however, imperative that we ensure that schools are accessible for all children. We should avoid a situation where, on paper, we have many schools, but they are all located in the cities. That is not what we want. So there should be equal distribution of opportunities to get education. For the third Five-Year Development Plan we should be able to give equal opportunity for all our children aged seven to 12 years old to go to elementary schools, even though, right now, we are certainly are not yet able to provide equal opportunity to attend junior high or; and when it comes to university education, of course, we all realize that this is a far-off dream. We will have to get there step by step.

Next is equal opportunity to health services. Health is a very important thing. Healthy people will be more productive. That is seen from the economic point of view. However, healthiness is also an individual goal. Productivity aside, we should still strive to make people live in a healthier way. Equity in health services is the way to achieve this. This can be done through the community health centers (Puskesmas), and traveling health centers aboard ships, small boats or vehicles, as well as auxiliary health centers, with the additional support of strategic deployment of doctors, paramedics and specialists, in such a way that during the third Five-Year Development Plan, hospitals in regencies will have specialists, including pediatricians. By so doing, equity in health services will become a reality.

The availability of drinking water is closely related to health. One of the reasons why people are not healthy is the lack of clean water, both in urban and rural areas. Provision of clean or potable water requires a lot of facilities such as water pipes, water pumps and so on. This program is a huge one and will result in the full realization of equity in health services.

The following elements — equity in income distribution and equity in working opportunity — are often inter-connected. Equity in income distribution is closely linked to working opportunity, because people can only have income if they can work. By expanding working opportunities we can achieve equity in income distribution. This is one factor we are all well aware of. All people must deal with this matter seriously in every program, through each of their actions and in every step they take.

Take the investment sector as an example; if there is a choice between using capital, equipment or manpower, the use of workers should be given priority. This can only take place when each one of us understands the underlying reasons that this is necessary. However, just realizing the importance of this is not enough. There is a solid basis for why things should be done that way. We should be able to alter the cost comparison of capital and labor in such a way that the use of equipment will be more costly than that of employing workers. If we import capital goods today, the exports will be relatively more expensive than they were last year. All of this constitutes an attempt of sorts to promote labor intensive investment.

This is also true of credit activities. If our understanding of investment is limited to the purchase of capital intensive equipment, and if we are less than careful, we will end up encouraging the use of tools and discouraging the hiring of workers. Therefore, we need to rethink — even in this credit sector — the differences between investment credit and working credit, making note that working capital is an oddity created out of convenience. In major projects or production drives, manpower can be put into better use in the production process; hence resulting in the need for more working capital but less investment capital. We need to give more thought to this matter of how to create wider employment opportunities, as well as business opportunities. The same applies to other fields; but the issue of job opportunities calls for our most serious attention.

Next, is equity of opportunity to take part in development, particularly for the younger generation and women. This is something which is quite clear. Our younger generation needs to take part in development, they should not have to wait; but they must be inspired to do so. How do we motivate them? By giving them opportunities to participate.

This is also the case for opportunities for women in development. Women make up the bigger part of the Indonesian population, comprising more than 51 per cent; so they are the majority. Of course, they must also be perceived as important capital for development and we need to push their potential further, so that they can be truly valuable to the development effort.

Recently, I have sensed an encouraging development, especially in rural areas, where the role of women has been impressive in various programs, including PKK (Education for Family Welfare). For example, when it comes to making use of their yards at home. House yards can be a magnificent source of food, supplementary nutrition for the family, when put to use for growing plants, or for fish ponds. People have started to do exactly that and this is quite heartening.

In light of this, the thought arises that maybe we have been paying too much attention to urban areas. Yet, it is clear that rural areas are also undergoing major change; due in no small part to the role of women. And yet another proof of the effective role of Indonesian women in development can be found in the Family Planning Programme. Today, the family planning programme in Indonesia has become a model for developing countries worldwide. This is not just lip-service; it is a fact.

Next is equity in the distribution of the development process across the archipelago, especially in relatively disadvantaged regions. Regions such as Irian Jaya, the islands of East Nusa Tenggara, and East Timor, as well as parts of Sulawesi and Southeast Maluku are begging for our attention. However, there are also pockets with relatively better economic conditions ,which also require attention. For example, the southern coast of Java island also needs our attention because it is an area that is relatively more backward than other areas.

Then, there is the last element of equity on this list: equality before the law. This is an issue that also needs our attention. We need to have clear cut programs that will ensure that justice is served in a timely manner for all who seek it and in accordance with the sense of fairness inherent in the minds of the people. The same goes with justice in the economic field. One example that needs our serious attention is the issue of land, including land ownership, land use and land acquisition or possession. As it is now, a person may have legal title to a piece of land, but not be able to posses or occupy that property.

Corrections are in order so that ownership and acquisition/possession of land will adhere to existing regulations without any irregularities, so that we can truly uphold social justice in our country.

These are some of the things that should be noted in relation to the equitable distribution program.

NOTE

[1]   Comments by the Minister of Economics, Finance and Industry and/Chairman of BAPPENAS made at the 1979 KADIN (Chamber of Commerce and Industry) Congress. This article is translated by Harry Bhaskara.

23

FOSTERING SMALL SCALE ENTERPRISES (1977)[1]

Introductory Note: *The development of small scale enterprises is an important part of the efforts to create jobs and equity in the distribution of the development process. It also has much to do with the enforcement of social justice. Much has been done in our country, as well as other countries, in the world. But the challenges are massive indeed, and certainly very difficult to overcome. Therefore everything should be considered and reviewed carefully. On the other hand, good regulations exist, but they are not widely known nor adequately exploited for the benefit of small scale enterprises. Therefore, this situation requires extensive and persistent rectification in order to effectively promote the development of small scale enterprises.*

The development of small-scale enterprises is an inseparable part of establishing the equality and equity in the distribution of the benefits of the development process that can lead to social justice. Therefore, it is imperative to pay attention to the development of small-scale enterprises. The important thing is how to determine how best to do this and what steps should be taken to realize this dream.

Thus, it seems prudent to make a review of what we have done during this New Order era: What has been successful, what has been less than successful and what has failed; in order that we can decide on the necessary steps to be taken. We can also learn from past experiences prior to the New Order era. Likewise, we can learn from the experiences of other nations in developing their small-scale enterprises.

Currently the People's Consultative Assembly is drawing up the new Broad Outline of the State Guidelines. The third Five-Year Development Plan will be formulated based on those guidelines. Hopefully this symposium will provide our representatives in the People's Consultative Assembly with materials to consider for the drafting of the State Guidelines, which will then be articulated in the third Five-Year Development Plan.

A review of what we have done in the past few years will unveil various problems rooted in the regulations and the laws that seem to have hampered the development of our business world, especially the small-scale enterprises. We need to review the rules and regulations, be they laws or government decrees or decisions. We need to work based on the existing regulations. However, if we find any rules that are incompatible to the current economic conditions, we will need to revise them.

An example of this is the situations experienced by certain quarters of our business circles prior to and after the Tertib Operation (crack-down operation) were launched. Before the operation, one of the frequent complaints among businessmen was the rampant collection of illegal fees. The burden of illegal fees added to production costs, causing many to define it as a high-cost economy. The Tertib Operation is still being carried out now and is expected to effectively curb the illegal fees over the long term. The elimination of the illegal fees, however, has given rise to another complaint: Everything has become slower. This is because all parties must now follow all of the procedures, which takes time. Previously, when illegal fees were being imposed, the business people would most often not have to follow the correct procedures. That means that the existing procedures now need to be reviewed and improved. The Tertib Operation aims at making all things proceed in order, with the illegal fees removed and procedures followed appropriately. However, if following the rules proves to take too much time, hence becoming an obstacle, it is certain that the procedures must be streamlined in order to get rid of any constraints.

One example of the kind of review of regulations that should be done pertains to capital investment. One month ago, on 3 October 1977, the government issued a Presidential Decree on investment procedures for both domestic and foreign investment. The stipulation reflects the determination to ease procedures in order to facilitate business. It has been decided that the authority of various government institutions is to be transferred to the Investment Coordinating Board (BKPM) so that investors only need to deal with BKPM. Decisions on taxes, import duties, business permits and so forth have been transferred from the respective ministers to the BKPM Chairman, who is authorized to make decisions on behalf of the ministers. This is one measure to ensure that the stipulation on investment procedures will assist businessmen rather than turning it into a burden. The business world will surely be able to judge whether the new stipulation will make facilitate businessmen in their following of the investment procedures.

In this context, I would like to draw your attention to the fact that small-scale enterprises are not yet fully benefiting from the Domestic Investment stipulation. Actually this stipulation is meant to apply to the entire business community, but those who have been able to make the best of it, are those who ask for and receive tax relief facilities, import duty abolishment and other facilities. These are mostly companies that do not fall into the category of small-scale enterprises. The problem now is how small-scale entrepreneurs can also benefit from the Domestic Investment stipulation. This is an issue that we all need to address together.

Another issue is business sites. In the past several years there has been a trend toward constructing new market places or shopping centers, which are meant to provide good sites for running businesses. Such sites have often been developed within the context of city beautification. The development of these new, more modern markets has turned out to be a source of various problems.

One of them is the eviction of small-scale traders from the sites at which they used to run their businesses, with bigger traders moving in and often permanently displacing them from the newly constructed or renovated markets. The weak, really small-scale traders are being pushed into the suburbs. This is the reality we have seen.

Therefore, several measures have been taken. First, a review has been undertaken to find out the reason behind this phenomenon. It turns out that there are two contributing factors. The first is that the cost of renovating or reconstructing markets is really high. The local administrations generally do not have enough funds. They have to borrow from banks on the basis of standard investment credit terms, or end up making construction loan agreements with contractors who allow them defer payment for the work done for two or three years at high interest rates.

Second, there are indications that the construction cost is often excessively high due to overly pricey designs and high construction costs. Because the high price of construction has to be covered and loans repaid in a short time, the business sites in those markets are often reserved for those who can afford to buy them or rent them for a number of years in one go. This means the traders with bigger financial means. The result is that the smaller traders, who originally occupied the old markets, are being pushed into the suburbs. Occasionally, small-scale traders win the opportunity to rent or buy business sites or kiosks in the newly built markets, but because of the high rents or prices for services there, they finally opt to sell their opportunities to other traders with more extensive financial capacity.

Several measures have been taken to solve the problem of providing appropriate business sites for small-scale traders. Long term loans of ten years, which allow a two-year term grace period without any interest, are offered to regional administrations. The loans are to be used to renovate or build market places on the condition that their design and construction should be modest so that the cost will not be too high. The spaces and kiosks in the markets are not for sale, but for rent only. Rents should be low, and upfront payment for a period of several years in a row may not be imposed. Furthermore, traders who have rented the spaces or kiosks are not allowed to sublet them to other traders. Thus are some of the provisions currently stipulated.

Now we need to review whether or not the stipulations have been truly really effective and what further measures are needed to improve them. What matters is that the small-scale traders will make the best of the numerous facilities so that they have a place to run their business.

Another problem often faced by our business community, especially the small-scale enterprises, is a lack of capital. Apart from their own capital, traders also get bank loans to run their businesses. Currently the cost of capital in our economy is relatively high, but what matters most is the question of whether capital from the bank is available for small-scale traders. Actually, there are programs available that allocate funds or capital for small-scale traders. The latest is a programme for the provision of credit for small-scale traders in villages. We need to review the effectiveness of the existing programmes. Are there any stipulations that continue to hamper the implementation of those programmes? If so, how can we improve the situation?

In this context, the Bimas (Community Development) Credit programme comes to mind. This programme provides credit for farmers at an interest rate of 12 per cent per annum. Several years ago, only farmers who owned land were entitled to this credit because they could use their land as collateral. However, problems would arise if the land certificates were still being processed.

According to bank regulations, the certificate offered for collateral must be a currently valid and intact document issued by the agrarian authority. But in many regions, either the farmers do not have any papers issued by the agrarian authorities, or they do not have a finished document because their land has yet to be measured.

Furthermore, how about the farmers who do not have land, but till other people's land? Could they get the Bimas credit? They are, after all, small-scale entrepreneurs as well. They run their business and face a range of risks, including price fluctuations, prolonged dry seasons, plant diseases and so forth. Therefore, in the Bimas credit programme, it was decided that the collateral could be made more flexible and farmers who do not own any land can now obtain credit with collateral that does not necessarily have a direct relationship to their livelihood.

Meanwhile, another problem has arisen due to the presence of brokers in the credit scheme. Farmers often obtain and pay back loans through brokers. If the broker fails to pay back the debt to the bank, the bank regards the farmer as having a bad debt and the farmer cannot obtain new credit. There have also been brokers who did not hand over the loans to the farmers seeking them. Therefore, a provision has been made to stipulate that brokerage is not recognized in the Bimas Credit programme. Farmers have to deal directly with the banks, in this case the village units of BRI bank. Certainly, although this approach protects the farmers, this regulation has meant more work for the bank and procedural steps for the farmers. Yet, this is an experience which needs to be heeded. If we are not careful, small-scale traders will continue to fall prey to credit brokers.

Furthermore, in the case of Bimas Credit, there is another problem related to default on outstanding debts. This is caused by, among other things, the existence of the brokers as I have explained earlier, but is also due to logical causes like crop failures or diminished harvests. Some farmers experience total harvest failures. In Indonesian agricultural lingo, this is called *puso*, meaning that the damage is 85–100 per cent. In such cases, the government lends a hand. Farmers who experience harvest failures do not have to return their credit and they can obtain new credit. Those who experience 50–80 per cent harvest failure can get an extension on their loans and still obtain new credit. However, there has been another consequence. Reports of *puso* have increased substantially because of the debt write-off. Therefore we need to be watchful to determine whether or not full crop failure has actually occurred.

All of these elaborations and examples show that there is a need for interaction between the business community and government officials. It is necessary to have a working method that allows the government to know what happens in the community and consider it while on the other hand the entrepreneurs can understand all of the government regulations. As a matter of fact, the government always tries to revise and improve its regulations. Therefore it is really important to get feedback from the business community. In the case of feedback, it is necessary to get the details about the real conditions in various business sectors and in various regions. What happens in one sector might not necessarily be what is happening in other sectors. What happens in one region might not happen in other regions. If we are not cautious, a broad sweep regulation might become an obstacle in the development of a certain sector or in a certain region.

NOTE

1 A talk as Coordinating Minister for Economics, Finance and Industry/ Chairman of National Development Planning Board at the Symposium on Small Scale Enterprises held by the Trade and Industry Chamber, 7 November 1977. This article is translated by Harry Bhaskara.

24

FOOD, FAMILY NUTRITION AND INTERSECTORAL COOPERATION (1978)[1]

Introductory Note: *The improvement of family nutrition is a very important endeavor. In 1978, I gave a message to the working conference of the National Programme for Family Nutrition Improvement Efforts. Nutrition improvement efforts are activities that involve various sectors so that they should be undertaken through cross-sector cooperation, as is the case with the program for food production promotion, the programme for family planning and various other programmes.*

It is important for the nutrition improvement efforts to benefit from previous experiences in multi-sector cooperation. I have described such multi-sector cooperation experiences here to serve as examples to be utilized by the nutrition improvement programme. Among the important instances cited are communication among the various central government agencies, among regional agencies, and between the central and regional agencies, and on the other hand information, reports or feedback from regions to the central government. Through the utilization of knowledge gained from these experiences in multi-sector cooperation in relation to various different activities, the nutrition improvement programme is expected to proceed smoothly.

Mr Chairman and distinguished participants of the national conference, first of all I would like to offer congratulations on the holding of the National Conference on Family Nutrition Improvement Efforts, a matter that we are all well aware is of major importance. This conference will hopefully provide important input for us in executing our respective duties.

Second, I wish to make it clear that I think there is probably not much I can convey to the participants of the national working conference this morning. Above all I believe that the conference participants are far more specialized than I am in the fields of diet, nutrition, health and other areas connected with nutrition, so that not much is left for me to contribute as thoughts to this meeting. Likewise, I believe this morning we all listened to the message of the President to this national working conference and the President's speech contains directives we need to observe. Therefore, as a contribution of ideas, I wish only to put forward a few things that may be relevant to this meeting today.

If I am not mistaken, this working conference will further discuss measures to strengthen the implementation of the national programme for Family Nutrition Improvement Efforts within the framework of a 1974 Presidential Instruction. For this purpose, I will set out and analyze the experiences gained so far so that all of us can carry out this task in the best possible way.

As aptly pointed out in the implementation manual for the National Programme for Family Nutrition Improvement Efforts (UPGK), the problem of nutrition, the problem of diet, is not a matter focused in a single sector, but involves various sectors, various fields, and therefore requires synchronization in planning and preparation, as well as proper coordination in its implementation. And, as I believe that we all well understand, this is a valid starting point.

In this context, nutritional improvement is only one of the various fields in which appropriate cross-sectoral activities based on the best possible methodology are vital. The Mass Guidance (Bimas) and Mass Intensification (Inmas) programmes in food production are just two examples of this inter-sectoral or cross-sectoral approach. The family planning programme is another that involves a wide variety of aspects and has been expanded to cover not just planned-parenthood, but also the problem of population as a whole.

And still another example of cooperation between sectors is the transmigration effort. Most recently, cross-sectoral cooperation has gotten underway in the fostering of economically needy groups, mostly indigenous populations. Therefore, it will be useful for this meeting if the various experiences already gained in nutritional improvement and other fields like Bimas, transmigration, family planning, and so forth, are utilized within the framework of our efforts to improve the operational methods in the field of nutritional improvement. Thus far, our experiences indicate that cooperation between sectors is, indeed, vital, but its implementation is a complex, and not entirely easy, undertaking.

The first thing is that the central government, with its various agencies, requires in its cross-sectoral activities is consistency; a common understanding of the objectives, relevant measures, and/or responsibilities. The impact of activities in any given sector must also be considered in relation to the others involved.

We must also take into consideration the level of synchronization and coordination, which involves provinces, regencies as well as districts and also villages, occurring at the regional level. We should think about some ways to facilitate this.

Then there should be consistency between the decisions made by the central government and their understanding as well as the realization of this understanding at the regional level. This does not always happen as expected; because we are all aware that there may be various interpretations, as perceptions may vary from place to place, creating confusion at the regional level.

In the same way, consistent feedback from regions to the central government is also necessary, so that the government can avoid making poorly based decisions. We need to watch out for this. In this context it may be beneficial for the participants if I relate some experiences in the field of food production promotion, for instance. The fostering of food production (under Bimas) has encountered a lot of problems.

First, of course, is the problem of counseling of farmers by agricultural officials, which is partly based on the research and development being carried out at various research centers.

Then there is the problem of irrigation systems of varying sophistication, ranging from simple to highly technological; and involving primary, secondary, and tertiary channels.

There is also the problem of means of production, which covers fertilizers, pesticides, high-yielding seedlings and so forth. This covers manufacturing done in the industrial sector, distribution by the trade sector, and funding by the financial sector. In this case, three institutions, with their varying responsibilities, are already involved.

We also have the problem of prices for the rice in the husk sold by farmers. We need to ensure that farmers receive proper income or compensation for their hard work. For this purpose, floor prices have been set for this type of rice, and purchasing is done through rural cooperative units (BUUD), which are fostered by cooperatives. The Logistics Affairs Agency (BULOG) or regional logistics depots (DOLOG), as separate institutions, then purchase the rice from the rural cooperative units. So, what is happening in the agricultural sectors influences a lot of other sectors. Perhaps this can be seen most clearly in the case of the large number of low-income farmers who cannot afford to pay cash for fertilizers, and are, therefore, provided with loans called Bimas credits. A mechanism, created and implemented through Bank Rakyat Indonesia, is required for the loans. To this end Bank Rakyat Indonesia has set up village units in all Village Unit Regions.

There are also a number of other institutions connected with the problem of increasing food production besides the Ministry of Agriculture; among these are: the Ministry of Trade, the Ministry of Industry, the Ministry of Finance, the banking system (Bank Rakyat Indonesia), the BULOG Logistics Agency, the Ministry of Manpower, Transmigration and Cooperatives and the Ministry of Home Affairs. This cross-sectoral activity has taken place for several years, but continuous improvements and enhancements of coordination are needed. This is very important because the process keeps going and always needs betterment. In addition, many problems remain beyond our full control, such as weather conditions, and new issues are arising all of the time, requiring constant improvements.

The same is true of transmigration, land reclamation, housing construction, school establishment, public health clinic development, road and drainage channel building, migrant transportation, and the provision of food supplies for migrants in the first several months of relocation, pending the planting and harvesting of crops. As well, the agricultural counseling in the regions requires the role of various central government and regional institutions.

This demands very close cooperation between different agencies, such as the Central Bimas Control Agency, the regional Bimas Promotion Boards in the provinces, and the Bimas Executing Boards in regencies and districts. In the case of transmigration, there are central, provincial and regency Transmigration Development Boards, which require very close cooperation. However, continuous improvements and better operational methods are always required or various problems will emerge.

If we examine the Bimas activities, there are the problems of fertilizer distribution, loans, irrigation and the purchase of rice in the husk from farmers. All of these factors affect each other and sometimes there is the tendency among us, when something fails to operate properly, to cast the blame onto another sector or another place. This should be avoided, because in taking the easy way of pointing out someone else's faults, we overlook our own errors or problems. This must no longer occur in the implementation of our cross-sectoral programmes.

Likewise, we need to deal with the information from regions submitted to the central government with care. Let us take an example of several years back — I cannot recall the exact year, but it is already some years past. At that time, a regency in one of the regions had to determine the best place to apply the Bimas programme, which required data on the area of irrigated paddy fields, and the area of paddy fields already properly irrigated. The data coming in from the regency turned out to be highly varied depending on whether it was originating from the irrigation office, the agriculture office, or the regional administration. Why? This was because the agencies were reporting to their respective superiors, who were not communicating with each other on this matter. In fact, this could have been prevented if the relevant regional officials had communicated — even just meeting informally or speaking over the phone — to compare each other's figures. The mismatches in the date should have been pinpointed and everything rechecked, so that only one correct version would have come from the three agencies. Due to this experience, a system was later adopted so that a joint report signed by all supervisors had to come from the irrigation office, the agriculture office and the regional administration. This system is quite simple, but can, indeed, be effective.

The same applies to instructions issued by the central government agencies to the regions. The tone of such instructions from the individual agencies may vary; each with a slightly different emphasis, so that their interpretations in the regions may also vary. This results in regional debates over what the instructions mean, with different perceptions by different officials. Therefore, the policy of issuing joint instructions or joint decrees has been developed and applied. With joint decrees, or joint instructions, a single document speaks with one voice. Although interpretations can still vary, this method does, at least, reduce the level of confusion.

So, in inter-sectoral or cross-sectoral operations, it is very important to pay attention to communication among central government agencies, communication among regional agencies, communication from the central government to regional agencies and from the regional agencies to the central government agencies. This is something of great importance.

Now the question is how to facilitate this communication. In this case, we should take care to avoid making the means an aim, because when this means becomes a goal, we will forget its main objective.

In maintaining communication, sometimes there is the tendency among us to create a detailed organizational structure; so detailed that it is likely to reduce flexibility, inducing rigidity. Every time a decision must be arrived at, a meeting is made mandatory; otherwise no decision can be made.

Difficulties will arise if this happens. It is true enough that some matters need to be decided in meetings where all officials are present, but quite a number of other things can be more immediately resolved by the officials from the various sectors without going through any formal meeting. This phenomenon of over-organization should be avoided. Indeed, we need communication and we need good cooperation, but we must never sacrifice our working flexibility to such organizational complexity.

Sometimes a look at meeting schedules surprises me; officials seem to be attending an inordinate number of meetings — they meet to communicate this and that; then go on communicating and meeting. Thus, their time for reading and writing good analyses, performing counseling work, and so forth is overwhelmed by such routine. Meetings at different levels are necessary, they are important; but we must remember that the ideas for program implementation are more important and that things that can be done without meetings should go ahead.

This is only one aspect of this problem. These meetings and dealing with the detailed organizational aspects, involves considerable costs. There is a clear tendency to spend a lot on organizing things, on meetings, on travel, and so forth. The meetings in districts consistently require follow up in meetings in the regencies, then in the provinces, and finally with the central government. We must avoid this trend as well.

Once again, such meetings are important, but they are not our aim. They are merely a means, so we should take great care. We have all experienced this frequently. We need to learn from these past experiences. Therefore, I offer these comments on what we must do to effectively and optimally implement our cross-sectoral programmes.

Another thing that I wish to emphasize on this occasion is that in realizing programmes there are, of course, certain things requiring our attention; in particular the fact that the programmes we are implementing may have unforeseen side effects. Some side effects are already calculated for, others are not, and some side effects can be predicted, while others cannot. Therefore, in formulating and developing our programmes, it is very important for us to study a number of matters. Therefore, I think it is important for us to take a serious look at what is now known as the Trilogy of Development:

National stability; fairly high economic growth; and equity in development, with equitable benefit for all stakeholders.

They are the three points in the Broad Outlines of State Policy that we must be aware of and fully comprehend.

The concept of national stability naturally involves various facets, including political stability and economic stability. In the economic sector, economic stability primarily means the stability of the economic situation, particularly price stability so that prices will not become volatile; rising and then falling, soaring again, then dropping. Prices are not intended to remain unchanged, but no increase should be drastic, and there should be no cycle of plunging prices during the harvest season, followed by skyrocketing prices in the planting season. In the harvest season, prices are, of course, going to be lower than those in the planting season, but there should be no massive fluctuations. This is what is meant by economic stability in the sense of price stability, and certainly for the purpose of nutritional improvement, the prices of food should not be fluctuating. This is an important aspect.

And then, regarding fairly high economic growth, there is a tendency, not only in Indonesia, but worldwide, to consider economic growth unimportant as an indicator. In this context, it must be noted that high economic growth certainly implies a fairly high increase in production levels; the importance of which we can surely all understand. However, once productions rates increase to an appropriately high level, we tend to find it less urgent as an issue. So if we come to perceive something as a given, or a matter of course, we usually no longer deem it an important focus.

So, when our food production increased steadily by four per cent annually, we considered the production increase unimportant. However, when our food production fails to increase by four per cent per year, as has been the case in Indonesia over the past two years, we experience it as an anomaly and feel forced to import food in large quantities. Swelling imports mean bigger foreign exchange spending. Imagine what could happen if we could avoid this huge foreign exchange expenditure; we could use our savings for other purposes, such as laboratories, hospitals, education facilities, and so forth.

Production increase is, thus, clearly important, and economic growth is also important. However, it is true that production increases and economic growth are not the only important aspects. However, any production of goods or expansion of services has to register continuously and at fairly high rates of increase to have the intended impact. Therefore, the trilogy of development, comprising stability, growth and equity, must be applied.

Equity is what we are all aware of and consider important today, and this, in itself, involves various aspects. Some of the aspects of equity are: equity in development, equity in development gains and equity in the development burden, as well as the implementation of development equally all over the country; all of which are meant to ensure the equitable distribution of the fruits of development across all sections of society nationwide.

In this context, it is, therefore, appropriate for us to pay particular attention to the problem of equity because the equitable distribution of the benefits of development is not an automatic process. In our experience, even if economic growth is high, development equity will not always ensue. It certainly is not something automatic; rather, equity based activities and equity based efforts have to be undertaken. Equity for all segments of society, as well as equity for all regions within the territory of our country, has to be consciously brought to fruition, for which the development of certain programs is required. This matter requires our serious attention.

For instance, investment loans are made available to our business sector. Yet, this provision of investment loans itself does not yet guarantee the utilization of the loans by small-scale business units. Only large-scale companies may be in a position to utilize the loans because of banking requirements. Therefore, the program for Small Investment Credits, better known as KIK, has been developed. It is clear, that we will have to consciously provide further direction in this matter, instead of only supplying loans.

Similarly, in the sector of education we need equal access to educational opportunities. Therefore, the programme for education prioritizes primary education because the lack of access to a primary school education certainly makes it impossible to expect people to achieve higher levels of education throughout Indonesia. Efforts are thus being made to ensure the availability of primary schools through the construction of Presidential Instruction (Inpres) Primary Schools. These schools are being built not only in cities, but in all parts of our country. These are programs for equity.

So in undertaking all these efforts, we need to devote our attention to the problems of stability; growth, or production increase; and the problem of equity. None of these is more important than the others; they are all equally important, and they have mutual impacts on each other, so that in the effort to improve nutrition, including the diet improvement programmes and so forth, we need to observe the effects of the programmes being developed. For example, the programme for diversification of foodstuffs, which is designed to encourage gardening in house yards and homestead crop plantations, is in my view something very important. It will be very important toward meeting nutritional needs, and also very vital for food stocks.

The experiences of the last two years have shown us signs prolonged droughts occurring in various regions, provinces and regencies. Some regencies have been severely affected by the droughts, while others experiencing the same dry conditions are not suffering as much. Why is this so? There are indications that the regencies being ravaged by the drought had focused too much on the cultivation of paddy, and done little about the development of house gardens or homestead crop plantations; so the cultivation of fruit and other useful trees and plants was not fully fostered. This may well be due to the fact that their rice fields were so well maintained, with proper irrigation systems. Conversely, in the other regencies facing the same severe dryness, people are still able to earn income from the crops they are raising in their own house yards. It seems that the people in those regencies have long been accustomed to the cultivation of homestead crops.

So, these experiences teach us important lessons worthy of consideration. Some regions have a long tradition of paddy planting, and other regions are used to crop rotation, growing both paddy and secondary crops as the seasons change from wet to dry. This practice has had considerable impact. It is clear that the food diversification programme directly affects the availability of food materials and also directly affects the pattern of food production. Such things appear to be simple but require our proper attention.

Then there is also the aspect involving nutritional food production, which can, perhaps, be called fortification. In 1974, in Kebayoran, this matter, covering the fortification of various simple foodstuffs, was also discussed. Now, we need to examine how extensively this plan has been realized, and, if not much has been accomplished as of now, we should determine the reasons for this. We need to find out if this problem also influences prices, making food expensive, as production costs become higher with the addition of certain substances. There used to be various fortification plans, involving wheat flour and other foodstuffs. It should also be ascertained if this is affecting the public's purchasing power. There used to be various fortification plans, involving wheat flour and others.

There is another matter we also need to examine; the problem of salt, including its iodization. The iodization was started with the programme for goiter control. But there has been a problem because there are two primary salt producers, PN Garam (state owned enterprise) and smallholders; a large group of impoverished people. In truth, it might just be simpler and easier to have iodization done by the large state-owned company. What about the salt produced by the smallholders, then? If it is, indeed, more difficult to ensure the iodization of the salt produced by the smallholders, and consumers require iodized salt to be healthy, then wouldn't it be appropriate to simply ban the sale of salt produced by smallholders? Yet, if they could not sell their salt, how would they earn a living? Salt producers are already among the poorest of the poor in Indonesia.

In Indonesia the impoverished people are the salt producers, landless agriculture sector coolies, fishermen, and craftsmen. In fact, we have long intended to draw up a special poverty eradication programme to assist those people with low incomes. So, if we decided to ban the sale of smallholder salt in certain regions and only allow the sale of iodized salt from PN Garam, our target of salt iodization would be achieved; however, the side effect — the impact on the smallholder salt producers — would still have to be taken into account, and a solution to their plight sought out. Therefore, we must strive to find methods to enable the appropriate and responsible iodization of the salt produced by smallholders. Currently, the methods employed center around balance, because, in reality, we need to seek balance, as well as harmony, in all of our undertakings.

Distinguished participants of the National Working Conference on Family Nutrition Improvement Efforts, I wish you to consider two main points from all of this:

- The first is how we should improve our operational methods so that they can be truly effective, because the nutrition improvement programmes are an integral part of the Second Five-Year Development Plan (Repelita II) and, today, we are entering the last year of Repelita II. The operational methods must then be improved on the basis of our experiences thus far, not only in the field of nutrition, but in all sectors.
- The second is that in developing these programmes we should really pay close attention not only to the achievement of targets, but also to accountability within the framework of all the objectives covered in the Trilogy of Development. We must closely observe all impacts to determine what things we had failed to predict, and what side-effects have emerged. In this way, in the coming periods; notably, of course, Repelita III, we will hopefully really benefit from the experiences we have had to date.

NOTE

[1]   A message delivered to the working conference of the National Programme for Family Nutrition Improvement Efforts on 18 January 1978. This article is translated by Harry Bhaskara.

25

REDUCTION OF POVERTY: THE INDONESIAN EXPERIENCE (1994)[1]

Introductory Note: *On the occasion of the 50th anniversary of the World Bank and the International Monetary Fund (IMF), the two multilateral institutions invited me to give a presentation on poverty reduction at the IMF-World Bank Conference "Fifty Years After Bretton Woods: The Future of the IMF and the World Bank" in Madrid, Spain, on 29–30 September 1994. The presentation, "Reduction of Poverty: The Indonesian Experience", was delivered on 29 September 1994 and published in Fifty Years After Bretton Woods, James M. Boughton and K. Sarwar Lateef (eds-), International Monetary Fund and World Bank Group, Washington DC, 1995, pp. 176–182. The presentation centered on: (1) What lessons can be drawn from Indonesia's experience in achieving a rapid reduction of poverty, (2) What can or should the international community do to assist developing countries in achieving poverty reduction.*

Let me first say how honoured I feel to be invited to speak on the topic of sustainable poverty reduction in this conference on the occasion of the fiftieth anniversary of the World Bank and the International Monetary Fund. I would like to express my good wishes to the IMF and the World Bank Group on this most important event. The choice of sustainable poverty reduction as a topic for discussion reflects the commitment of the two institutions to support developing countries in their endeavours to reduce poverty and improve living standards.

As to poverty reduction, I am familiar only with the experience of Indonesia. Therefore, my contribution to this conference will be limited to poverty reduction in Indonesia only. Let me start with a few statistics. *The 1994 Annual Report of the World Bank* indicated that:

> "Among regions, East Asia and Pacific stands out as the one that has made the most impressive gains in poverty reduction, as well as being the fastest growing. ... The most impressive gains have been made in Indonesia, where the percentage share of absolute poverty has fallen from 60 to 15 per cent of the total population over the period (1970–90), and China, where it fell from 33 to 10 per cent".

The analysis of poverty over time is difficult and controversial. Nonetheless, estimates on poverty in Indonesia has reached a fair degree of consensus: poverty has fallen rapidly over the past twenty-five years. The proportion of the population below the poverty line fell from about 60 per cent in 1970 to about 29 per cent in 1980 and to about 14 per cent in 1993. The absolute numbers of those in poverty fell from about 70 million in 1970 to about 26 million in 1993. Total population in 1993 was almost 190 million. More than 110 million live on the island of Java, which has an average density of more than 800 people per square kilometer. Of the 26 million below the poverty line, 15 million, or 58 per cent, are in Java.

What explains the sharp drop in poverty in Indonesia? The most important factor seems to be sustained rapid economic growth, which was broadly based and labor intensive. The effects of this growth were reinforced by an array of policies that improved the health and education of the poor, reduced population growth to manageable levels, and provided infrastructure. In economic terms, the rate and pattern of growth generated a strong demand for labor, while the policies in education, health, and infrastructure enabled the poor to take advantage of this demand to improve their incomes.

Let us first discuss the growth process. Between 1970 and 1993, real GDP increased by about 6.5 per cent annually. With population growing by about 2.2 per cent on average, per capita GDP grew over 4 per cent per year. Of key importance to poverty reduction in the 1970s and early 1980s was the high rate of growth in the agricultural sector, on which most of the population and the poor depended. Production of rice, the most important crop, grew by nearly 5.3 per cent a year between 1971 and 1983.

The sources of rapid growth in rice production have been a combination of the rapid spread of irrigation, the provision of key inputs, and the spread of high yielding varieties. At the same time, investment in rural infrastructure, as well as price policy, public procurement, and price stabilization, increased the level and stability of the prices received by the farmer. This early emphasis on agriculture played a decisive role in breaking the downward cycle of poverty, population growth, and environmental degradation.

In the second half of the 1980s and the 1990s, a different process became important in generating high growth and reducing poverty — the rapid growth of exports of labor intensive manufactures, which generated employment growth in manufacturing of about 7 per cent per year after 1985. In addition, the growth in manufacturing employment was accompanied by rapid growth of construction and employment in the construction sector.

During the three-years period from 1984 to 1987, Indonesia's total outstanding debt increased from US$31.2 billion to US$50.2 billion, an increase of 60 per cent. Its annual debt service payment increased from USS4.2 billion in 1984 to US$6.9 billion in 1987, an increase of 64 per cent.

The very sharp increase in both total debt outstanding and annual debt servicing was mainly due to the realignment of world currencies, in particular the rapid depreciation of the US dollar against the Japanese yen and other major currencies. However, a substantial proportion of Indonesia's debts was denominated in yen and currencies other than the US dollar. It has been estimated by the International Monetary Fund that more than 80 per cent of the increase in the stock of outstanding debt and about two-thirds of the increase in debt service payments were attributable to the valuation effects of the depreciation of the US dollar.

The impact of the sharp depreciation of the US dollar on Indonesia's development was even worse because of its timing. It coincided with the sharp decline in the international price of oil in 1986. Indonesia's development was thus receiving a double blow: the sharp fall of oil prices and, at the same time, the sharp depreciation of the US dollar.

As a response to the new challenges, Indonesia embarked on a comprehensive set of economic reforms, policy adjustments and restructuring. These measures included the postponement of major capital intensive projects, devaluations, flexible exchange rate management, prudent fiscal and monetary policies, tax reforms, financial sector reforms, waves of deregulation of foreign trade and industry, the rollback of non-tariff barriers, tariff reform, improvement of the climate for investment, development of the stock exchange, and an all-out effort to capture foreign markets for non-oil exports.

All these measures, which were implemented in a consistent manner, resulted in a substantial growth of exports, employment, and investments. Instead of capital flight, the country had a vigorous capital inflow.

An issue that attracted wide-ranging interest was the question whether all those economic reforms, policy adjustment, and restructuring did not result in an ever-increasing burden for the poor. A number of studies carried out to measure the incidence of poverty and its trend concluded that the incidence of poverty declined from 22 per cent in the 1984 to about 18 per cent in 1987, implying an absolute decline in the number of poor Indonesians from about 35 million in 1984 to about 30 million in 1987.

The success in reducing poverty during the difficult adjustment period in the 1980s was due to three factors:

- *First,* the development efforts before the adjustment period was directed at establishing a strong rural economy and establishing an extensive network of social and physical infrastructure, such as primary schools leading to universal primary education; integrated centers for health, nutrition and family planning; and rural networks of roads, irrigation facilities, and support for flood control.
- *Second,* the economic reform and policy adjustments introduced contained elements geared toward sustaining progress on poverty reduction. Budgetary expenditures in poverty-related sectors — such as agriculture, human resource development, and transfers to regional governments — were protected relative to other sectors.
- *Third,* the combination of trade and industrial deregulation and real exchange rate adjustments led to a rapid recovery in investment and employment in manufacturing and agriculture.

These policy changes were supported by the World Bank, the IMF and bilateral donors. The inflow of funds from the sources cushioned the fall in oil prices, allowing Government spending and aggregate demand to be maintained while avoiding high levels of inflation.

In summary, rapid, sustained and labor intensive growth was a major factor in reducing poverty in Indonesia. This close linkage between growth and poverty reduction is reflected in Indonesia's particular growth process: initial rapid growth in agriculture followed by rapid growth in labor-intensive manufactures — and in the policy packages that generated it.

Let me now turn to another important factor accounting for poverty reduction in Indonesia: the slowdown in population growth. Annual population growth rates in Indonesia fell from 2.5 per cent in 1970 to about 1.7 per cent at present. This drop was the result of a pronounced reduction in fertility rates at the same time as mortality rates fell rapidly. A successful family planning programme, as well as rapid educational and employment gains among women, played a crucial role in reducing population growth. Indonesia's total fertility rate was nearly halved in two decades — from 5.5 in 1970 to 3.0 in 1990. Child survival rates improved, owing to the provision of health care, especially through programmes such as universal child immunization, improved nutrition, and rapid gains in female education. The gross enrollment rate for females in primary education increased from about 73 per cent in 1970 to 114 per cent in 1990,[2] and in secondary education from 16 per cent in 1970 to 45 per cent in 1950. The effect of these factors on reducing population growth is now well recognized.

In sum, as I have tried to illustrate, Indonesia was able to reduce poverty rapidly, first, through sustained, broad-based and labor-intensive growth based on rapid growth of agriculture, and then through rapid growth of labor-intensive manufacturing exports. Second, the poor were able to participate in that growth because of substantial improvements in education and health and investments in infrastructure. Third, population growth fell sharply.

What lessons can be drawn from Indonesia's experience in achieving a rapid reduction of poverty? First and foremost is the need for a true commitment to achieving it. It has to be a true commitment as opposed to adhering passively to possible fashions in the development debate. Such a commitment has to be translated into operational policies and programmes to be implemented in a consistent manner. These policies and programmes have to be internally designed and self-imposed rather than being parts of conditions attached to loans or grants. The test of a true commitment arrives when the availability of resources is rapidly declining: whether to forego other claims or to yield to pressures and sacrifice the poverty reduction programmes.

Another critical requirement is the development of capabilities, both individual and institutional, to identify problems and opportunities and to design and implement poverty-reduction policies and programmes. However, poverty reduction should not be postponed until such capabilities are completely developed.

The Indonesian experience with poverty reduction also shows clearly the important role of broadly based labor-intensive economic growth, together with the rapid growth of primary education and the effective delivery of health care and family planning services. It follows that the pattern of growth pursued in a country is of great importance for achieving the objective of poverty reduction. Broad-based labor-intensive growth in Indonesia was primary in agriculture during the 1970s and shifted toward labor-intensive manufactured exports in the 1980s and 1990s.

Education and health are ends in themselves, but they also have a great effect on the pace of labor intensive growth of the economy. In particular, the education of women is of a great social and economic benefit.

Finally, what can or should the international community do to assist developing countries in achieving poverty reduction? Needless to say, poverty reduction is the responsibility and, therefore, the homework of the individual country concerned. However, to be successful in carrying out a poverty reduction programme, there is *a serious need for an enabling external environment* — a world economic environment that is supportive. The following are some examples.

Volatile exchange rates between the major currencies can have a devastating impact on a developing country's economy. Thus, the rapid depreciation of the US dollar against the yen could have wiped out Indonesia's endeavours in poverty reduction. The two economic superpowers in the Pacific certainly did not intend to harm another country in the Pacific, but in trying to find solutions to their problems, they did not take into account the impact of their actions on the developing countries. The establishment of a stable and predictable exchange system can be achieved only by the major developed countries.

Another important enabling external environment is related to market access. Manufactured exports of developing countries, such as textiles and garments, are facing non-tariff barriers in accordance with the MFA (Multilateral Fibre Agreement). Everybody is happy that the Uruguay Round was agreed upon by all countries, but the MFA will remain in force for another ten years. We have to wait ten years before there will be real market access for our textiles.

The burden of debt repayment can be very severe for developing countries. Let me describe Indonesia's experience with debt. When there was a change in government in 1966, Indonesia had a huge debt in relation to exports, reserves, and GNP. At that time, Indonesia had arrears, and what it did, of course, just as any other developing country, was to go to the Paris Club and negotiate a rescheduling. We came out with an agreement, namely, rescheduling for eight years with three years' grace period for the amount due in one year. Following that agreement, we had to go to the Paris Club every year for another rescheduling. In addition, we had to negotiate at that time with twenty-two creditor countries. There was complete uncertainty about what would happen the following year. That was very much in our mind. If you ask people working in a country to take care of poverty problems while worrying about the payment of debt the next year, I think that is too much to ask.

What happened next was that the Paris Club agreed to ask a third party to study the problem of Indonesia's debt and come up with a proposal for a solution. After some time, we agreed to ask the late Dr Hermann Abs of the Deutsche Bank — which at that time was not one of Indonesia's creditors — to make a study of Indonesia's debt problem for the Paris Club and for Indonesia. In his work, Dr Abs was assisted by many able officials from the World Bank and the Fund.

Dr Abs came up with three proposals. *The first* was that the settlement of the debt should be a once-and-for-all settlement that did not have to be repeated every year. Once done, that was it; no more negotiations. The *second* principle was that Indonesia must be able to pay; the settlement was to make Indonesia creditworthy so that it could have normal financial relations. Creditworthiness was the objective. And *third*, there should be a nondiscriminatory treatment of all debt.

Indonesia was lucky because the Paris Club countries agreed at that time to these three proposals. Unfortunately, the Paris Club said that this was a unique case that could not be used as a precedent for other developing countries.

This history is just to give you an example of the big difference it made to Indonesia to have its debt settled — and settled in a way that can be called a final settlement. Because of that, we were able to concentrate all of our efforts on the development of the country and on poverty alleviation. The settlement of Indonesia's debt on the basis of the principles put forward by Dr Hermann Abs *(once-and-for-all settlement, creditworthiness as an objective, and the principle of nondiscrimination)* could be considered more generally for the settlement of debts of other developing countries.

NOTES

[1]   Presentation at the 50th anniversary of the World Bank and the IMF in Madrid Spain on 29–30 September 1994.
[2]   "For some countries with universal primary education, gross enrollment rates may exceed 100 per cent because some pupils are younger or older than the country's standard primary school age" (World Bank, *World Development Report 1994*, p. 243).

PART VI

INDONESIA AND THE WORLD

26

IN THE MUTUAL INTEREST OF
RICH AND POOR NATIONS (1982)[1]

Introductory Note: *Every year the European Economic Forum organize the Davos Symposium at Davos, Switzerland, which usually are attended by many present and former cabinet members of developed and developing countries as well as important business leaders. Many officials from developing countries use the opportunity to attract foreign investment into their countries. I was invited to attend and address the Davos Symposium in 1982. While I highlighted some pertinent aspects of Indonesia's development and the opportunity they offer for mutually advantageous business and industrial cooperation, I spent some time explaining on how we in Indonesia agree with the view that the current state of the world economy was freewheeling into stagnation. The persistent crises of the world economy are symptomatic of a structural malfunctioning of the international economic system and a basic imbalance in international economic relations. It is indeed in the mutual interest of rich and poor countries:*

- *to increase the availability of financial resources to the developing countries through bilateral and multilateral channels to alleviate debt burdens, meet liquidity needs and ensure continued development;*

- *to increase world food production and to assure international food security;*
- *to achieve greater stability and predictability in the supply of raw materials at prices remunerative to producers and fair to consumers;*
- *to halt and reverse the present dangerous slide towards more protectionism;*
- *to provide the multilateral financial institutions with the necessary capabilities to play a greater role in channeling financial resources to the developing countries.*

I am genuinely pleased to be able to participate in this 1982 Davos Symposium and would like to thank our hosts, the European Management Forum, for providing me the opportunity to highlight some pertinent aspects of Indonesia's national development and the opportunity they offer for mutually advantageous business and industrial cooperation.

Before doing so, however, allow me to say a few words on how we in Indonesia see the current state of the world economy, for I think you will agree with me that in the world in which we live today sustained economic progress can only be made at the national level if it can be assured at the global level.

I am not a pessimist by nature. However, I cannot but fully support the view of an imminent European statesman, our chairman Mr Edward Heath, who stated that the international economy is freewheeling into stagnation.

Indeed, the industrialized countries are presently continued to be plagued by high inflation, unemployment, sluggish growth and reduced industrial output. These conditions, in turn, are causing havoc to the more vulnerable economies of the developing countries. The problems of mounting debts, of rising balance of payments deficits and steadily worsening terms of trade faced by the developing world have recently been further aggravated by high interest rates, declining commodity prices and an alarming wave of new protectionism in the industrial countries.

But there is an even more distressing part of this picture. Instead of resolutely joining in an integral and comprehensive attack on these global problems, a number of major industrial countries appear to be moving in precisely the opposite direction: by adopting inward-looking policies and stop-gap measures, oriented towards short-term interest rather than the long-term, global requisites for the revival of the world economy.

The North-South dialogue continues to be bogged down and prospects for an early breakthrough appear to be dim. In the meantime; a new chill has descended on East-West relations, threatening to trigger an even more wasteful and irrational new round in the global arms race.

Together with others in the — developing world we believe that the persistent crises of the world economy cannot solely be ascribed to temporary or cyclical phenomena. They are indeed symptomatic of something much more fundamental: A structural, malfunctioning of the international economic system and a basic imbalance in international economic relations as well as in the functioning of international institutions.

Their solution, therefore, cannot and should not be sought in piece-meal action or in short-sighted policies. Their solution requires global cooperation, supported by farsighted concepts and structures, designed to forge a new kind of partnership among nations, based on equality, equity and genuine mutuality of interest.

It is, therefore, indeed very heartening that on the eve of the Cancun Summit Meeting Mr Heath expressed his stern warning against the view as if "… all major initiatives to galvanize the economic growth of the South must await the rejuvenation of the northern economy.[2]" He stated bluntly: "This is nonsensical. Given the interdependence of North and South, it is quite impossible for the North to escape the consequences of stagnation in the South. Indeed, the development of the Third World could provide a major impetus to the restoration of growth and employment in the North itself." Indeed, the developing countries provide increasingly important markets for the exports of the industrial countries. At the same time imports from developing countries, which are much cheaper than similar goods produced in the industrial countries, can contribute positively in controlling inflation in the industrial countries. It seems very clear, therefore, that the development process of the South should not be shelved while waiting for an upturn of the economy of the North. Rapid development of the developing countries is part and parcel of a comprehensive attack on global problems for the revival of the world economy.

Thus, it should hopefully become increasingly obvious that it is in the mutual interest of both rich and poor nations to increase the availability of financial resources to the developing countries, through bilateral as well as multilateral channels, in order to alleviate debt burdens, meet liquidity needs and ensure continued development. At the same time such-flows will prevent the further contraction of the world economy and the concommittant loss of exports and employment opportunities for the industrial countries as well as the risk of defaults for the international banking system.

It should further be in the mutual interest of all to increase world food production and to assure international food security, just as, it would be in the global interest to reduce uncertainty about the short-term and long-term prospects of oil and other sources of energy.

It should be in the mutual interest of all to achieve greater stability and predictability in the supply of vital raw materials, at prices remunerative to producers and fair to consumers, through equitable international commodity agreements and the establishment of a viable Common Fund for Commodities.

It should be in the mutual interest of all to halt and reverse the present dangerous slide towards more protectionism, so that world trade can continue to flourish within an open, expanding and freer trading system.

We know that protectionism is a complex phenomenon involving a number of often quite sensitive economic and political factors and causes. In the final analysis, however, it is a self-defeating exercise. Industrialized countries cannot expect to overcome problems of excess industrial capacity or maintain their exports to developing countries if at the same time the earnings and hence the purchasing power of the developing countries are reduced by closing or restricting access to the markets of the industrial countries.

It should also be in the mutual interest of all that the multilateral financial institutions are provided with the necessary capabilities to play a much greater role in channeling financial resources to the developing countries. For this purpose it is imperative that a beginning has to be made in introducing major reforms in the decision making arrangements within these mutilateral financial institutions in order to reflect the realities and needs of a changing world. Such reforms will not only constitute the beginning of a genuine sharing of responsibilities in the management of the world economy, but will also be very instrumental in channeling available surpluses in developing countries and in matching savings and investments at the global level.

Of late it has been suggested that developing countries ought to rely less on the flow of official development assistance from industrial countries, but instead should rely more on "the magic of the market place". To this I would like to say that I know of no developing country that denies the importance of trade or of private investment in national development. But the facts show that no private enterprise can be expected to build irrigation canals or mount a programme to eradicate illiteracy or malaria, for the simple reason that there is no private earnings in those type of investments. In this respect another eminent European statesman, Mr Willy Brandt, in assessing the results of the Cancun Summit Meeting, stated among others : "It was disappointing that so much time was spent on matters where no real disagreement exists. Why should one discuss the merits and the necessity of private investment? In our report (the Brandt Report) we emphasized that official development assistance has always played a marginal and subsidiary role in financing investment in developing countries. It has never been a question of choosing between aid and private investment. The problem rather is whether private investment alone is enough, and whether it is forthcoming in the first place." When one reviews the record of development over the past generation the most successful countries have benefited from a mixture of private investment and aid; the rest had too little of both[3] I don't think I have anything to add to Mr Brandt's statement.

The record of the past few years shows that in the face of continuing worldwide economic hardship and the sharply reduced performance of the industrial countries, a number of developing countries have been able to register continued, substantive growths, some of them even spectacular growth. Thus, instead of retrenchment, there is evidence among the developing countries of conscious and vigorous efforts to maintain the momentum of development, to diversify production and exports, and to enhance overall economic capabilities and management.

In this respect, a case in point is the economic performance of a group of countries in Southeast Asia, belonging to the Association of Southeast Asian Nations, better known as ASEAN, comprising of Malaysia, Philippines, Thailand, Singapore, and Indonesia.

As far as Indonesia is concerned, the country is at present facing a most exciting and promising decade of its history. We have not been immune to the effects of global recession and world inflation, but we have fared better than most. Indonesia's economic growth in real terms was 9.6 per cent in 1980. During 1981 the rate of inflation was 7 per cent.

The country's debt-service ratio is presently 11 per cent and net official foreign exchange reserves amount to seven months of imports.

Being primarily an agricultural country, the major emphasis in national development has been in rural and agricultural development. A major effort was mounted since 1968 to increase rice production, rice being the main staple food. A major breakthrough was achieved in 1980: rice production increased by a record 13.3 per cent during that year. In 1981 the increase amounted to about 10 per cent.

The rapid increase in rice production enabled the country to reduce substantially imports of rice from 2.6 million tons in 1979 to only 0.5 million tons in 1981. Even more important, the increase in agricultural production led to rapidly increasing rural and agricultural employment and income. This, in turn, became a major force in the creation and rapid expansion of the domestic market for the country's manufacturing industries.

Meanwhile major investments are taking place to expand the production of commercial crops, such as natural rubber, palm oil, copra, tea, coffee, sugar, and pepper.

In the field of oil and gas, the production of crude oil amounts to 1.6 million barrels per day, of which 1.2 million is exported. Natural gas production amounts to over 1,000 billion standard cubic feet, of which about 40 per cent is exported as LNG (liquified natural gas). To ensure a steady supply of oil and natural gas, exploration activities have been stepped up. Expenditures, for oil exploration increased from US$ 340 million in 1979 to over US$ 1 billion in 1981. Existing plants for the liquifaction of natural gas are being expanded and in another two years LNG exports will be double the present volume. Moreover, major investments are being made in oil refineries as well as in petrochemical industries, such as the development of an olefin center, an aromatic center, nitrogenous fertilizer plants and a methanol plant.

Great emphasis is presently being given on diversifying sources of energy. For this purpose major investments are taking place to develop coal on the islands of Sumatera and Kalimantan, as well as geothermal energy and hydro-electric power.

Major expansions are under way in the manufacturing sectors, such as sugar processing, plywood manufacturing, production of heavy equipment and diesel engines, construction of foundries, steel plants and machine shops and the manufacture of machine tools and automotive components.

Substantial improvements are also being made in the nation's infrastructure to support the rapid growth in agriculture and industry: the road network is being vastly extended, seaports and air terminals being modernized, transportation systems improved, modern telecommunications systems installed and electric power facilities greatly expanded.

We realize that our development goals can be met only through a coordinated effort by the public and private sectors. For this reason, we have sought through our policies to foster the creativity and adaptability of the country's entrepreneurs. We also encourage the establishment of joint ventures in many areas where access to foreign capital and expertise can speed up the development process.

There are many opportunities for international business to join in Indonesia's future growth and prosperity. What we ask of international business is that they recognize that we in Indonesia seek "partners" in the fullest sense of the word. All parties in a partnership must benefit for the relationship to be a successful and happy one. We seek today investors whose business goals and operating methods are compatible with the economic and social objectives we wish to achieve in Indonesia. This, I suggest, is a legitimate and reasonable aspiration.

As we in Indonesia stand on the threshold of an exciting economic era, we look forward to evolving partnerships and new avenues of cooperation with the international business community.

NOTES

[1] Address to the European Management Forum Davos Symposium in 1982, Davos, 30 January 1982.
[2] Edward Heath, "The Common Interest of Rich and Poor", *Euromoney*, October 1981.
[3] Willy Brandt, "Progress by the milimetre at Cancun", *The Economist*, 28 November 1981.

27

INDONESIA CHAIRED THE OPEC CONFERENCE IN BALI AT A TIME WHEN IRAN AND IRAQ WERE AT WAR (1980)[1]

Introductory Note: *Professor Subroto served as Minister of Energy and Mining for ten years. Later he became Secretary General of OPEC for six years. OPEC is the Organization of Petroleum Exporting Countries, whose members include Saudi Arabia, Iraq, Iran, Kuwait, Libya, Algeria, Venezuela, Angola, and Indonesia.*

When he was no longer Minister of Energy, the energy ministers of OPEC member countries all together requested that Professor Subroto assume the post of Secretary General of OPEC because for ten years they had known Professor Subroto as a very wise gentleman and a figure who had always succeeded in bridging the divide between OPEC members infamous for their mutual opposition.

In 1980, when Professor Subroto was still Indonesia's Minister of Energy, something happened that could never be forgotten by the energy ministers of the other OPEC countries. In their meeting early that year, it was agreed that the OPEC session of 1980 would take place in Bali, Indonesia.

However, the Iraq-Iran war broke out in that same year. A decision was then required as to whether the session would remain slated or be put off. The OPEC annual sessions always set the prices of petroleum produced by OPEC countries. New prices would determine the growth of crude oil prices in the world. If the session were to be postponed, there would be no world oil price consensus. This situation could create chaos on the world crude oil market. If the OPEC session in Bali was to get underway as planned, the Iraq-Iran war would likely continue in Bali. The decision to proceed with or delay the OPEC session was left to the host, who would preside over it. What was Indonesia's decision and what happened?

In 1973 Professor Subroto became Minister of Manpower, Transmigration and Cooperatives and, in 1978, he was appointed Minister of Mining and Energy, a post which he held for ten years through 1988. He gained a great deal of experience as Minister of Mining and Energy, which covered the sectors of petroleum and natural gas, various other fields of mining and electricity development for the population, as well as for the support of industrial growth.

In the petroleum sector, Minister Subroto kept striving for the continuity of Indonesia's crude oil production and exploration, the growth of domestic crude oil processing and the continuous development of crude oil exports. The same was true of the nation's natural gas production capacity. The domestic market for petroleum in the form of fuel always received his endless attention in order to achieve a balance between the public demand for oil fuels and the public capacity to bear the burden of subsidies through the state budget of income and expenditure. One aspect he keenly observed was the need for oil and gas export revenue to be fully accommodated by the state budget of income and expenditure for utilization in line with the development programmes. Similarly, the supply of fuel for the public was always under his control. Among the challenges he faced was the problem of distribution of cheap kerosene for the public because this fuel was also utilized by some industries. In fact, the industries could use other types of oil fuels without subsidies or with low subsidies. Thus was the dilemma he faced as there were increasing signs of the smuggling of highly subsidized oil fuel into the export market.

Apart from crude oil, the extraction, processing and marketing of other mining products also demanded his attention. So did the expansion of electricity production and distribution, which was highly significant for the improvement of public welfare and the boosting of industrial production. In this case, the conflict between the benefit and burden of subsidies was always under his watchful eye.

As a net exporter of crude oil, Indonesia is one of the member countries of OPEC (Organization of Petroleum Exporting Countries). Within the OPEC framework, Minister Subroto always alertly and closely observed the situation in order to ascertain that world crude oil market developments truly provided equitable benefit for producing countries and consuming countries. The sharp acumen of Minister Subroto as Indonesia's representative was highly appreciated by the oil ministers of other OPEC member countries. His impartial attitude in the face of strong opposition between OPEC countries (such as between Saudi Arabia and Iran, or between moderate Gulf countries and hard-line Libya, as well as Algeria) made these other OPEC oil ministers even more convinced of the wisdom of Minister Subroto in handling controversies among them.

One example of the high level of confidence that the oil ministers of OPEC member countries placed in the man they called "The Wise Minister Subroto from Indonesia" was the following occurrence:

In 1980, a very nerve-racking incident occurred. Early in that year the OPEC member countries had agreed to convene a ministerial session in Bali, Indonesia, at the end of the year. But in September 1980 a war broke out between two important members of OPEC, Iraq and Iran. If the session was to be postponed, OPEC would not be able to adopt a common stand on crude oil price developments at that time. This could constitute the beginning of an OPEC rift with all of the potential consequences on the economies of OPEC member countries. Conversely, if the session was to be held, it carried the great risk of triggering an armed confrontation between the two warring nations during the meeting, with the effect of OPEC being unable to make a decision for the control of crude oil market developments.

The burden for overcoming this dilemma was shouldered by the Chairman (or President) of the OPEC Conference, Minister Subroto. After profound consideration, the Indonesian government decided to carry out the OPEC session in Bali with all its consequences. It was the task of Minister Subroto to prepare the session in the best possible manner. This meant doing two things: preventing the outbreak of any armed incidents during the session; and seeing to it that the session would adopt the appropriate decision for facing crude oil market developments.

It was also far from simple to convince the other OPEC member countries to attend the session. They had to be made to realize that any failure in the OPEC session would mean the failure of OPEC, with all of the potential consequences and impacts on the economies of the crude oil exporting countries. On the other hand, they were asking each other if Indonesia was capable of controlling the session so that no fighting would occur between Iran and Iraq within or outside of the meeting venue.

Minister Subroto and President Director of Pertamina State Oil & Gas Company Piet Haryono were busily preparing for the session along with security officials. Once all of the OPEC member countries were convinced that these efforts were adequate, they sent delegates representing their respective oil ministries. The downside of this was that these representatives all felt it necessary to be accompanied by fully armed guards.

Several days before the session began, something even more alarming happened. Iran's oil minister was seized and held hostage by Iraqi soldiers during his inspection of an Iranian oil region that was a battle zone at the time. It was very propitious for OPEC that the government of Iran continued to send a delegation led by its deputy oil minister. The delegation brought along a very large photograph of Iran's oil minister and placed it on the seat meant for the chief delegate from Iran. This was intended to remind participants of the session of the Iranian minister's detention by Iraq.

It had long been the practice in OPEC sessions for delegates to sit side by side according to the Roman alphabet of the English language. The order was thus always: Indonesia, Iran, Iraq, etc. If this order were followed, an incident might occur, or even a very big clash.

Minister Subroto, as chairman of the session and host, had anticipated this. The English alphabetic sequence was "changed" so that the order of seats for delegates became Iran, Indonesia, Iraq. The Indonesian delegation, realizing that the delegates of Iran and Iraq carried arms that could be used for fighting at any time, calmly occupied the places between the two delegations for the sake of a successful session, which was very important to the economy of Indonesia, as well as the economies of countries all over the world. Bapak Piet Haryono said at the time:

"The Indonesian delegation acted as Shatt-Al-Arab (the strait between Iran and Iraq that was being fought over)."

The OPEC session in Bali was opened with a speech by President Suharto, which received a warm reception from the participants. They expressed gratitude for the wisdom of the Indonesian government so that the unity of OPEC countries could be maintained.

It turned out that the OPEC session in Bali proceeded smoothly despite the various strong statements made by the delegations of Iran and Iraq against each other. Minister Subroto, as chairman of the session, managed to control the meeting so that the atmosphere remained peaceful. After the meeting had been completed with good results, and all the delegations had left Bali, Minister Subroto and Bapak Piet Haryono took deep breaths and congratulated each other.

Prof. Subroto served with complete dedication as Minister of Mining and Energy for ten years: 1978–88. When the oil ministers of OPEC member countries became aware that Prof. Subroto was no longer serving as minister, they urged him to become the Secretary General of OPEC, the highest office in OPEC, a post normally held for three years. However; owing to their high confidence in him, they requested that Prof. Subroto continue to serve into a second term, so his service to OPEC in this capacity lasted a total of six years.

In his position as Secretary General of OPEC, he handled various issues with success. First, he eased tension among the OPEC member countries. With great patience, he created an atmosphere of peace and agreement among them, by calling to mind their common goals that were far more important than their individual interests or differences. Second, he initiated ties between OPEC and non-OPEC petroleum exporting countries, including Mexico, Norway, Britain and the Soviet Union. Third, he promoted relations between OPEC and crude oil importing countries, including both industrialized countries (the US, Japan, and the European countries) and developing countries (India, Brazil, and Ghana, etc.). He also worked hard to establish contact between the Secretary of OPEC and the International Energy Agency, which had been set up by the industrialized countries and was based in Paris.

By building and strengthening effective information networks, the OPEC ministers obtained a great deal more complete information for discussion at the organization's meetings and for further processing by the OPEC Secretariat with its considerably increasing capacity. In this way, the countries affiliated with OPEC could make decisions on the basis of more reliable information.

Many circles have conveyed their appreciation to Professor Subroto, including the OPEC member countries, the crude oil importing countries (industrialized and developing countries), as well as various other oil circles and research institutions. When Prof Subroto was preparing to leave the city of Vienna (where the Secretariat General of OPEC was based), President Thomas Klestil of Austria honored him with the conference of the "Austrian Grand Cross of Merit".

Upon his return to Indonesia, Professor Subroto continued to intensively take an interest in energy affairs through his role as Chairman of the Bimasena Mines and Energy Society. Meanwhile, he again became engaged in the education sector when he accepted the offer to become Rector of Pancasila University.

NOTE

[1] "Indonesia Memimpin Sidang OPEC di Bali, Sementara Iran dan Irak Saling Berperang" adalah tulisan sambutan dengan judul asli "Memang Benar Tak Kenal Lelah" dalam buku *Subroto Tak Kenal Lelah*. Penerbit: Yayasan Bina Anak Indonesia, Jakarta, 2004, hal XVII–XXVI. This article is translated by Harry Bhaskara.

28

FIFTEEN WORLD ECONOMIC PHENOMENA THAT STOOD OUT DURING THE DECADE OF THE 1980s (1989)[1]

Introductory Note: *Throughout the 1980s, the world experienced dozens of dazzling economic phenomena. A difficult recession occurred in the early years of the decade. Afterwards, industrial countries enjoyed a rapid growth simultaneously for seven years. Then the worst stock market crash since 1929 struck. In 1985, the U.S. dollar depreciated sharply against the yen, mark and other currencies. This development, coupled with a sharp decline in oil prices, hit Indonesia's economy like a one-two punch. During the 1980s, the world had to cope with an environment of high real interest rates. Another important symptom was a U.S. balance of payments suffering from a budget and current account deficit. This led to a huge surplus in Japan and West Germany. Also in the 1980s, capital moved from developing countries to developed ones. This was the result of the huge amount of debts owed by the developing nations. The debt crisis troubled many economies in Latin America. In the Southern Sahara Desert in Africa, the level of people's welfare dropped considerably. In contrast, the economies of South Korea, Taiwan, Hong Kong and Singapore grew swiftly. Another prominent economic phenomenon in that decade was the emergence of protectionism on the basis of a variety of excuses.*

Now it is 1989, just months away from entering the 1990s. To help foresee economic developments in the next decade, it would be good to turn back the clock and observe what has happened to the world's economy in the 1980s. There were quite a few occurrences, but we will focus on the fifteen most prominent ones.

First, we still remember the exceptional recession in the early 1980s. That hard-hitting recession took place from 1980 to 1982. The recession was so grim that some called it a depression, just like the one occurring in the 1930s.

Second, after the recession, a recovery process began in the industrial countries. These countries recovered and enjoyed economic growth. Their economies have not only recovered, but have expanded substantially and continuously from 1983 until now, 1989. This has resulted in an economic growth spurt of seven straight years, which is a rarity in the history of the world's economy.

As we are all aware, the world's economy develops in cycles. There are downs and then ups, which are called recoveries. So the economy improves and grows. And then it slows down again. This cycle occurs every several years. Sometimes it happens every three or four years, and sometimes every five years, but this time it's up to seven years. The world has witnessed a world economic recovery and continuous growth for seven years twice since the end of World War II.

This leads to a question, will this phenomenon be sustainable in the coming years or will this be followed by a slowdown. If we stick with the cycle theory, obviously after a growth, there will be a downturn. When will this cycle take place; when is the downturn going to hit: in 1990, 1991 or 1992?

We need to be prepared for that, as it has become clear that the economic growth in the industrial countries will not go on forever. In time, a slowdown will hit. Yet, when it does, will it repeat the massive recession of 1980–82, along with its severe consequences, not only to the industrial countries, but also to most developing nations? This is the sort of preparation that we have to do.

The **third** phenomenon in the 1980s was **the exceptional stock market crash in 1987**. It was the worst crash since the end of 1929. Despite this massive crash, its impacts have so far remained under control. The question remain, however, as to whether a crash similar to that in the stock markets in 1987 could hit again; starting in New York and spreading to other financial centres in many countries.

The **fourth** occurrence was the **extraordinary turbulence in the world's major currencies**. In particular in 1985, when the U.S. dollar sharply depreciated against other main currencies, notable the yen, Deutsche mark and others.

In 1985, US$1 equaled with around 260 yen. In mid-1987 US$1 was equivalent with around 130 yen and then 125 yen; extraordinary depreciation. Then it appreciated again at the end of 1988 and into 1989 to stand presently at 143 yen.

That was an extraordinary phenomenon. A longer way back, in the 1970s, US$1 equaled to 360 yen. What is happening currently worldwide is that the main currency, that of the U.S., whose economy is large and strong, has experienced an exceptional shift. What has been called currency stability, much lauded since the end of the World War II, has proved to be unmanageable. Things have shifted and the stability has shattered into pieces. The impact has been immense. Even in Indonesia, we have suffered from it. Our yen-denominated debts, if calculated using the U.S. dollar, have become larger. In reverse, when the U.S. dollar recently strengthened from 125 to around 140 yen, our dollar debt lessened. If the U.S. dollar stayed at 140 yen, rather than 125, our debt payment in one year would be cut by US$500 million; a significant amount. But if the U.S. dollar weakens again, our burden would become heavier.

What are the prospects for the coming years? Many have tried to predict them. Try as one may, however, projections are never entirely accurate. For instance, there are prominent economists saying that the objective of the U.S. dollar depreciation was to improve the U.S. balance of payments. If that is true, then it is not enough to simply make the US$1 equal to 125 yen. This step should be taken even further, but to what level? There are opinions suggesting that the U.S. dollar needs to weaken from 125 yen to eventually reach 100 yen. This was the opinion of someone who once headed the Economic Advisory Board of President Reagan. So we may need to take this into account, although there are experts with different opinions.

The **fifth** occurrence in this decade that has had major impacts on the world's economy, including Indonesia, is the **decline, or more precisely, the plunge of the oil prices in 1986**. At the end of 1985 and the beginning of 1986, oil prices were about US$25 per barrel. In June 1986, the prices went down to US$8 per barrel. An extraordinary drop, and we all suffered the consequences. The prices then slowly moved upward in the beginning of 1988. In mid-1988 the prices went down again to US$11–US$12, and have only recently returned to an upward trend to stand currently at around US$18.

What will happen to the oil prices in the coming years; will they fluctuate again to trade at US$18, US$15, US$12 or US$25? This will have a major impact on the Indonesian economy. Obviously the price of a product depends on supply and demand. Demand for oil in 1989 and beyond is predicted to increase, but not significantly. The industrial countries, with their growing economies, will need more oil of course, but this will be more or less compensated for by their efforts to curb the use of oil, leading to a reduction in demand. On the contrary, the developing countries will need a lot of oil to fuel their economies. So from the demand side, overall there should not be any major change. There will be a change, but not a significant one.

What about from the supply side? There are two big groupings of oil exporters, namely OPEC and non-OPEC. Non-OPEC groups together many countries, including Mexico, China, Angola, the Soviet Union, the U.S., Britain, and Norway. The production level of the non-OPEC grouping continues to increase, but it is not going to be high. In the 1970s, when the oil prices jumped, members of non-OPEC increased their production enormously, by around 50 per cent. Now the increase in production every year is very small. Some of the members have even experienced a decline in output. One of the large non-OPEC producers experiencing an output decline is the U.S., while Britain's production remains stagnant. One member, whose production is still on the rise, is Norway.

So the supply from the non-OPEC group cannot be expected to increase rapidly. What about OPEC? OPEC is a grouping of countries whose members predominantly boast exceptionally abundant production potentials. Not only Saudi Arabia, Kuwait, United Arab Emirates, Iran and Iraq, but also Venezuela, have recently found large oil reserves. However, not all OPEC members have abundant reserves. Others have smaller reserves.

What about OPEC's oil supply and demand on the world's market? Among its members, OPEC upholds an agreement to limit production. The idea is to keep the volume of oil sold on the market far below the production potentials of OPEC members. In reality, however, not all OPEC members can control themselves. There are members who sell more than their set quotas. There are others who comply.

Nowadays, with OPEC imposing limits on production, oil prices could climb to around US$18 again. What about in the next few years? Demand is expected to remain largely unchanged, perhaps increasing slightly. With the non-OPEC supply likely to stay the same, this will depend more on the OPEC members. If the demand rises — albeit a little — then the prices will go up. The problem is that there are OPEC members with large reserves who want to increase their exports. If they do, then the prices will not rise. On the contrary, with a limit on supply, the prices will move up. That's why there is a difference of opinion between two groups of countries within OPEC. Countries with plentiful reserves wish to increase their exports. If quotas are raised, then the prices will become stagnant. On the other hand, countries with smaller reserves, such as Libya, and Algiers, wish to retain the current quotas in order to push the prices up. So whatever is going to happen to oil prices in the coming years will greatly depend on the decisions and actions of each members of OPEC, in particular those with large reserves.

The **sixth** phenomenon in the 1980s was **the decline in prices of most export commodities from developing countries**. This has hit developing countries really hard, especially countries depending on only one or two commodities.

The **seventh** problem in the decade was the **high real interest rates**. The real interest rates rose throughout the 1980s. The real interest rate is defined as the margin between the interest rate and inflation. If the interest rate is 10 per cent and inflation is at 3 per cent, then the real interest rate is around 7 per cent. This is what has happened in the industrial countries and has brought about severe impacts. The question is, at a time of high real interest rates, will the growth in the industrial countries be sustainable? This rate environment is greatly affecting indebted developing countries. Their commercial debt burden is getting heavier because of it. The high real interest rate is also influencing the flows of capital in the world.

The **eighth** phenomenon impacting the world's economy has been the **huge state budget deficit suffered by the U.S.**, as well as the current account deficit in its balance of payments. This huge budget deficit is also having a great impact on the world's economy.

The **ninth** occurrence, in addition to the U.S. current account deficit has been **the extraordinarily huge amount of surplus enjoyed by Japan and West Germany**. At present, what has become known as the Japanese surplus recycling is happening. We recall the term recycling from the 1970s, when the petrodollar, a significant share of the dollar revenue gained by oil-producing countries that had been stashed in international banks, was recycled in the form of commercial loans to many developing countries. Eventually, because of the rise in real interest rates in the world, those countries failed to repay their debts, creating a debt crisis. Now we see another big surplus in the world; not in the Middle East, but in Japan. The surplus in Japan is so huge that it urgently needs to be recycled back into the world's economic system. Yet, how do we recycle this big surplus in Japan in such as way as to avoid the failure experienced in recycling the petrodollar? How can we exploit the Japanese surplus recycling to benefit the world's economy? That is the challenge these days.

The **tenth** phenomenon, and this could in fact determine the direction of the world's economy, is **the movement of capital flows from one area to another, from one country to another**. During the 1970s and 1960s, the capital flows moved from industrial countries to developing ones. This was not only in the form of relief funds; commercial bank loans also moved from the industrial to developing nations. In the 1980s, it has been the other way around; capital flows have moved from developing countries to industrial ones. Why has this happened? This has been caused by the huge debts owed by the developing countries. The repayment of debts, along with the interest, means that there has been more capital flowing into industrial countries than into developing ones.

Changes also have occurred within the industrial countries, namely the huge amount of capital flowing from Europe and Japan to the U.S. How did this happen? This was caused by the high interest rates in the United States. What was the cause of that? It is caused by the enormous U.S. budget deficit, which is financed by borrowings achieved through the selling of government bonds carrying an obviously attractive interest rate. Because of inflation concerns — a big deficit always exposes the threat of inflation — monetary policy, for example, setting interests rates so high, then becomes the instrument for controlling inflation. So, as long as the U.S. deficit, which brings about the danger of inflation, is not fully under control, the interest rates will remain high in order to keep inflation in check.

With the interest rates being high in the U.S., the surplus in Japan and Germany has flowed into the U.S. This is recycling, but the U.S. has become the destination. Consequently, developing countries are lacking in capital. The amount of capital flowing into the developing countries is getting smaller. This needs to change. Capital flows from industrial countries to developing ones need to be boosted. This can happen only if the huge flows of capital from Europe and Japan to the U.S. can be stopped, or at least reduced. And that will only be possible when the U.S. manages to control its budget deficit. So in the end, it's very important to keep a close eye on developments in the U.S. budget deficit in the coming years. This is one of the key indicators for the world's economy.

Now we can look into the **eleventh, twelfth, thirteenth** and **fourteenth** phenomena, which all involve developing countries. Throughout the 1980s, the developing countries worldwide have exhibited varying symptoms.

The **eleventh phenomenon is the foreign debt crisis**, in particular for countries in Latin America. Practically almost all countries in Latin America have suffered from a debt crisis. They cannot afford to repay their debts: and some have announced that they cannot pay up at all, while some said they could repay the principal but not the interest, and some said they could pay the interest, but not the principal, and others that said they could only pay part of the interest, and so on. The result has always been the same. Immediately after the Latin American countries made such announcements, the capital flows to that particular country would stop, creating a serious problem for trade, and an even more serious one for investment. All the efforts being done — since 1982 when Mexico announced they could no longer service their debts — up to now 1989 have come to little avail. The solution applied in Mexico, and most recently in the Philippines, is not necessarily applicable to other countries. The countries suffering most from this debt trap Latin American and African nations, for instance Nigeria, while the Eastern European nations of Hungary, Poland, Rumania, and Yugoslavia are also feeling the pinch.

The **twelfth** phenomenon involved the developing countries in the **Southern Sahara Desert in Africa**. This area has once again witnessed **an exceptional human tragedy**. The standard of living in those countries has dropped significantly, and there is extraordinary suffering on that continent.

The **thirteenth** phenomenon occurred when, at a time when the fierce recession hit in the early 1980s, in other parts of the world there were four countries enjoying rapidly growing economies, which earned them the title of **newly industrialized countries**. They are South Korea, Taiwan, Hong Kong and Singapore, and are often referred to as the

"Four Dragons" or "Four Tigers". They are developing countries, but their economies have been developing rapidly, in sharp contrast to those of Latin America, or Africa. South Korea had huge debts, but has managed to accelerate repayment. So they were not only able to repay all the money in time, like us, they even managed to pay off a segment ahead of time. This raises a question, what is going on in the world? There are developing countries that cannot repay their debts and are suffering massive levels of human suffering, but there are also others who have been growing at a rapid and steady pace.

The **fourteenth** prominent occurrence in the decade, or more precisely in the late 1980s, has been the **possibility of the emergence of new "dragons"**. There are countries predicted to have the potential to become new dragons. In most opinions, these countries are Thailand and Malaysia. Then there are some who have mentioned — whiles others have disagreed — two more countries; the Philippines and Indonesia. So, for some people, we are considered as eligible to become a candidate for the dragon category. Indeed, there have been people suggesting that Indonesia is a country that talks a lot, but has yet to make the right steps. However, there are others saying that the steps taken by Indonesia in response to challenges have proven to be consistent. The private sector has stepped up and has begun to grab a share in the world's markets. Those are just opinions. Whether or not we would become a dragon eventually will, of course, depend entirely on ourselves.

What is obvious is that when compared to the first four dragons, the four candidate countries seen as having the potential to become new dragons, have abundant natural resources; in particular Indonesia and Malaysia.

The **fifteenth** phenomenon in the 1980s can be seen in **the growing signs of protectionism worldwide**. This tendency has not only emerged in the form of tariffs, but also, in particular, in the form of non-tariff barriers based in various regulations for which a myriad of excuses have been made.

There were, of course, many other phenomena occurring in the 1980s, such as a the stronger integration among several countries, including the targeted "1992 Project" toward a unified European market with whatever implications may emerge, as well as the U.S.-Canada free trade plan, and the effort in the Pacific by Australia, Japan and the U.S., which want to undertake some sort of cooperation. How this is going to turn out, is also something we need to think about. However, the above phenomena discussed are the fifteen symptoms we can most appropriately think about, study and look back at before predicting what the upcoming 1990s will be like.

Our world indeed keeps changing. If it did not, it would no longer be an interesting place. Yet, those changes sometimes put us in difficult situations. Yet, they also often present opportunities. Basically, all are a form of a challenge, and it turns out that there are countries successful at addressing those challenges; namely the Four Dragons. There are also others, such as Brazil, Mexico and Argentina, which have failed to fully manage and address those challenges despite the fact that they are advanced industrial forces. There are also countries, like those in Africa, which have totally failed at meeting those challenges. There are also developing countries like Indonesia that have carried out changes and economic reforms; all in answers to those challenges. Currently, what is happening in the East Europe is unique, uncommon, not only in the field of politics, but also in economics. China has also reformed its economy to adjust to the world's development, allowing it to become a member of the IMF, World Bank, and the Asian Development Bank.

A massive change is indeed happening in the world's economy. We are not alone in this world and we need to deal with all the challenges this presents properly.

NOTE

[1]   A deliberation at the National Working Meeting of Golkar Businessmen, 20 August 1989. This article is translated by Harry Bhaskara.

29

PERCEPTION OF INTERDEPENDENCE BUT LACK OF MEANINGFUL ACTION (1984)[1]

Introductory Note: *In 1984 the Yomiuri Shimbun, one of Japan's leading dailies, invited me to deliver a keynote address at the 1984 Yomiuri Symposium on the International Economy. The keynote address was delivered on 17 May 1984 and published in the Daily Yomiuri of 18 May 1984. In the address I refered to the increasing perceptions in the world of the growing interdependence of the world economy which, however, are not translated into meaningful actions. I further encouraged Japan — which had the highest growth rate, the lowest unemployment rate and the lowest inflation rate among the industrial countries during the years of severe recession — to be more assertive in taking up new initiatives to respond to the economic crises facing the world.*

The organizers of the 1984 Yomiuri Symposium on the International Economy are to be congratulated for their choice of the overall theme of this symposium: "Human Development in an Era of High Technology

— Implications for an Interdependent World Economy". This overall theme has been further divided into three sub-themes: (1) "Revitalizing the Economies of the Industrialized Nations", (2) "Strengthening the Infrastructures of the Developing Economies", (3) "Towards Human Development — North-South Interdependence".

I am impressed by the emphasis given by the organizers on the human aspects of these problems. They believe that "human constraints" can be a serious or even disabling obstacle, which is to be overcome by "human development" — the development of the abilities of people in the widest sense of the word. In particular with respect to the topic on "North-South Interdependence" the organizers of this symposium stress the importance of overcoming human constraints, particularly the international perception gap existing among national leaders.

Indeed, a significant evolution has taken place in international perceptions concerning interdependence in the world economy. A number of years ago the interdependence between the North and the South, between the economies of the industrialized countries and the developing countries, was not yet widely recognized. The countries of the Third World were considered to be on the periphery or at the margin of the global economy and there was only a one-way relationship with the industrialized countries in the center.

At present there seems to be a growing awareness of the economic interdependence between the industrialized North and the developing South. The increased "presence" of the developing countries on the world economic scene, the increasingly important markets provided by the developing countries for the exports of the industrial countries, the significant industrial capacities and the growing potential for competitive exports of manufactured products in a number of developing countries, the increased strength and cohesion of some of these countries through a gathering momentum of regional cooperation such as the ASEAN, all these had a significant impact on perceptions concerning economic interdependence.

In recent years the developing countries absorbed more than 35 per cent of the total exports of the United States, more than 40 per cent of the total exports of Japan, and about 40 per cent of the exports of the European Economic Community, exclusive of intra-trade. The huge increases in payments surpluses of the oil exporting developing countries became a significant source of financial resources for the international capital market and when oil prices began to weaken, these countries remained as major holders of substantial investments in the industrial countries.

On the other hand, the crisis in development taking place in the developing world had a significant negative impact on the industrial North: the debt crisis in a number of developing countries who were major borrowers in the international capital market, the substantial cutbacks in investment programmes and the severe curtailment of imports by practically all developing countries, all signify the reverse dependence of the industrial world on the developing countries.

Apart from the growing awareness concerning the interdependence of the economies of the industrialized countries and the developing world, there is also a rapidly increasing realization of the intricate interdependence of economic issues: the interaction between trade and exchange stability, between interest rates and cutbacks in development programs, between budgetary deficits and exports.

More recently another kind of interdependence received a growing recognition:

the interdependence between economic events and political processes. The *ad hoc* measures insisted to overcome the debt crisis of a number of developing countries imply rigid conditionality leading toward substantial economic retrenchment. Such insistence has finally started some degree of concern among industrial countries as to its social and political implications.

The growing realization of the intricacies of interdependence between the North and the South, between economic issues such as finance and trade, and between economic measures and political processes, signify an increasing perception of the challenges facing the international community.

On the other hand, it is also indicative of a very severe "human constraint" in that such a change in perception came about only after some high drama took place on the world economic scene: the dramatic collapse of international debt and the dramatic increase in the relative prices of crude oil.

"Human development" directed to overcome "human constraints" in narrowing the perception gap in the international community has indeed still a long way to go. While there is an increasing perception as to the growing interdependence of the different segments of the world economy, these perceptions are unfortunately not translated into meaningful actions and constructive policies.

There have been many meetings at the highest levels — Summit Meetings, Ministerial Meetings and other meetings — in which there were strong expressions of commitment to the goals of international development cooperation, to the need for an open trading system and to adhere to the principles of multilateral economic cooperation. Nevertheless none of these international economic meetings have succeeded in arriving at a breakthrough in regard to international economic cooperation. Indeed, in whatever forum the North-South dialogue is taken up, there is at present a sense of a stalemate, an impasse, a sense of falling back, a weakening of earlier commitments.

A multilateral approach to international economic problems has been since years a cornerstone of international economic relations. There seems, however, a serious erosion of the commitment to multilateralism in general. In the field of trade, for example, there is not only a proliferation of restrictions but also a growing trend of bilateralism. The basic rules of an open trading system still prevail and are still considered suitable. The basic problem is that these rules are simply not observed and are of limited application. To many developing countries these facts and the continued insistence of the industrial countries on "graduation" and "reciprocity" have created a growing perception of a credibility gap.

A fundamental problem facing the developing countries is access to the markets of the industrial countries. This market access has been progressively restricted. These restrictions are only partially related to the severe recession. Even the arrival of economic recovery has not resulted in a reduction of these restrictive measures. These restrictions are basically not of a cyclical nature but rather a consequence of structural rigidities which can only be overcome by deliberate steps toward structural adjustments. In developing the international trading system it is, therefore, imperative to take account of the link between such structural adjustment and the future trading system.

The urgency of adequate market access is even more pronounced for a number of developing countries faced with the problem of resolving their debt crisis. Only with an adequate access to the markets of the industrial countries will they be able to overcome their debt problems. In this light the problem of overcoming structural rigidities in the industrial countries becomes indispensable not only to counteract the high levels of unemployment in these countries but also to enable the global economy arrive at an effective solution of the international debt crisis. In this regard overcoming "human constraints" in the process of structural adjustment through "human development", such as finding flexible responses in the educational system to a changing industrial structure, have indeed global ramifications.

In reviewing the present state of the world economy one cannot but struck by the fact that while the world economic recovery is at present underway, many countries in the developing world are in the process of retrenchment and of cutbacks in investment, in development activities and in imports.

Earlier I referred to the growing perception in the developing world of a credibility gap, a perception of a lack of effective leadership in the world economy. During the years of severe recession the Japanese economy has consistently shown the highest rate of economic growth among the industrial countries, at the same time the lowest rate of unemployment as well as the lowest rate of inflation. It is therefore most logical if there is a growing expectation in the world that Japan will be prepared to be even more assertive in taking up new initiatives to respond to the economic crises facing the world.

NOTE

[1]   Keynote address at The Yomiuri Shimbun Symposium in Tokyo, 17 May 1984.

30

ADVANCING MUTUAL UNDERSTANDING AND MUTUAL CONFIDENCE (1996)[1]

Introductory Note: *In 1996 Nihon Keizai Shimbun, the leading economic daily in Japan, established the Nikkei Asia Prizes to promote understanding among countries in the Asia Pacific region. The Nikkei Asia Prize for Regional Growth was awarded to me. In my acceptance speech during the award ceremony in Tokyo, Japan, on 15 May 1996, I said that I considered the honour conferred upon me "... as an expression of appreciation and confidence in my country, its people and its government. ..." and that "My role has been limited to contributing in a small way to advancing mutual understanding and mutual confidence." Referring to Indonesia's history of the last thirty years, I enumerated a few requirements to bring about a fundamental economic transformation: "... a national resolve, a determined leadership, clear directions, and full commitments to put your own economic house in order and to live in peace with your neighbours. The next requirement is a sympathetic understanding by other nations and a readiness on their part to develop an effective and mutually advantageous economic cooperation."*

Nihon Keizai Shimbun under the leadership of Mr Takuhiko Tsuruta has established the Nikkei Asia Prizes to promote understanding among countries of the Asia Pacific Region. It is a great honour for me to be awarded the Nikkei Asia Prize for Regional Growth and I would like to take this opportunity to express my deep appreciation to Nihon Keizai Shimbun.

My profound thanks also goes to all members of the Selection Committee under the chairmanship of Mr Gaishi Hiraiwa. To be chosen by the distinguished Selection Committee from among so many eminent persons in Asia who left their marks in promoting regional growth is truly an exceptional distinction for me.

Allow me to look upon this distinguished honour conferred upon me as an expression of appreciation and confidence in my country, its people and its government for their endeavours to promote regional growth and regional cooperation. My role has been limited to contributing in a small way to advancing mutual understanding and mutual confidence.

On this auspicious occasion perhaps I could share with you some of my thoughts on regional growth and regional cooperation. In developing a vision of the future it seems appropriate to ask ourselves what can be learned from the past. Looking back at Indonesia's history of the last thirty years, the first lesson is that a fundamental economic transformation of a country and its economic relations with other countries can indeed be accomplished. In order to bring about a fundamental economic transformation, a few requirements are to be met. These are, first of all, a national resolve, a determined leadership, clear directions, and full commitments to put your own economic house in order and to live in peace with your neighbours. The next requirement is a sympathetic understanding by other nations and a readiness on their part to develop an effective and mutually advantageous economic cooperation.

Here the relations and economic cooperation between Japan and Indonesia comes to mind. During the middle of the 1960s Indonesia faced a myriad of problems, including widespread food scarcity, hyperinflation, stagnant industries, substantial unemployment, rapidly deteriorating infrastructure, and a balance of payments crisis. At that time many international analysts and observers held out little hope for Indonesia's future. The turning point came in 1966 when the new government of Indonesia adopted an economic stabilization and rehabilitation programme, a balanced budget, and a competitive exchange rate. At that time the country was confronted with a severe foreign debt crisis.

Debt payment due, including arrears, exceeded exports earnings. In September 1966, at the initiative of the Government of Japan, the first meeting between the new government of Indonesia and its creditors took place in Tokyo. That first meeting, convened at the initiative of the Government of Japan, provided Indonesia the opportunity to announce and explain its new economic and financial policies. Three months later, in December 1966, the Tokyo meeting was followed-up by the Paris Club meeting which agreed to reschedule Indonesia's foreign debts. After two months, in February 1967, the first meeting of the Inter-Govemmental Group on Indonesia (IGGI) took place in Amsterdam at the initiative of the Government of the Netherlands. Both the Paris Club meeting on Indonesia's foreign debt and the IGGI meeting would not have taken place without that crucial Tokyo meeting in September 1966.

Many occasions of effective economic cooperation between the two countries followed. In 1970 a plan for a final settlement of Indonesia's debt crisis was worked out in the Paris Club. Initially, the plan did not receive the support of the Government of Japan since it was contrary to the provisions in the existing laws of Japan. Had the Government of Japan at that time continuously opposed such a settlement in the Paris Club, no agreement with any creditor could have been reached. But instead, the Government of Japan and in particular the late Mr Takeo Fukuda, who was then Minister of Finance, made a determined effort to overcome such legal impediments by successfully introducing an amendment to the existing laws. In today's language of development cooperation, it was an act reflecting the true spirit of cooperation between partners in development.

The second lesson of Indonesia's recent economic history is related to the existence of so many uncertainties and unpredictable events. On the world scene, events such as what happened to the Berlin Wall and to the Sovyet Union are cases in point. We may be tempted to say that in today's world the only certainty is that there are numerous uncertainties. One example of uncertainty in the past was the two external shocks experienced by the Indonesian economy during 1986. The sharp appreciation of the Japanese yen against the US dollar and at the same time the very rapid decline of international oil prices were a double blow to the Indonesian economy. But here again, the Government of Japan reacted positively and immediately. Such a deep understanding of the predicaments of a developing country is indeed quite rare in the present world.

What we also learn is clearly that through national resolve and determination a country can achieve a high a degree of resilience in facing the challenge of uncertainties. In a world full of uncertain and unpredictable events we must be able to firmly establish national resilience and to work together towards achieving regional resilience as well as global resilience.

Here comes the role and the responsibility of the mass media. In facing this uncertain world it depends very much on the ability and the efforts of the mass media to promote mutual understanding between nations. It is very heartening to note that the present initiative of the Nihon Keizai Shimbun to establish the Nikkei Asia Prizes is a reflection of that spirit.

NOTE

[1]   Acceptance speech on the occasion of the Nikkei Asia Award Ceremony in Tokyo, 15 May 1996.

Index

About the Author

Widjojo Nitisastro was born on 23 September 1927 in Malang, East Java. Right after graduating from the Faculty of Economics, University of Indonesia *cum laude* in 1955, he was appointed Director of the university's Institute for Economic and Social Research succeeding Professor Sumitro Djojohadikusumo.

From September 1957 to March 1961 he continued his study in Economics and Demography at the University of California at Berkeley, California, USA. He received his PhD in economics with a dissertation titled "Migration, Population Growth and Economic Development: A Study of the Economic Consequences of Alternative Patterns of Inter-island Migration".

He was only 34 years old when the University of Indonesia appointed him as full professor of the Faculty of Economics on 1 June 1962. The title of his inaugural lecture was "Economic Analysis and Development Planning", delivered on 10 August 1963. From 1964 to 1968 he served as Dean of the University of Indonesia's Faculty of Economics. In addition, he served as Director of the National Institute of Economics and Social Sciences of the Indonesian Council for Sciences. He was also an instructor at the School of Staff and Command of the Army and at the Military Law Academy. Cornell University Press published his book *Population Trends in Indonesia* in 1970.

In 1966 he was appointed Team Coordinator for Economy and Finance of the Staff of Personal Assistants of the Chairman of the Cabinet Presidium of General Soeharto with the following members: Professor Mohammad

Sadli, Professor Subroto, Professor Ali Wardhana and Professor Emil Salim. In 1968 he was appointed to chair President Soeharto's economic advisory team with a larger membership.

When he was 39 years old he was appointed Chairman of Bappenas (National Development Planning Agency) on 20 July 1967 and retained the office for 16 years until 1983. In addition, on 9 September 1971 he became Minister for Development Planning and from 1973 to 1983 he was Coordinating Minister for the Economy, Finance and Industry.

From 1967 to 1983 he headed delegations to many international meetings, such as Inter-Governmental Group on Indonesia (IGGI), Paris Club (1967–70), and others. Since 1983 he has been the government's economic advisor.

He was also member of the South Commission (headed by President Julius Nyerere) and the Policy Board of the Inter-Action Council (under the Chairmanship of Chancellor Helmut Schmidt).